THE TOOLS WE NEED TO BUILD RELATIONSHIPS
AND REPAIR THEM WHEN THEY BREAK

The
Toolbox

VANESSA LONDINO

THE TOOLBOX

Copyright © 2021 by Vanessa Londino

For information contact: www.vanessalondino.com

Book and Cover design by Linda Bourdeaux, thedesigndesk.com
ISBN: 978-1-73638-131-1

This book is dedicated to all who are on the healing path,
who realize the work keeps going,
who need second, third, fourth, and umpteenth chances,
and who are committed to pursuing a path of love.

Disclaimer

All names and circumstances in this book have been changed or altered to protect the privacy and confidentiality of my clients. The essence and desires behind their conflicts are universal.

Table of Contents

Introduction

~

July 30, 2005.

My mother stood in the threshold of my apartment on the Upper West Side of New York City with a large, rectangular, white box tucked under her arm. I looked up from my perch on the far corner of my sofa, curlers in my hair, a steaming cup of coffee in hand.

It was my wedding day.

She paused for a moment of dramatic silence in the doorway, gazing at me intently before she walked in and set the box down on the coffee table. "Vanessa, before I give you this gift, I want to know: do you have the right to wear white today?"

A pang of guilt shot through me.

"Yes," I lied.

Having confirmed my mother's fantasy — that her twenty-six-year-old daughter was, in fact, a virgin on her wedding day — I was permitted to open the box. Inside was an elegant, cream-colored negligee and matching robe. I expressed my gratitude for her thoughtful and tasteful gift, swallowing my guilt and a pounding heartbeat that had suddenly lodged itself in my throat with a large gulp of coffee.

The Toolbox

You see, in my mother's fantasy world a girl became a woman on her wedding night. Men were gallant, noble knights – gentle and strong. Women were objects of beauty – dainty, feminine, and adoring of their men. They cooked, cleaned, sewed clothes for the household, and raised children who were never dirty, messy, or loud. And, like the Virgin Mary, they were always innocent and chaste. According to Mom, I could look forward to sex that was slow and romantic. There would always be a warm breeze blowing gently through the sheer white drapes in our bedroom, where rose petals fell continuously from dimmed, crystal chandeliers.

To prepare me for life as a wife and mother, my mother taught me to … guess what? Cook, clean, sew, decorate, arrange flowers, and dress beautifully. I interpreted her lessons on traditional feminine domesticity through my own romantic, dramatic lens and entered adulthood as a flirtatious, striking, culinarily-skilled young woman. I fancied myself the "complete package" and didn't anticipate needing to know much of anything else. I was prepared for a marriage that would look exactly like the last scene of every satisfying romantic movie.

Two weeks prior, I'd sat in the backseat of my parents' car, voicing my doubts about my impending nuptials.

"This doesn't feel right!" I cried. "He doesn't *get* me!"

"Vaness'," Dad piped in, "Just relax. This is normal. It's called cold feet. You'll get past it."

I was wasting my breath. Several minutes spent trying to convince them, especially him, that this wasn't a case of cold feet, that I was seriously doubting whether or not this was the right man for me, were spent in vain. I was young and naïve, and my parents had been married for over thirty years by that point. Dad's authority as both my father and a three-decade marriage veteran won out. I ignored my gut, shut my mouth, and commanded my heart to get on board.

You see, in my father's fantasy world, relationships "aren't that complicated."

"You meet someone, you fall in love, you get married, you stay together; it's not complicated. Don't overthink it."

In his fantasy, the woman was a ravishingly beautiful (this part was actually true of my mom) temptress. All that feminine fire would keep him intrigued and be waiting for him when he came home from work, a warm meal on a well-appointed table. But it was to be a fire that would never burn him. In Dad's world, women should be feisty and exciting but not too difficult and definitely not dramatic.

Mom raised me to be a domestic goddess. The goal was to serve, entice, and impress your man.

Dad raised me to be enjoyable and easygoing. The goal was to be interesting, entertaining, and uncomplicated.

My wedding day came and went, and I spent the morning after weeping on a bench in Central Park, alone. Nothing felt right, neither the wedding nor the match, but here I was: married.

The strongest part of my relationship with Christopher was the intellectual connection. We had fascinating, lengthy, in-depth conversations about every topic imaginable. The weakest part of our relationship was... everything else.

Emotionally I was fire; he was ice.

Sexually I was insecure and largely inexperienced; he was impatient and unattuned.

Spiritually I was curious and seeking; he was agnostic and resolved about it.

Socially I maintained a strong, devoted circle of friends; he was a loner.

I was a naïve, overly romantic, emotionally impulsive

young woman.

He was a scared, guarded, emotionally unavailable young man.

And yet... we *did* fall in love. And it may have worked... but neither of us had a clue how to build and maintain an intimate relationship. My parents' relationship rules were for the cinema and the Eisenhower era, not real life. Relational hardship was to be endured, not cured.

"But we're *miserable!*"

"But you're *married!*"

So went the logic.

Christopher's parents divorced when he was seven, and the rule he extrapolated from their demise was: keep your cards close to the vest, give just enough, and it should work. Neither of us had witnessed or experienced true intimacy or healthy conflict. Neither of us were told the real story of what love really is. I saw commitment, not closeness. He saw civility, not commitment. My expectation was too much connection; his was too much distance. I was trying to live out a fantasy; he wouldn't give more than the bare minimum. None of our parents voiced any concerns. The kids are in love! That was enough.

The marriage lasted a little over five years.

• • •

July 26, 2011.

I stepped outside into the frigid winter air. The square outside of the courthouse was bustling with energy and conversation. I paused for a moment, noticing the faces coming and going through the revolving doors. I imagined the situations that had brought them to the courthouse that day. I wondered if anyone else was there to upend their life as I was.

Introduction

At eight-thirty that morning, I walked in married.

One hour and a judge's decree later, I walked out divorced.

It happened fast. Too fast. I felt stunned.

I had erroneously assumed that the pain and inner conflict I felt in the months leading up to the court date would lift once the legal piece was finalized, but I was wrong.

There are five sub-divorces in every divorce: emotional, physical, mental, financial, and legal. The emotional divorce starts long before the legal one is even on the table. This is a withdrawing of the heart, resisting communication, limiting access to our vulnerable inner world. The physical divorce is the slowing down and eventual stopping of affection and sex. The mental divorce is the withholding of thoughts, dreams, and a sense of partnership. We're no longer "in it" together. The financial divorce is the separation and division of assets. And finally, when the sub-divorces are all in motion, the legal one is finalized. Ironically, the legal divorce is the easiest; all it requires is a judge's order. The others, particularly the mental and emotional divorces, are grueling and can last a long, long time.

The weeks and months following that cold January day were among the darkest in my life. The fantasy I had been taught and sought had shattered by my own doing. The crushing weight of it all bore down on me, each pound of pressure an unanswerable question:

Will anyone love me again?

Will I always be alone?

Will I have children?

How will I make it on my own?

Will my family ever forgive me?

Can I ever forgive myself?

Those dreadful months became fruitful, productive years. I started and completed graduate school. I traveled often and alone. I spent weeks in silent retreat learning to hear my own voice, trusting it for the first time. I looked closely and bravely at my family history, owning where and how their dysfunction had become my own. I discovered a depth of strength and a new creativity I'd never known before. I was writing the story of my own life and claiming every page.

But I needed to make peace with the past.

About a year after the divorce, I reached out to Christopher with a request that he might have understandably denied but graciously accepted. I wanted to hear from him, in his own words, about what I'd done wrong in our marriage. Those unanswerable questions early on had only led me to more questions:

What had his *experience in our marriage?*

What could I have done differently that would have fostered a healthier relationship?

What did he need that I provided?

What did he need that I couldn't provide?

Had I hurt him in ways I hadn't yet had an opportunity to address and heal?

I had examined my actions and motives with gut-level honesty during the months following the divorce, but I wanted to hear from the man whose heart had been intertwined with my own. I knew, without a doubt, that if I didn't learn from my own failures in the marriage, I was bound to repeat them. We talked. He was brutally honest, even harsh. I allowed it. The conversation was long overdue and brought with it a new wave of grief. Why hadn't we been this honest with one another before? Why hadn't we just *listened* to each other? Tears were shed, apologies offered, and forgiveness covered what was left unhealed.

My marriage was finally over, and a path opened for self-discovery.

I was more determined than ever to understand why my story had played out as it did. I had been taught a specific set of behaviors that would ensure a successful marriage: serve your man and family, be easy going yet entertaining, and so on. They hadn't worked. I sought out answers as to what had gone wrong and I found some, but... was there a *better* way?

As my work as a therapist progressed, I began *to notice* a pattern. Just like myself, the individuals and couples I saw in therapy had entered their relationships with their own assumptions about what would make it work. And just like me, these lessons – passed down through spoken words, unspoken expectations, and family culture – translated into behaviors that became patterns their relationships.

Mine looked like this:

LESSON	BEHAVIORAL PATTERN
"Always look beautiful, and keep a beautiful home."	Prioritizing appearance over authenticity
"Don't be too cold or too available."	Engaging and withdrawing to maintain control of the attraction
"Don't be too needy or too emotional."	Suppressing needs and emotions

The Toolbox

LESSON	BEHAVIORAL PATTERN
"Don't overthink it."	Ignoring gut instinct

My clients' looked like this:

LESSON	BEHAVIORAL PATTERN
"Make enough money to keep her happy. Happy wife; happy life."	Working like a dog to maintain a lifestyle that wins you approval, even if it's killing you
"The way to keep a man faithful is to give him sex whenever he wants it."	Tolerating resentment and fear
"Keep your vices and failures private. Your spouse doesn't need to know."	Telling your partner only what you think they need to know, lying to protect yourself
"Have a baby; that'll fix things."	Avoiding relational dysfunction by focusing on the family's needs
"Make sure you agree on matters of faith."	Ignoring how disconnected you feel by taking comfort in a "higher" purpose

LESSON	BEHAVIORAL PATTERN
"Don't make waves."	Avoiding conflict whenever possible
"Don't let anyone push you around."	Growing louder and more aggressive when necessary

And so on.

As my clients and I inventoried their lessons and behavioral patterns, we noticed that these behaviors functioned a lot like tools. They laid dormant until one or both partners felt threatened or afraid. Then they unconsciously drew them out like weapons of survival. When we examined whether or not these tools were effective for building a loving, safe relationship, we admitted that while some worked well, most were problematic. The cause was clear: these tools were designed for self-protection, not connection. We needed better tools.

The Toolbox was born.

As we introduced healthier tools, something else became evident. Even though my clients were showing great courage and willingness to examine their engrained behaviors, there seemed to be a block when we talked about implementing new ones. They were more than willing to change and adjust but didn't have sufficient understanding of healthier tools. They had never seen them in action.

"I don't know what you mean, Vanessa."

"I don't know how to do that."

It dawned on me: the challenge was not a lack of

willingness. It was a lack of knowledge.

When I talked about Compassion (Chapter 6), there was general knowledge of the concept but a lack of understanding about how it works in intimacy.

When I talked about Validation (Chapter 4), I heard protestations like, "How am I supposed to validate her when I don't *agree* with her!" There was clearly a lack of understanding about what validation actually means.

When the word Confrontation came up (Chapter 10), it always seemed to be viewed as a dreaded problem rather than an opportunity for connection.

All of these words and concepts have tremendous power to build and repair relationships, but we have zero chance at utilizing and harnessing their power if we fail to understand them or their practical use. These are the behaviors associated with healthy connection, but we are seldom taught these by our parents. We either experienced them or we didn't. Most children don't receive education and instruction around concepts like Empathy (Chapter 9), Listening skills (Chapter 2), or how to set healthy Boundaries with others (Chapter 7). Children simply learn how relationships work by *being* in relationship with parents, siblings, other adults, and peers. If those relationships are healthy and safe, we will naturally emerge as adults who seek out relationships that feel similarly. If those relationships were dysfunctional and toxic, well then, we seek those out too. We then become adults who repeat the same behaviors as our parents – healthy and unhealthy – and we pass them on to our children.

So what do we do if we didn't learn healthy tools? Is there any hope? First, we need to understand *why* a healthy relationship is healthy. What behaviors are consistently present in relationships deemed to be enjoyable, satisfying, and enduring? Without definitive knowledge, we are playing Russian roulette with our romantic lives! We just hope that falling in love will mean we are compatible forever. We can and must do better than that.

Second, we need to take a look at our current behaviors in our relationships. Without realizing it, we all entered adulthood with our own "toolbox" relationally speaking. These tools may be healthy or unhealthy, but either way they're engrained by now. When a relationship works, we aren't thinking about *why* it's working, we just enjoy it. But when things start to unravel, we reach for whatever tools we have. If shutting down and closing up kept us safe as children, we pull out the tool of Withdrawal. If voicing our preferences was met with silencing and/or shaming, we pull out the tool of People Pleasing. If we had to shout to be heard, we draw the tool of Aggression like a pistol from a holster. We are reenacting behaviors and using tools in our relationships every day, productive and unproductive. We need to know which tools we are currently employing and whether or not they're working so we know which tools need to be replaced.

When I started using the metaphor of a "toolbox" with my clients, I began naming the tools I observed in session aloud. When a relationship was in distress, I was witnessing tools like Defensiveness, Avoidance, Exaggeration, Blame, the Silent Treatment, Deception, Aggression, and Deflection. These tools are highly effective for self-protection, not for connection. They build walls, not bridges.

When I started pointing out my clients' habitual tools and suggested we learn and practice new ones, a shift took place. Anger and frustration were eclipsed with hope. New connections were formed, and patterns that had been in place for years were finally being interrupted and replaced with more useful, connective ways of relating. We learned to slow engrained reactions long enough to give us a chance to choose something different. Much in the same way we choose a flathead screwdriver over a Philips head, depending on the screwhead, we were beginning to see the importance of knowing which tool was the right tool for the moment.

Just as our professions require that we possess knowledge and skill with numerous tools, whether that's a scalpel for a surgeon, a hack saw for a carpenter, or an investment tool for a financial planner, our relationships require that we possess knowledge and skill with relational tools.

"Does Everyone Need a Relationship Toolbox?"

Yes.

A plethora of psychological research and life itself teach us that the best marker of satisfaction in life is quality relationships. If people have satisfying, fulfilling relationships with others, they show higher levels of sustained happiness than those who have successful careers with poor or lower quality relationships. Our lives take on joy when we share them with others in meaningful ways.

We are all in relationships. We are in relationships with ourselves and others. Sometimes those relationships are enjoyable and enriching, and sometimes they cause us great stress. If you are a human, you need a good relationship toolbox. Whether you are reading this book married, single, happily married, happily single, unhappily married, unhappily single, searching, or on the verge of giving up, you still need a solid relationship toolbox. At some point, you will be building or repairing a relationship, and you'll need the tools to do it.

This book is not meant to be exhaustive. On the contrary, these chapters will serve as a primer of these essential and vital relational concepts. In fact, many books have been written on each subject! What this book *will* give you, however, is a working understanding of each tool. Some knowledge is better than no knowledge. Every chapter will describe the tool, how its presence or failure affected us as children, and how to use it in our relationships today. This book is about the relationship skills we need *now* as adults. Ideally, we would have learned how to use these tools through experience and by name in childhood, but likely we didn't. We emerged as adults with some combination of healthy tools for connection and many for self-protection. It's time to acquire a healthy tool set. This book is a start.

As we learn, practice, and develop skill in relationships, we deepen our experience and therefore our understanding of each tool. Just as a basic construction toolbox contains a hammer, a couple of different sized and shaped screwdrivers, a measuring tape and such, this relationship toolbox is a basic one. Just as we need familiarity and practice with basic construction tools, we approach relationship tools with the same attitude and understanding.

We all have relational gifts depending on our personalities. Some of us are better peacemakers, and some are better leaders. Some of us tend toward empathy, and some of us thrive in direct confrontation. The good news is: all of these natural-born gifts are useful in our relationships. The other piece of good news is: we can learn new skills. What we have, we hone. What we lack, we learn. What generally drives us into stalemates and unproductive conflicts is using self-protective tools or insisting on using the same tools in every situation. When they don't work, and they won't work all the time, we grow frustrated and may blame ourselves or our partners. This is like throwing a screwdriver against a wall because it can't hammer a nail into wood.

We simply need the right tools at the right time.

"Where and how do I start?"

The Toolbox

Start by reading this entire book. Notice which tools in the relationship toolbox you tend toward naturally. Perhaps Humor (Chapter 8) resonates with you. That's likely a strength. Perhaps the chapter on the Right Mindset (Chapter 1) brings up feelings of anxiety at the very outset. These internal feelings of ease or tension are signaling that one tool is a strength while another needs some practice and skills training. Be very mindful of the chapter(s) you want to dismiss. This is likely a blind spot, and this tool will need a lot of practice.

Use the discussion questions at the end of each chapter to deepen your understanding of yourself and your partner, if you are in relationship. No one is born with relational mastery, so we need not feel shame. We are on a journey together of learning how to foster and facilitate deeper connection. We can heal our wounds and grow closer once again, but we need to make a start. If you are not presently in a relationship, notice which tool seems most interesting to you. Which chapter got your attention? Begin to practice using that tool with friends and family members.

After you finish the entire book, pick one tool. Just one. You'll have plenty of time to work on other tools over the course of your life and relationships, but pick one to start. If you do not know which tool to pick, ask your partner. My guess is they'll have a strong opinion!

When we pick up a new tool, we need a realistic expectation of how long it will take to gain mastery. A youngster learning to use a hammer is going to hold it and wield it differently than a seasoned carpenter. Likewise, a person practicing the tool of Apologizing (Chapter 11) is going to sound and feel very different than someone for whom this comes naturally or someone who has been practicing. We must give ourselves and our partners grace and patience! We are all trying.

Next comes practice and humility. No one learns a concerto in five minutes, nor do we perfect our golf swing in one day. We practice again and again. We fail then try again. These tools are no different. If we want to transform our relationships for good, we need to pick up these tools, familiarize ourselves with them, take them out for a spin, and commit to practicing until we gain skill. When we get it wrong, we simply own it, refocus, and try again. We don't need to parade around our homes in self-flagellating humiliation nor do we quit because it doesn't come naturally. We are learning, and learning requires practice and humility.

For example, if I am working on the tool of Deep Listening (Chapter 2), I become aware when my partner is opening up. I stop what I'm doing, I turn and face them, I take a deep breath, and I release other thoughts and agendas from my mind. If I lose focus, I simply say, "Hey, I lost focus, and I really want to hear what you are saying. I'm working on listening right now. Would you mind repeating that?" When we create an atmosphere of genuine effort and humble learning, our homes lose an edge of judgment and impatience. Instead, we grow in our respect for one another. Nothing softens a heart more than someone making a sincere effort.

Over time, through practice, failure, commitment, and determination, we develop not just skill but mastery. These skills may not come naturally, but they can be learned and acquired. Our toolbox grows as we remain committed and humble.

We all want successful relationships. We are *made* for it. Yet, so many of us simply weren't taught how. We thought falling in love was enough. We entered adulthood prepared in many ways but unprepared for the most important job of all: loving. It's time to learn. It's finally time to train ourselves for the relationships we want.

Alright then. Let's start assembling our Toolbox.

CHAPTER 1

The Right Mindset

Doug and Patricia came to therapy with one question on their minds: should we stay in this?

They began their marriage like most young people do – eager, optimistic, full of dreams, and convinced that the person standing beside them at the altar would be the perfect companion to build a life filled with happiness and satisfaction. Doug was a dedicated and gifted professor; Patricia ran a non-profit. They met in graduate school, and both described their attraction as a meeting of the minds. Sharing a strong passion and purpose for their professions, they were mutually impressed with the other's altruism, drive, reputation, and potential. At the outset, their respect for one another was deep. As their relationship progressed from meeting to dating to commitment then engagement, they blissfully submerged themselves in conversations about starting a family, raising children, and how to live out their dreams.

Their relationship took on a reputation of its own among their friends, families, and professional circles. "What a power couple!" "Those two were meant for each other." Even the pastor who married them chimed in during their marriage ceremony: "These two are world-changers."

Their love was strong. Their potential was inspiring. They rode the wave.

Their assumption seemed reasonable at the time: *we'll have a happy marriage because we're both good people and we're in love.*

It's a simple formula... if only it worked!

The joy of their wedding day was followed by two to three years of newlywedded bliss. They worked hard, traveled during Doug's summer breaks, and kept dreaming about the future.

"So what changed?" I asked.

This talented, bright, promising couple sat on opposite ends of the sofa in my office, staring at me with three feet of tension between them.

"We fight about everything now. No matter what it is, we fight about it. For the entire time we dated and the first two years of our marriage, there wasn't a single disagreement, but now it seems constant," Patty said through tears.

"Doug?" I invited him to contribute.

"That's all true. I thought we were compatible. I'm not sure anymore," he said coldly.

"What do you believe made you compatible?" I asked.

Doug answered quickly and definitively, "We were both on the same track. We were focused on our careers. We got married because we understood one another. Now it feels like I'm living with a stranger."

I noticed the expression of hurt on Patty's face as Doug described her that way.

"Patty, what has changed for you in the marriage? What's been lost?"

Patty paused for a moment then spoke quietly, her tone carrying the weight of her sadness, "I feel like I've lost the friend I had in Doug. We were so like-minded when we met, and over the years, I think I've grown and he's grown, but I just don't think we've grown closer together."

They both seemed resigned to the state of things.

"How is the reality of your marriage different from the expectations you both had?"

Both partners looked at me thoughtfully, their mental gears turning.

"I didn't think it would be this hard," Doug said. "I figured we'd have ups and downs like all couples do, but I didn't think we'd ever lose the spark between us."

"Patty?"

"When we got married, I felt that Doug understood me. He got me. I don't know how this is possible, I mean it sounds counter-intuitive, but the longer he's lived with me, the less I feel he knows me."

Now it was Doug's face that registered hurt.

"So part of what I'm hearing is a sense of shared disappointment. Reality isn't what you expected. Is that right?"

They nodded.

"It sounds like you both had an expectation of married life that didn't pan out, and faced with the reality of where things are today, you aren't sure if this is the marriage you want. Let's back up and take a closer look at your expectations. Let's make sure they were and are aligned with reality. Then you can decide if what you have is worth holding onto."

Doug and Patty had built their relationship on a faulty foundation. They rode the wave of love and promise but were naïve to the challenges marriage brings.

"Our love is different," the couple in love insists.

No, it's not.

When the path got rocky, they were surprised instead of prepared. Rather than accepting the struggles they faced as normal, they surmised they'd made a poor choice in a partner.

They lacked the most basic tool in the relational toolbox: the Right Mindset. Before any other relational tool can be used, we need a sober view of the path before us.

Our first tool is the Right Mindset.

• • •

THE DOPAMINE WEARS OFF

Butterflies in the stomach, lightheadedness, quaking, shaking, insomnia, loss of appetite, increase in appetite, rushes of creativity, high anxiety, visions of beauty, crushing depression, feelings of grandiosity, spontaneous works of art… Is this a list of symptoms of a psychological malady or the effects of LSD? No, it's just a short list of what humans describe when they believe they've met their Soulmate, the Perfect Other, the One. It's the most famous subject in the world. Countless songs, poems, books, films, plays, and ads have been written about one singular human experience: falling in love.

When we fall in love, we experience a cascade of dopamine in the brain that literally feels like we are high. *All the time.* The natural and healthy interpersonal differences we experience in other relationships collapse for a period of time with our beloved, and the effect is that of merging into the other. We experience feelings of unity, bliss, and connection like never before, and we think we have met our Other Half. We have a sense that this person completes us in ways no one else can, and we form our romantic relationships around the usually unconscious belief that this feeling is real and will continue indefinitely. In premarital counseling sessions, it's common and predictable to hear young and/or immature couples insist that while other people fall out of love, they never will. They're different. Their relationship is immune to the common pitfalls that plague others' love lives.

Indeed, this is a glorious fantasy – that love can be so strong, so pure that it will blot out pain.

Emotional pain is the experience of disconnection from self and/or others. The deepest desire of our hearts is to live in the safety of a loving bond, and yet our first experience of life is separation. We are born, separated from the bodies of our mothers, and we breathe in our own oxygen for the first time. The warm, dark, cocoon of the womb – where we are safe to grow, change, and develop – must be left for the harsh outer world where we will experience cold, want, need, and separation. Every need is met in the womb without us asking. We are given space, time, nutrients, and safety. We experience the perfect combination of solitude and intimacy. In the outer world, we will have to learn to identify our needs and wants and verbalize them to people who can meet them, but in the womb…we are *satisfied*.

Romantic love provides us with a near perfect springboard to live out the fantasy that we can somehow recapture that state of perfect, uninterrupted oneness. The idyllic fantasy is that our beloved will know us and love us with such complete knowing that we can be like fetuses again. Every need is met. We don't have to try or ask. In other words, the relationship requires no work on our part.

The Toolbox

We are safe again, whole again, *one* again.

We believe that our love is uniquely special and immune to the pain of separation. Others fall out of love, but not us. Others may suffer through the heartbreak and heartache of disconnection, but not us. Our love is different. We were meant to be, and that sense of destiny and purpose buoys our hopes above the water line of mediocrity. Our fantasy is twofold: (1) this feeling is real life and (2) it will never go away.

But the dopamine wears off.

Dopamine is not secreted when we feel connected (that's mostly oxytocin) but when we feel pleasantly *surprised*, and falling in love is indeed a string of new and exciting experiences that elicit feelings of wonder, delight, and novelty. We are delighted with unexpected gifts, outings, experiences, qualities of character, and exceedingly pleasant moments. One after another, we create experiences with and for one another that keep the dopamine flowing steadily. If the relationship is a flash in the pan, the dopamine stops suddenly, and we believe the love has died. This was not love. This was dopamine, and we were high. The high simply wore off.

If we remain committed to the partnership and it develops into a long-term commitment, the surprises slow down into the inevitable patterns and routines of daily life. The mundane replaces the novel, responsibility replaces spontaneity, and the dopamine… slows… down.

We may find ourselves bored. Restless. In the absence of dopamine, we come to believe something is wrong with the relationship, and we grow distant. This inhibits the flow of oxytocin, that lovely "cuddle" hormone responsible for countless hours in one another's arms, and we begin to feel lonely.

This was a mistake, we think.

The Right Mindset

When we enter our romantic relationships with the mindset that the high will last, we are in near or total fantasy. We are dreaming of a situation in which our every need is met, like embryos and infants, and we will never have to mature, change, compromise, or suffer.

Indeed, fantasy is simply imagining a situation that doesn't require the pain of growth.

No one fantasizes about a relationship where our strength, courage, and will are put to the test. No one fantasizes about crying bitter tears of disappointment and learning to forgive. These aren't fantasies because they involve self-examination and maturation. Fantasies never involve pain; they are imagined scenarios in which our every need is met perfectly. Whether we have been in relationship for a short or a long period of time, if we find ourselves fantasizing about who our partner could be or should be, or even fantasizing about another relationship, we are typically avoiding the personal growth our current relationship requires.

When we enter relationship in fantasy, reality can be a bitter pill to swallow, and yet reality is where real love, intimacy, connection, and union occur. Fantasy relationships – those in which we are playing roles, not bringing our true selves to the relationship, and coasting on "high" feelings – result in less satisfying outcomes. The crash and burn are inevitable. Those who pursue reality, with realistic expectations, know real love.

And so, the first element of the Right Mindset is being realistic. Our feelings of bliss will not last, but they can deepen into a trust that forms a bond stronger than iron. Our connection will not go uninterrupted, but we can know one another more deeply and intimately on the other side of disconnections and conflict. Conflict will come, and we can learn its unique potential to draw us closer to one another. We are not the exception. We will know fear, anger, and shame in our most intimate relationships. What might be exceptional about our relationship is not that we don't experience these difficult emotions, but that we use them to grow closer. We need not fear when the dopamine slows. This opens the space in our minds to really know our partner rather than idealizing them to fulfill a fantasy.

THE FUTILITY OF BLAME AND THE POWER OF ACCOUNTABILITY

Blame is a funny thing. It accomplishes very little relationally speaking, but its presence is pervasive. We experience an unpleasant emotion, and before we've asked a question or had a moment of self-reflection, we've pointed a finger. Blame is a lot like kudzu, that invasive vine that covers everything in its path, hogging the sunlight, starving and destroying every plant in its wake. Blame chokes healthy relationships.

Why is blame so toxic?

Well, let's define blame before we discuss whether or not it's a healthy relational tool. Blame is defined as the act of assigning responsibility to someone for a wrong that has been committed. Sounds innocent enough, right? I mean, we should hold people accountable for their actions, shouldn't we? Yes, of course we should. But the function of blame in relationships isn't about holding others accountable.

In relationship, blame is used to offset unpleasant emotions. It's how we react when we dislike what is happening at the moment, and we need a place to dump our negative feelings. The energy of blame is usually angry, accusatory, and immediate. When we blame someone, we are generally blind to whatever part we may have had in the outcome. We are seeing an unpleasant situation as an isolated, unwanted event rather than the result of a system or cycle. Blame places the fault squarely at the feet of another. We are innocent; our partner is at fault. Period. End of story.

The problem with blame is in its simplicity. A relationship is a complex dance of interactions. When we blame someone, we shrink the complexity of emotions and interactions into a one-sided perception: "It's your fault." We don't want to take the time to soothe our own feelings of anger or frustration and give the situation the reflection and consideration it deserves. We want release – now. We are heavy with anger, and blame is the dumping ground. The person who is blamed generally feels shamed and can become defensive. After all, they will have their own version of the story. If the blamer holds a lot of power, the relationship is a one-way street of accusation. One person is right and innocent; the other is wrong and a failure, at least for the moment. If both partners have equal power in the relationship, blame ushers in a painful conflict. We now lobby the blame back and forth, back and forth, until someone eventually gives in.

Blame sees relational difficulty through a lens of unmet expectations, devoid of compassion and self-awareness. Blame's job is to throw a dagger of fault and subsequent guilt, and once it hits its mark, we may have successfully accused our partner into remorse and possibly changed behavior, but we are no closer to one another. This is the futility of blame. Much energy is expended, but disconnection persists.

There is a better way.

Self-accountability is the keystone of the right mindset. Self-accountability is the perspective that gives us a much more realistic view of ourselves and therefore the situations in which we find ourselves in our relationships. When we are self-accountable, we do not suspend our expectations of ourselves when our partner does wrong. Instead, we are able to say:

- *"I've done the same thing."* This self-aware humility invites our partner to take more responsibility for their actions.

- *"We all make mistakes."* This neutralizes blame and opens the door for deeper disclosure.

- *"I had a part in this too."* This creates a bond of equality and fosters trust.

- Maybe we just ask: *"What happened?"*

We have expectations. We make and receive promises. Sometimes we fail. Sometimes others fail us. We need not ignore wrongs, mistakes, or even harms, but instead of resorting to blame which only leads to standoffs and defensiveness, we can respectfully and thoughtfully ask, "What happened?" This question is more powerful than we realize. Blame demands answers. We bark out questions like, "What were you thinking?!" "How could you forget to do that?!" "What's wrong with you?!" If this is how we are opening the dialogue when something goes wrong in our relationship, we need to be realistic about how it's going to go: terribly. This is what self-accountability is all about. Self-accountability accepts that if we allow ourselves to start a conversation with blame, we are responsible for communication going down the drain. Yes, even if we are wronged. Yes, even if we are angry.

When we ask: "What happened?" we are opening ourselves to learn about how our partner thinks, how they make decisions, and what is important to them. This question flows from the <u>presumption of good intent</u>. This powerful stance in our relationships means we are working from the assumption that our partner is loving, good, and doing their best. It means we do not assume their failures derive from a lack of love or good will. The right mindset is the presumption of good intent. Many difficult moments devolve into unnecessary arguments when we make the almost-always erroneous assumption that our partner failed us in some way because they do not love us or want the best for us. After thousands of hours of couples counseling sessions, I can honestly say I have almost never observed malice, which is the intent to do harm. More often than not, challenging moments in relationships are due to negative interpretations of actions rather than the actions themselves. When we ask, "What happened?" we are giving our partner an opportunity to self-reflect, own their actions, and explain their thinking. The intent is almost never to do harm. Yes, the impact can be hurtful, but the intent must be heard. We can balance our hurt with the intent, and move forward from there. We do not confuse self-protective actions, which we all do from time to time, with malice. This is the right mindset.

Accountability is a habit. So is being a victim, blaming everyone else for our misery. So is being a martyr, blaming everyone else for our exhaustion. So is narcissistic pride, only seeing the faults of others without looking in a mirror. When we are accountable, we are concerned with our own behavior.

Often, in couples counseling sessions, I will ask the members of the couple what they want from the other. The answers vary but always reflect a desire for more positive interactions. I hear requests for things like grace, more fun, satisfying sex, honesty, compassion, and emotional connection. I often follow up with, "Are these accurate descriptions of yourself? Do you bring these things to the relationship?" Sometimes it's a yes, and sometimes there's a long pause. If the person is self-accountable, they'll immediately see the point: we must be the change we want to see in our relationships.

Couples often stay in cycles of misery and conflict because they continue to take cues from the other. As long as one partner continues a behavior, the other partner will keep reacting to it. The cycle continues; the relationship is stuck. The right mindset means we take full responsibility for ourselves. If our partner raises their voice in anger, we remain calm. If our partner becomes harsh with hurt, we remain gentle. If our partner is aloof in self-protective fear, we remain available. We stop blaming our unloving behavior on our partner, and we begin to accept the power of accountability.

When we are self-accountable, we believe the following: It does not matter what my partner does; I will hold myself responsible for *my* behavior. Their behavior – good or bad – is not an excuse for mine

GROWING UP

Our mindset about our actions and self-accountability, thus our impact on others, starts in childhood. The mindset we had during childhood will carry over into adulthood. How we were taught to engage and think about the tasks of childhood will inform how we think about our responsibilities now.

Infants and babies communicate through body language, facial expressions, and sounds. The onus is on the caregiver, usually the mother in early life stages, to intuit and attend to the needs of the baby despite the lack of language. Parents first learn the different cries of their baby, each cry signaling a different need. When babies start learning words, parents become masterful interpreters of baby talk. Each word is both a delight to hear and a wonderful challenge to discern. As the baby progresses to toddler age and singular words are strung together into early sentences, parents are in no rush to correct the child's language quite yet. The expressions of the child are too adorable to alter. But eventually as the toddler grows into early childhood, there will be ongoing instruction on correct grammar and pronunciation. Parents will encourage their child to "use their words" rather than acting out. As late childhood ensues, language skills advance and parents rightfully and naturally shift the responsibility of communication from themselves to the child. This gentle passage from infancy to childhood means that the child takes on more and more ownership for making their inner world known to their parents. Eventually, the child is a preteen then an adolescent then an adult, and the hope is that the ability to self-express will mature with the child.

Let's take potty training as another example of this shift in responsibility. Changing the endless diapers of the baby is eventually replaced with instruction on using a toilet and a schedule of toilet use every few hours. Next the child is taught to voice their needs, and parents can increasingly rely on the child to express their need to use a toilet without prompting from the parent. Finally, we have an older child, preteen, adolescent, and then an adult who is able to regulate their need for a restroom entirely on their own.

This passage from infancy to toddlerhood to childhood to adolescence and finally adulthood can be summed up as one process: from dependency to self-sufficiency. The categories of this process are as varied as adult responsibilities. Leisure, work, financial stability, hygiene, cleanliness, cooking, laundry, and all of the eventual tasks of adulthood begin in childhood in the form of play, schooling, allowance, brushing teeth and bathing, tidying up one's room, chores, and so on. How we experienced this passage from dependency on our parents to self-sufficiency as adults will have a significant effect on our mindset about our life and relationships.

If we didn't get sufficient instruction as children, we may be fearful as adults. Children must face the size and scope of the adult world in increasing measure throughout their childhood. This is called growing up! It is the responsibility of the adults in their lives to help them digest this in manageable doses. If too much was expected of us too soon in any of the tasks of life, we may find that as adults, we tackle the responsibilities of adulthood but deep inside, we are afraid of getting it wrong. We felt overwhelmed and alone as children, and we still feel overwhelmed and alone today. We don't ask for help because we are used to being on our own. We might find that we lack real self-confidence. We get by, but we wonder if we are doing it "right." We chase success because we fear abandonment.

If we were coddled, we had parents who did too much for us past the age and stage we needed the help. We were capable of more than was expected of us, but as kids we didn't know better. We accepted the "babying" and didn't develop resilience, the ability to fail and try again without losing heart. We may live with exquisite shame, unable to stomach it when we fail. We may work hard to keep up appearances. We don't care about the process; we value results. We don't know our own power because it was never called out of us. We may struggle with integrity – willing to cut corners to keep up the show.

If our parents were impatient, demanding, or ungracious with us as children, we didn't have the opportunity to learn in peace. The pressure was on! Do it right and do it now. We may live with deep anxiety. There is a drumbeat inside of us, unrelenting and unforgiving. We may be hard on ourselves and hard on others. We disallow failure in ourselves and everyone around us. Our mindset is harsh and without grace. We chase perfection because anything less is unacceptable.

If our parents were generally forgiving and understanding of us as children, if they were more often patient than not, if they had realistic expectations of us as we grew up, we likely carry that sense of balance now. We can be patient with ourselves as we learn, and our failures do not derail us. We can accept responsibility for ourselves without shame. We do not over-function for others because we learned the value of personal accountability. We do not place impossible standards on ourselves or others. We don't chase perfection. We are okay with an earnest life, albeit a bit messy.

The key is in the connection between actions and consequences. If we had punitive consequences without proper instruction, we were likely fearful as children and will be fearful as adults. If we were able to get away with improper behavior without appropriate consequences – through parenting that was too lenient, negligent, or absent – we will not easily accept responsibility for our actions as adults. The flow between good behavior and desirable consequences and poor behavior and undesirable consequences was interrupted.

We cannot relive our childhoods nor can we change how we were parented, but we can change how we think about these things now. Some of us have been running on fumes for years because we have been accustomed to stress for far too long. Some of us do not take risks because we don't know how to fail. Some of us were never allowed to be free, spontaneous children, and our adult lives are too heavy. Some of us take too little responsibility for ourselves because our parents didn't expect enough out of us. Some of us blame others because we are used to taking blame.

The right mindset means that we are learning the balance between accountability and grace, maybe for the first time. It means we have realistic expectations of ourselves first, then others. It means we are not shocked by consequences when our actions led us to them.

THE RIGHT MINDSET IN ACTION

Relationships require an investment of our time, resources, and energy. When we meet someone and fall in love, we are generally not thinking pragmatically about the investment of self the relationship will require in the long run. We are riding the wave of feeling! We may assume all will be smooth sailing because we are high, but eventually reality sets in. Whatever strengths, relational propensities, and growth we've accumulated thus far will be required. Whatever we lack will come sharply into view.

The right mindset means that there is room in our lives for this person. Couples who both work excessively long hours should think carefully about having a relationship and even more carefully about having children or even pets. If we want our time and our activities to reflect our own priorities and desires, it's likely not the time for an intimate relationship. If our careers or hobbies come first, our relationship will never thrive. On the contrary, when we are ready, willing, and able for relationship, there is space in our schedules and in our hearts.

The right mindset means that there is room in *us* for growth and change. If we are rigid in our ways and don't think we should have to change anything to be in relationship with another human being, we are not only unready for a relationship, we may be toxic to others! Relationships are not static agreements; they are fluid exchanges of energy and self-revelation. As we grow and change, the relationship must grow and change. The commitment we make to one another is not a commitment to love who this person is *right now*. It is a commitment to love this person *on the journey of their own life*.

Here are some scenarios in which we are *not* ready, willing, or able for romantic relationship:

- We are still married to someone else.
- We are not over an ex. We're either still in love or still in hate. (Yes, this is a thing.)
- We haven't worked through and forgiven the hurts and harms suffered in previous relationships.
- We fear being alone and are looking for a relationship to cure our loneliness.
- Our personal life is not in order: high debt, no job, chaotic living situations, etc.
- We are actively addicted to substances (drugs, alcohol) or behaviors (sex, gambling, work, etc.).
- We are miserable and don't know why.
- We depend on pornography to relieve our boredom and loneliness.
- Our schedule does not allow us the time to invest in a relationship.
- Deep down, we hate and distrust the sex to which we are attracted.
- We believe the right relationship will save us.

This list is not exhaustive, but we get the point, don't we? The right mindset is crucial to beginning a relationship on the right foot and giving it the best chance to thrive and succeed.

The reverse list looks like this. Read through this carefully and notice the readiness of this person for relationship:

- We are single.

- We have let go of and forgiven previous lovers.
- We are not holding on to a record of wrongs committed against us and have sought therapy or counseling to help us process and learn from them.
- We know how to be alone without becoming despondent and depressed. (It's possible.)
- Our life works well (not perfectly) financially, professionally, relationally, and logistically.
- We are independent, financially stable, and wholly responsible for our obligations.
- We are in recovery if we are or have been addicted to substances or behaviors.
- Generally speaking, we love our life and the direction in which it's headed.
- We soothe difficult emotions in healthy ways (exercise, friendship, spirituality, self-work, therapy, 12-step programs, yoga, etc.).
- We have the time, energy, and desire to give a relationship the investment that it needs to thrive.
- We do not harbor feelings of hatred or distrust for others, even though specific people may have harmed us in significant ways. We have worked through that harm, forgiven them, and our heart is open and able to trust, in general.
- We are proud of the life we are building and have built.

Let's look at that last statement a little more closely. This is an important element in our mindset and an essential foundation for our relationship toolbox! A healthy sense of self-pride. This should not be confused with arrogance. Arrogance stems from a desire to be separate from and above others. Healthy pride is an outward glow and radiance as a result of realized inner intent. We have set goals, accomplished some dreams, and our faces show it. Arrogance about our lives places us alone on an island of self-congratulatory smugness. Healthy pride places us in community with imperfect people who are celebrating one another's victories and accomplishments in spite of odds and obstacles. When we are building a life we truly love, we come to relationship with a sense of security, confidence, and a healthy wholeness within us. We are not asking another person to complete or save us. We are inviting another person to share the experience of a life we already love, a life *worth* sharing with someone else.

Let's be honest with ourselves. Do we *love* the life we've built? For where we are developmentally – age and maturity – is our life one that we can show to another with pride? If not, which areas do we wish we could hide? Which areas need work? Which areas bring us the most joy? We don't have to have every category of life in perfect condition to have a healthy relationship, no one does, but we do need to know what we want and be working toward that with intention and energy. Living in complacent misery, habitual chaos, or unaddressed frustration will only filter down into our relationship.

Our relationship mindset is *our* responsibility, *our* work. The quality of life we have attained is going to play a large part in the peace or conflict the relationship experiences. Our inner peace is our outer peace, and our inner conflicts become our outer conflicts. The investment of time and energy we have made in ourselves will be mirrored in our relationships. It starts with us. This is why the right mindset is crucial.

Do you want a healthy relationship? Be a healthy individual.

It is essential for us to be moving in a healthy direction with momentum for us to feel a healthy sense of pride. It's not about a finished product. We are all works in progress.

It's about the motivation with which we are pursuing a healthy, satisfying life. The right mindset means we are (1) realistic and (2) willing to accept full responsibility for ourselves. A good place to start is with an honest self inventory.

- How are my relationships?
- How are my finances?
- Do I like my living situation?
- How is my career going?
- How is my physical health?
- How is my mental health?
- How is my emotional health?

(A more thorough self-inventory can be found in Appendix A.)

These questions are not the basis on which we can or should form judgments about ourselves or others. These are some of the categories of life that we all need to address periodically and make choices to change, maintain, or improve. When we take full responsibility for our life, even if a category of life is in a terrible state, we can maintain our dignity and healthy self-pride if we are aware of it and are working on it. Maybe it's not a priority right now, but we're aware. We will get to it, depending on how urgent it is. Our worst enemy is denial. Denial is the intentional or unintentional act of *not seeing*. We must look at our lives honestly if we are going to be ready, willing, and able to have an honest relationship. This inventory is an important tool for self-awareness, which we'll cover in a later chapter, but it can be useful whether we are looking for a relationship, in a relationship, or intentionally single.

To look at ourselves with courage and compassion, to stare down the shame and disappointment we feel because parts of our life are not where we want them to be… this is real courage – the guts to face ourselves. Just that exercise in courage alone will promote a humility and confidence in us that will form the foundation for a healthy sense of pride. These are the brave and vulnerable parts of the self that we bring to another in intimate relationship. Not the polished "I have it all together" lie, but the *real* journey.

"KNOW THYSELF"

Socrates' ancient dictate is the best advice for a healthy relationship.

"Wait! Isn't it more important to know my partner?"

No.

The process of knowing ourselves requires time, patience, curiosity, and compassion. Wouldn't it be lovely to bring those qualities to our partner? First, we must bring them to ourselves. We cannot give what we do not have. We must come to our relationships – whether they are new or established – with a working knowledge of who we are as people. We will not know what we feel, need, or want if we do not know ourselves. We are then placing our partners in the impossible position of an archer in the dark. We leave the hard work to them: *you must learn who I am and then meet my needs. Hit the mark!* Friends, it is far more mature and frankly more efficient if we take the time to learn ourselves first. We need to know our feelings, wants, needs, blocks, healthy tools, unhealthy tools, and patterns. Conflict is smoother and less dramatic when two people have done the hard work of self-knowing. Why? There is far less blame.

We will know our strengths and weaknesses, so we will know what we are bringing to another person. To have a healthy relationship, *we need to be aware of both.* This kind of awareness does not lead us to platitudes like "no one is perfect" or "I guess I'm just a regular guy."

We will know ourselves more specifically. The right mindset is a self-informed mind. It might sound like this:

"I am naturally warm, loving, and nurturing Sometimes I miss boundaries that I need to set, and I can become resentful and aggressive as a result. I'm working on that by really going slowly in relationship so I know I'm taking care of myself in healthy ways as we go."

"I'm very strong-minded, so I usually have a gut sense of what the best course of action will be. That's been great for me professionally, but sometimes in relationship, I can tend to be too harsh and demanding, so I work on that by asking my partner what he thinks before I fly ahead making decisions for both of us."

"I made a series of really impulsive financial decisions after my divorce, and I got myself into some pretty stupid debt. It took me about a year to come to my senses, but I'm in the process of cleaning all that up, so I'll need to lay off expensive outings for a while."

This kind of self-awareness says:
- I've looked at myself.
- I see my strengths, and I can see my flaws too.
- I don't chase perfection; I've dealt with that shame.
- I don't hide or lie.

When we have a healthy humility and a healthy pride about our life, it'll drastically change the energy we bring to our relationships. Instead of insecure and defensive energy that wants to impress at the expense of authenticity, we'll be able to bring someone into our world – with all of its beauty and flaws – with *peace*.

Recall that quintessential scene that appears and reappears in so many movies featuring a bachelor or bachelorette. Someone unexpectedly comes to the door and the surprised bachelor races around, hurriedly throwing clothes into a hamper, a pizza box from last week is shoved under the sofa, empty beer cans and cereal boxes are scraped off the kitchen island in one fell swoop into an already overflowing garbage can, all this while the patient and likely horrified guest simply stands in the doorway, watching their panicked date attempt to create a façade right before their very eyes. This is what happens in relationship when our lives are not in order. Someone arrives at the "door" of our life, and we launch ourselves into Operation Impress and Deceive, which often includes spending too much money on things we don't really care about to give this stranger to whom we feel some hopeful connection an illusion that we are who they want.

We must stop doing this. Let's get our lives in order. If we have previously enlisted ourselves in Operation Impress and Deceive and we feel like a new relationship means we have to launch into that panicked frenzy once again to (mis)represent ourselves favorably, let's take an inventory instead. When someone arrives at the door of our "home," which is our life, we should be able to open the door with ease, joy, and self-acceptance. Our "home" isn't perfect, but it's ours, and we can take pride in it.

• • •

Doug and Patty needed a new mindset. They needed to grasp that their struggles were actually a natural part of relational growth. Much of what created the despair they were feeling was the belief that their love was somehow tainted or flawed because of their emerging differences. As therapy progressed and they were able to find mutually satisfying and sustainable places of connection once again, they realized that disconnections, conflicts, and disagreements are simply par for the course.

"I think I've been unfair to you," Doug offered after several months of work. "I assumed you'd always see our world my way, which means it wasn't our world. It was *my* world. I think I have blamed you for being you."

"You did," Patty said with a laugh, "but I allowed it. I think I was afraid of our differences too. We didn't know how to broach them so we ignored them. I'm not as scared of disagreeing with you anymore."

Instead of judging the health of their relationship by the level of agreement, they started to view it through a lens of authenticity and acceptance. With this shift in expectations and a new definition of "healthy," the couple breathed a sigh of relief. Realizing that it's normal and even healthy to hit the inevitable bumps in the road and having the tools to navigate them made a huge difference in their levels of stress.

The habitual focus on the other and doubting their compatibility shifted to a healthy focus on the self: am I engaging this relationship in the healthiest way I know? How am I growing?

This is the Right Mindset.

TOOL TIPS:
THE RIGHT
MINDSET

- The dopamine, the "emotional high" of being in love, eventually wears off.
- Having doubts about our relationship is normal. It doesn't mean the relationship is not healthy, nor does it mean we are not compatible.
- A fantasy relationship never requires us to change and grow; real love does.
- We work on our relationship from the presumption of good intent. This means we assume our partner's intentions toward us and the relationship are good.
- We must be single, open, and willing to be ready for a romantic relationship.
- We accept total and complete responsibility for our actions in relationship. Whatever we do is our choice. We agree not to blame anyone else for our actions.
- We periodically take inventory and practice self-care. Our happiness is not our partner's job.

QUESTIONS
FOR
DISCUSSION

1. What are my strengths and weaknesses relationally?

2. Have I taken a personal inventory? How do I feel about doing this?

3. How do I want my partner to see me? How do I see myself? Are there discrepancies between how I want to be seen and how I see myself?

4. Have I engaged in Operation Impress and Deceive? Are there secrets? Have I ever used deception in my relationship(s) to appear more attractive, desirable, or competent?

5. What modalities for increasing my self-knowledge (therapy, meditation, reading/study, intentional solitude, certain religious practices) am I willing to employ? Which works best for me?

CHAPTER 2

Listening

Consuelo and Charles had put in the time. Twenty-three years of marriage and five children had forged a bond of shared history and responsibility, and yet here they sat, on the edge of ending it all. Consuelo was "done," and Charles was "baffled" that she felt that way. As she detailed the excruciating course of their relationship's demise, he sat in quiet, angry silence, tolerating her diatribe.

"He doesn't see me. He doesn't care." Her emphases pointed to the depth and length of emotional pain she'd been in.

Predictably, he countered. "What do you mean I don't see you? I see you every day! I've seen you in every situation of life! I cannot understand how you can say that!"

"Consuelo," I interrupted gently, "what do you feel Charles is not seeing in you?"

"Everything!" she erupted into tears.

Charles and I were silent as she cried. I held space for her feelings, and Charles seemed once again baffled. He neither understood her nor had a clue as to how to address her pain.

Slowly, in a voice quivering with the constrained

effort required to hold back a torrent of tears, she began to describe a marriage of strong commitment and weak connection.

"Charles, what are you hearing Consuelo say?"

"She's not happy with me. Nothing I do is enough," he muttered. "I've heard it a thousand times."

"I understand that is what you think you are hearing, but what did she say? Can you relay back to us what you actually heard?"

Charles stared at me for a long moment.

"What are you talking about?" he asked through confusion and frustration.

"I'm wondering if you heard Consuelo. She's said quite a few things just now, some of them very intimate and painful, and I know we tend to hear what others say through the filter of our own perceptions and feelings, but I'm wondering if you can repeat back what you actually heard her say."

He couldn't.

"Consuelo, what does Charles say to you about his discontentment in your marriage? What have you heard?"

"I'm a failure as a wife! He can't take the time to listen to a thing I say!"

"I never said that!" Charles roared.

I moved quickly to tame the explosion before we were all scorched. Tension was sky high, hurt was ignited, and anger was covering the scene like lava.

"Okay, okay, Folks... You have something in common from what I can see."

They both grew quiet.

"No one feels heard. You are both hearing messages

but apparently not what the other is communicating. I think we need to slow things down and work on simple listening. After all, we cannot resolve an issue if we don't understand the nature of it. Listening is where we start learning what the actual issues are."

Once again, quiet filled the room. Consuelo had assumed she was a better listener than Charles, but our little office experiment had proven otherwise. Both partners realized that day that they were making more assumptions about the meaning of the other – based on their own emotional state – than they were effectively understanding the other's position and perspective.

Our second tool is Listening.

• • •

A LEGITIMATE SHORT CUT

Listening is the most underrated tool in our relationship toolbox. Without listening, we are driving blind. Without listening, we are shooting in the dark. Without listening, we just opened a large box containing all the parts to a complex piece of furniture, and the assembly directions are missing. Good luck! We might be able to figure it out, but we're going to waste a *lot* of time.

Listening gives us a multidimensional lens into another's inner world. We don't need to follow our loved ones around, noticing their facial expressions, monitoring their habits and rituals, watching for patterns and exceptions, then deducing "what can this say about them?" We can simply *listen* to them.

Few actions convey love, respect, and dignity like truly listening to another human being. By listening, we communicate with our attention that another's words – the audible expression of their inner thoughts and feelings – have value. Consequently, this conveys that *they* have value as their external expression is a mirror of the internal self. When we listen, it is as if we are saying, "I am attuned to you and paying attention to you because what you think, say, feel, and know matters to me." The more intimate the relationship, the more intimate the disclosures, the more precious the listening.

Likewise, few actions can be as damaging and invalidating as failing to listen to our partner, yet so many of us struggle with the intentional application of this skill. In our world, multitasking is the norm. We lightly grasp what another person is saying, and we think it's enough. We tune out, distracted by the many thoughts and worries running through our minds, and we nod affirmatively while our partner talks, but if asked, we cannot tell you what they said. We perceive deeper disclosures as unnecessary, "heavy," or "too serious," and we keep things "light" and "easy" because we cannot sit with genuine human experience long enough to dignify its complexity by listening to it.

We rob our relationships of the simple and soulful bond that comes from two people engaged in meaningful, honest conversation. We grow bored with one another, not because we are boring but because we have stopped listening. We have a shallow understanding of another's position, and instead of drawing out the deeper layers, we settle for knowing nothing but the top soil of our lover. We want the emotional bond, the security, and the satisfaction associated with deep knowing. We want passionate, connected, mind-blowing sex, but we don't listen – really listen - to how their day went. It ain't gonna happen.

TALK IS CHEAP

Some of us will say, "I don't need to listen. I can see everything I need to know about another person by the choices they make." We lean on the aphorism that "actions speak louder than words." We trust sayings like "walk the talk" and "I'll believe what you do, not what you say." These adages have merit. Indeed, our words can bind others to us in honor and trust or they can break the very same bonds into fragments of distrust, skepticism, and downright dismissal when we fail to fulfill our words with our actions. While we can learn much about another person by the choices they make, we cannot deduce or know the deep truth of another person's heart by their actions alone. For example, the successful executive has us all fooled. We think she's satisfied because she "has it all," and we do not hear about her shame and sexual frigidity. We assume the energetic father of four is glorying in fatherhood, but he is secretly feeling crushed by the weight of responsibility. How many times have we tragically heard of a suicide by someone who "just seemed so happy?" Our outer lives tell part of the story, but they do not tell the whole story. When our relationships are rocky, we likely aren't being heard or *feeling* heard.

In couples counseling sessions, it is almost always pointless to spend time and energy making promises of how we are going to do this or that differently. While behavioral changes are needed, they will not be made through declarations of intent or the force of the will. These promises arise from fear, anger, or shame. We don't want to lose the relationship, so we make frantic promises to change! We do our best to follow through, we try hard to change our behaviors, and then we generally slide back into our previous habits sooner or later. Instead, we need to strengthen the bond and let new actions flow from deeper connection. Promising better behavior seems like a reasonable solution, but it rarely pans out.

Listening strengthens our bond.

How?

Listening is a choice to value another person. It is a loving action of the will to attune to another human being and take in who they are through the words they speak. It is not surprising to see couples breathe new air into their relationship after a session of simple, basic listening! Nothing says, "I see you, I respect you, I value you" like calmly, openly, willingly listening to our partner. When we feel heard, our bodies relax, our minds open, and our hearts feel a natural swell of gratitude. We innately deserve to be heard, and when we receive what our hearts need, we naturally connect to the giver. (Many emotional and sexual affairs begin with someone finally listening!)

When we are listening, we are conscious, present, and attuned. When we are talking, and another is attentively listening to us, we are more mindful of our words and the impact they might have. Many arguments, unnecessary escalations, and hurtful words are spoken in relationships where listening is weak or nonexistent. We feel we must speak more loudly or more strongly to get our point across. Gentle, effective language is replaced with words that cut, sting, or shock – all meant to get the attention of our partner. Listening is a wake-up call. The listener wakes up to the potential listening has: we have the power to connect, value, dignify, empower, and respect our partner. We have the ability to create feelings of closeness, trust, and connection, simply by listening well. If we are speaking, we realize the power of our words. We realize that our partner is truly listening, and therefore we must meet their attunement with careful, constructive, honest communication on our end. When one person decides to really listen, the energy in the relationship shifts.

"CHILDREN SHOULD BE SEEN AND NOT HEARD"

We hope this idiotic and harmful piece of garbage advice has run its course, don't we? We are living in a new era where child-rearing is concerned. The zeitgeist has evolved from the devaluation of the childhood years, marked by the abject dismissal of children's relational rights and wisdom, to an era where children are heard and valued on new and far more healthy levels. We are paying close and loving attention to them. We are finally listening. When parents listen to children, they communicate the same relational realities as adults do in adult relationships. When a child feels heard, he/she feels valued, dignified, and respected for who they are because their inner world – expressed in words – is being received. When parents tell their children over and over again that they have value, that they have worth, that they should be confident, but they do not *listen* to them, the child does not internalize the words. They internalize the actions. Why? Because actions convey value, not words. No child will know their worth if their parents do not value them enough to actually listen to them.

Were we heard as children?

The experience we had with listening during childhood will strongly affect how we listen and speak to one another as adults. If we had parents who took the time to sit with us, face us, absorb our words, and grasp our meaning, we will know the relaxing, affirming experience of being heard *in our bodies*, in our very nervous systems. If our parents taught us to listen by training us to sit still, make eye contact, and pay attention, both listening and speaking with intention will come more naturally to us. Conversely, if we were not heard as children, we may find it difficult to stop what we are doing, open our hearts and minds to our partners, and allow their words to reach us. And if we were not taught to listen with patience and attention, we may find it difficult to give another that kind of patience and attention now.

If we did not have parents who listened to us as children and conveyed our value and their love for us by taking us seriously enough to listen to us, we may have learned to withdraw or grandstand. We might find that this is our pattern in adult relationships. Perhaps we've chosen a partner with whom we replay the same dynamic that was present in our childhood. (This is almost always the case.)

If we are in a withdrawing pattern, we are accustomed to not being heard, so we don't press it. We live two lives – the outer person is agreeable, easy-going, and doesn't make too many demands. The inner person may be anxious, lonely, furious, exceedingly creative, or all of the above. We figure we aren't going to be heard anyway, so we let it go, whatever it is we want or need to express. While our relationship may appear peaceful, it is disconnected. We are still in our childhood pattern of devaluing our own voice because it was devalued for us. We develop the adult behavior (survival tool) of shutting down. We don't know how to self-assert because our parents didn't teach us how. We were allowed to be excessively quiet and complacent. We didn't ever argue our position or will, and no one asked us about it. No argument equaled a good child. We equate having our voice with disconnection.

Perhaps we aren't so complacent. Perhaps we didn't feel heard and developed a loud, aggressive personality as a result. "You're going to hear me, damn it!" is our way of functioning in the world. Our relationships might feel turbulent and intense as a result. The wound of childhood is still looming large and foreboding, and we are trying with all our might to recapture the connection we desired with our parents through volume and force. We can be overbearing. We can be too direct, too harsh, brutally honest, afraid that if we don't pound our words out, like driving a nail with a hammer, we will not be heard. We never experienced the power of gentleness expressed through patient listening. We see gentle communication as ineffective or even weak. We need to say it, say it now, say it clearly, and let the chips fall where they may. Listening to us, in our adult relationships, can be a painful experience for the listener. Instead of the natural flow of conversation, our partner may be half-listening out of self-protection in case our words become too harsh. Or maybe we create a home environment that is desensitized to loud, aggressive communication. Both are problematic.

Some of us weren't heard as children and became human radios. No matter where the dial is tuned, sound is emerging. Communication is a numbers game: the more words spoken, the greater the chance that something will seep in. We lack intention and direction with our words. We do not take a breath, we do not stop to check in with our listener, we just talk and talk and talk. And yet, we say so little. Underneath this compulsive behavior is the fear that what we have to say doesn't really matter so we have never learned to choose our words with care. We ramble instead. We hope, like a child learning to speak, that our lover will actually be able to glean what we are saying through our babble. The listener in this dynamic can feel exhausted and overwhelmed. They might tune us out, and the pattern that arose from feeling unheard is reinforced.

We need to check in on this relational skill, going back to our childhood. Understanding our history with listening and being heard will give us insight into how we do this as an adult. Children who are taught their value by being heard grow into adults who are proficient listeners.

But whether or not this was learned in childhood, it can and must be learned now.

LISTENING IN ACTION

Not all words or disclosures require the same type of listening. Like all skills, the application of it depends on the need at hand. Let's talk about two different kinds of listening: **light listening** and **deep listening**.

LIGHT LISTENING

Light Listening is for hearing and ingesting information that is not particularly emotional. It may be logistical and/or impersonal. For example, our spouse tells us that our daughter needs to be picked up at 5:00 PM after basketball practice. This information can be acquired and ingested in a variety of contexts. It might be shared while we're doing something else, which we refer to as multi-tasking. With Light Listening, we don't need to be listening in a way that respects the depth and/or sensitivity of the disclosure because there is little to none. In Light Listening, there may be no eye-contact, touching, verbal/nonverbal communication of support, or deep comprehension. When we are Light Listening, it's about information not intimacy.

"Can you grab an extra package of hamburger buns at the grocery?"

"The car needs gas."

"The party starts at seven."

Are these important disclosures? Yes, they are. This is information we share to keep our relationship connected in everyday life. Seemingly mundane disclosures are actually very important pieces of information that keep us knowledgeable and cooperative about what we need to bring to our shared responsibilities and activities, day by day. Without these bits of information, we lose a sense of togetherness.

The appropriate responses to Light Listening are communications of comprehension.

"Extra hamburger buns, got it!" on our way out the door.

"I'll put gas in the car after breakfast," while putting on our shoes.

"Ok, let's plan to leave at 6:30," we call out from the shower.

These responses convey the receipt of information, not necessarily participation in intimacy. They may be said facing one another or not, but a response is necessary.

DEEP LISTENING

Deep Listening is required when the disclosure is emotional, personal, vulnerable, or urgent. For example, our partner begins to share the details of a conversation with his boss that's left him feeling miserable. This is a deeper disclosure. This requires a different set of responses than Light Listening does. Deep Listening requires that we stop what we're doing and turn toward our partner. This is essential! Eye contact and turning toward our partner communicate that we are emotionally available, invested, paying attention, and that the information being shared is worthy of our time and energy. Deep Listening is not just about information, it is about comprehension first, then support, care, comfort, and empathy. It fosters connection. Deep Listening may not require solutions unless they are solicited. Often, Deep Listening is the solution.

"But I can't always stop what I'm doing to face my partner and listen..."

Of course we can't. If we cannot stop what we're doing in a moment when Deep Listening is required, *we do not try and offer Light Listening instead.* To do this is to insult the importance of the disclosure. Instead, we acknowledge both the depth of the disclosure and the limitation we currently have by saying, "What you are saying right now is important to me, but I can't stop what I'm doing to listen face-to-face. Are you okay if I listen while I do this, or should we circle back later?" If the speaker is comfortable with us multitasking, we continue on, glancing up from time to time to check in with their facial expressions and make eye-contact. If they are not comfortable and would like our undivided attention, we give a specific time frame to circle back. We might suggest, "Can we talk about this after the kids are in bed?" This communicates volumes! It says we are attuned, we are aware, and we are available.

Here we have the Three A's of Deep Listening:
- **Attuned**
- **Aware**
- **Available**

We demonstrate that we are **attuned** through eye contact, turning our shoulders to the other, and slowing our breathing. We demonstrate that we are **aware** through our reactions to our partner's disclosures. Our facial expressions and the emotions they convey are important. We allow ourselves to register what our partner is saying and let our nonverbal responses communicate our comprehension, concern, and love for them. We are **available** by putting down our phones, turning off the television, closing the laptop, or shutting the book we were reading. We are removing every distraction and offering our presence to our partner.

When we are Deep Listening, we are not only taking in the information, but we are learning how the events have impacted our partner. This is not about logistical information. This is about *subjective experience*. This is why solutions are often useless. The logistical facts are not the issue; the emotional experience is, and emotional experiences don't need to be fixed, they need to be *heard* and *validated* (Chapter 4).

To know which type of listening is appropriate, we ask:
- What is the nature of the disclosure?
- Is it logistical or personal?
- Is my partner emotionally neutral or activated?
- Is the information of an urgent nature? Are the stakes high?

Many hurts arise when we make the mistake of offering Light Listening when Deep Listening is needed. This communicates a kind of insensitivity and lack of attunement. We need to learn when to stop and turn toward our partner or when we can receive the information on the go. Different information requires different levels of attention. We need to know the importance of our eye contact. Our eyes are the windows to our soul, and when we offer our eyes to another person, we are offering access to our very soul.

DON'T PLAY RELATIONAL TENNIS

The game of tennis involves a ball crossing over a

net, again and again. The crowd seated at the center of the court gets the best view and the most rigorous neck workout. Their heads go back and forth, hour after hour. We follow the ball, and it never stays put until the match is over. We can play the same game in our relationships. We volley our emotions and accusations back and forth, from one to another, for hours, days, *years*, and nothing lands, nothing sticks.

"You said you were going to invite them."

"Well YOU said you'd remind me..."

"I DID, but YOU don't check your text messages!"

"I DO check my texts!"

On and on we go... back and forth, no one is listening, no one stops to really hear the other, and the tension never diffuses. While this kind of volleying makes for an exciting tennis match, Relational Tennis means we have a problem with listening. And it's exhausting.

Most of us are moderate to adequate listeners when the information is neutral to us. We can hear tale after tale about friends, coworkers, ailments, traffic jams, and shared activities and events, but when the disclosure gets personal – when it's about *us* – our ability to listen goes out the window, and yet this is when it's most important.

This is where the practice of listening becomes a skill.

When our partner needs to express painful or intimate feelings about the relationship, it is time for Deep Listening. What they are giving us is solid gold! They are giving us information about how certain aspects of the relationship are affecting them. They are telling us how they are experiencing the interactions we are having. Why would we resist this information? Because we might interpret this type of disclosure as a complaint, accusation, or declaration that we have failed. To "listen" with this lens is to strip our partner of their right to have their own experience of the relationship. We are making a dangerous assumption when we assume that our experience will be their experience, that our intentions will always translate into reality. We cannot and need not assume that our efforts are meeting their needs perfectly. This is a different human being with different DNA, a different personality, history, experience, and perspective. Rather than receiving relational disclosures with defensiveness and apprehension, we can invite the disclosures with curiosity and confidence. A disclosure of unpleasant emotions doesn't mean we are failing. It simply means our partner is experiencing some unpleasant emotions in the relationship. We need to know what they are, why they are happening, and what our partner wants or needs. All of this requires Deep Listening.

And a secure ego.

When we are insecure and our ego is driving the bus, we have very low tolerance for any kind of relational discomfort in our partner. We will view these disclosures as attacks, and we will go on the defensive. This means we aren't listening; we are formulating arguments in our heads while our partner speaks. This is Relational Tennis.

"I feel anger at how you acted toward my friends..."

"I can't believe you're mad at me! They were rude and obnoxious!"

"You aren't listening to me!"

"I am listening, and what you're saying isn't making sense!"

"You're not hearing a word I'm saying!"

"I HEARD YOU!"

Back and forth, the ball goes over the net again and again. Nothing lands. It's just a volleying of the ego, back and forth.

In order to prevent Relational Tennis, we must be mature and self-controlled. When we feel defensive words formulating in our minds and tension rising in our chests, we breathe... and we return to eye contact and *listening*. This is difficult at first and slowly becomes easier as we practice. If we are so emotionally activated that we can no longer listen with attunement, awareness, and availability, we communicate this, we step away to give our nervous system time to reset, and we return to the conversation when we are able to give the Three A's once again: Attunement, Awareness, and Availability. The more we breathe and return to listening, the more skilled we become, and the less we need to take breaks to calm ourselves. Once one person has been heard and *feels* heard, then it's the other's turn to communicate, and the speaker now takes on the role of the listener. We don't shift our position until the one speaking has been heard.

If we "listen" in conflict with the goal of hearing the flaws and holes in our partner's position, we are listening with the wrong aim. The goal of listening is not to point out the other's flaws and win the competition. A relationship is not a debate or a tennis match. The goals of listening are understanding and connection.

If we think we have listened in a conversation, we need to ask, "Do you feel heard?" If the answer is yes, we respond to their disclosure with our own thoughts and feelings. If the answer is no, we begin again. We do not engage in Relational Tennis.

We hold ourselves accountable (Chapter 1) for offering:
  - **Attunement**
  - **Awareness**
  - **Availability**

If we think we are good listeners, we need to humbly ask the people with whom we are the most intimate and receive their response without argument. There is no need for shame or worry. This tool can be mastered.

When we lack the tool of listening, we are relying on assumptions and subjective deductions to inform our decisions in the relationship. This is at best lazy and at worst dehumanizing. To assume that our own perception of a person is the sum total of that person is to place ourselves in the role of a god. Human beings are wells of wisdom, complexity, contradiction, and surprise. To engage in relationship without listening is to strip down that glorious mystery into a manageable piece of machinery. This might give us a sense of control, but we are limiting our ability to experience the beauty of the other. This is like missing a sky full of stars for a single light bulb.

Listening is the telescope.

• • •

Charles and Consuelo turned out to be good listeners after all. Years of unresolved conflict and fear of loss had sped up their interactions to a point where the communication was rapid and misfiring. They had been engaged in Relational Tennis for so long that they'd forgotten the power of simply listening. When their attention was refocused on hearing one another and nothing else, a miraculous thing occurred: they chose their words more carefully, and they began to understand one another.

"I didn't realize you felt lonely," Charles admitted in a session one day. "I would never have assumed you felt lonely! We have five kids!" Charles was beginning to see how listening was correcting assumptions, assumptions that arose from his experience of their family, not hers.

"It's funny, Charles. I feel like I've been saying that for years, but with everything and everyone else swirling around us, maybe it was easy to miss that in the midst," Consuelo offered generously.

"Whatever the reason, I didn't hear you. No, I wasn't *listening*," he corrected himself.

Charles and Consuelo decided that the best course of action for them was to start their day with coffee together, every morning in the living room. They needed to implement boundaries with the children who would need to understand that this was Mom-and-Dad-Time and not to interrupt unless it was urgent. This gave Charles and Consuelo protected time to talk, to listen to one another, and to start their day in a connected place. The behavioral change arose out of a desire to nurture the bond they'd begun to experience in their therapy sessions. This was not a promise born out of desperation, fear, or resentful acquiescence but a change of course born out of a mutual desire to connect and remain connected.

Listening was the essential first step in this process of healing.

TOOL TIPS:
LISTENING

- Listening may be the most important tool.
- Listening conveys love, respect, and dignity. Feeling heard forms and strengthens the bond between people.
- Listening is active and intentional. It requires conscious energy and focus.
- When children feel heard, they develop self-worth.
- There are two types of listening: Light Listening and Deep Listening. Light listening is for logistical, humorous, and unserious disclosures. Deep Listening is for personal, vulnerable, and emotional disclosures.
- The Three A's of Deep Listening are: Attuned, Aware, Available.
- Deep Listening is especially important when the disclosures are about the relationship itself.
- The goals of listening are understanding and connection.

QUESTIONS
FOR
DISCUSSION

1. Did my parents listen to me when I was a child? Did I get the sense that my thoughts and feelings were welcome? Was one parent a better listener than the other?

2. If I did not feel heard as a child, what did I do when my words fell on deaf ears? Am I still doing this?

3. Do I consider myself to be a good listener? (Hint: you do not often feel anxious or bored when others share their thoughts and feelings with you.) How will I know if I'm improving?

4. How do I feel about personal, deep, or vulnerable disclosures? Am I comfortable? Uncomfortable? Why?

5. What can I work on in order to become a better listener? How will I know I have?

CHAPTER 3

Emotional Expression

Scott came to therapy because his partner, Patrick, gave him an ultimatum. Their relationship had been on the edge of ending for many years, waxing and waning between a mediocre acceptance of their shared unhappiness and periodic outbursts of absolute misery. Patrick had wracked his brain, trying to figure out what was wrong with Scott, but eventually admitted to himself that trying to diagnose his partner wasn't improving anything. He contacted me for an "official" diagnosis, prepared with his best armchair therapist guesses as to the cause of Scott's inability to connect with him or their children on a meaningful level. Was it Asperger's syndrome, severe narcissism, or perhaps even sociopathy? I listened with acute interest and a bit of fear. *A sociopath? Who would be entering my office?* Patrick described outbursts of anger and severe impatience with the kids. He described feeling afraid of Scott's temper and avoiding conflict at all costs. Patrick had attended a lecture I'd given on emotional health and asked me with his last shred of hope and not a little desperation: would I please see Scott? Sure, I'd see him. My curiosity drowned any fear I had.

When Scott arrived for his first session, he carried

himself with the impatient, skeptical energy of a man who doesn't have time to waste. A successful executive in the finance industry, he had learned to ascertain within minutes if someone was worth his time, and this was no different. He was polite. Formal. Observing. Scott was a self-made man in every sense of the word. Raised in a working-class section of St. Louis with little resources at his disposal, he had worked hard in school, earned a scholarship to college, graduated with honors, and put himself through graduate school to earn his MBA. Success came easily as character traits learned in childhood functioned well in his career: keep your head down, make friends easily, don't let anyone see you sweat, and always stay ahead of the curve. He was well-liked and well-respected by his colleagues. Even though work was filled with stress and pressure, the outcome was worth the toil and the toll. Scott was very successful and had been promoted many times. He liked the pressure; it brought out the best in him. At home, however, the stress and pressure of his relationship were just as unrelenting, but there never seemed to be a payoff. He tried just as hard at home as he did at the office but never felt like he was gaining ground. The personality traits that worked at the office didn't work at home. He fluctuated between exasperation and confusion.

Scott initially described his childhood as idyllic. School years were normal and predictable with a healthy peppering of boyish pranks and stunts. Summers were spent at his grandparents' beach house on the Outer Banks. He had a special, nourishing relationship with his grandfather and I could see the warmth and nostalgia come over him as he described his "Pop." He adored his little brother and enjoyed a close and satisfying relationship with him into their adult years. Mom was depicted as a loving and affectionate woman who had believed in him every step of the way.

I kept exploring and listening. Something wasn't adding up. There must have been a dynamic or patterned situation that had habituated Scott's anger as a first line of defense. As his trust in me began to develop over time, he opened up about his mother a bit more…

"She was *always* there for me," Scott emphasized.

"And where was Dad?" Scott explained that they had divorced before he could remember, and he grew up without knowing his father.

"Did she remarry?"

"Oh yes. Several times."

"How did you feel about the men she married?"

Scott grew quiet and turned his gaze to the window. I'd hit a nerve, and silence filled the room until he was ready to speak again. Over the next few sessions, Scott told me more about his childhood. His mother had raised him and his little brother with a gentle touch in her right hand and a cup of beer in the left. Neither ever went dry. She wasn't an "angry drunk," and he never felt afraid of her, but she was not emotionally present either. She never outright abused him, but her emotional absence created a chronic state of neglect that left Scott with a deep fear that his emotional needs would not be met. She believed in Scott, and his success was her crowning glory. Unable to feel satisfied and proud of her own life and choices, Scott donned the mantle of the family hero. He accepted pressure as an obligation. He became everything a mother would want in a son: successful, married, stable, a father, a community pillar. The more we dug into his story, the more we uncovered his deep resentment toward his mother for her alcoholism and disastrous choices in mates. The men his mother chose were usually heavy drinkers themselves, sometimes violent, and often jealous of him. Throughout his childhood, Scott moved as many times as his mother remarried, and he resented her for that too. His own children had been raised in one house as a result. Scott wouldn't do to them what was done to him. He recounted a memory of mom driving him and his little brother drunk when the car drifted into the opposite lane, into oncoming traffic. Scott had grabbed the wheel and veered them away from probable death. He told me about laying in his bed, listening to violent dramas playing out in the living room between his mother and her lovers. He recalled desperately trying to protect his little brother from the reckless, unpredictable choices his mother made. We explored the changes to his personality as he started new school after new school, trying to build a social life then being uprooted again. The resentment ran as deep as his memory could recall.

When I asked Scott what he remembering feeling in the moment when all of these memories took place, the answer was consistent: nothing. He didn't feel anything. When I asked how he felt as an adult in his marriage, it was always some version of anger – frustrated, exasperated, annoyed. It would be some time before Scott knew that he felt anything else.

Our third tool is Emotional Expression.

• • •

WHAT ARE YOU FEELING?

People seek therapy because they are unhappy. We are experiencing unpleasant emotions (fear, shame, anger, despair, tension, etc.) more often than the pleasant ones (hope, joy, relaxation, satisfaction, etc.), and we want to change this pattern. If we cannot describe what we are feeling, the therapist has a difficult road ahead because there is no language to communicate experience. This is like going to a doctor and not knowing the parts of the body or how to describe pain.

"Doctor, it hurts."

"What hurts?"

"It hurts."

"Where does it hurt?"

"It hurts."

"Can you describe the pain?"

"It just hurts."

Without an emotional vocabulary, therapy can sound similar.

"I'm just not right."

"What are you feeling?"

"I don't know, I just know I haven't been happy for a long time."

"Well, if you're not happy, do you know what you are feeling?"

"No. I don't know."

Emotions are sneaky, powerful things if we are not aware of them. They come on strong, overtake the whole body, and yet we often don't even register what is happening inside. If we are unaware of what we feel, we simply *react*, we don't *respond*. Unconscious reactions (meaning we did not consciously choose our behavior) serve one purpose: to alleviate the pain of emotional distress. This is similar to the body creating a fever to eliminate a pathogen. Our goal is to eliminate the pain.

Perhaps we rage in anger. This reaction may serve to dispel the intense energy of anger, but it is not a healthy relational response. The receiver of this rage will not trust us.

Perhaps we shut down in fear. This keeps us safe, like an animal freezing in camouflaged terror when a predator appears, but it will not bring us any closer to another human being. We cannot create safety in a relationship until we admit to ourselves and another that we are afraid.

Perhaps we hide behind work when we feel shame. This may give us the illusion of being busy, important, or helpful, but we have not come face to face with our own feelings of inadequacy. The shame remains.

As long as we remain unaware of our emotions – we do not consciously feel them or name them - we will react unconsciously. Emotional unawareness creates relational chaos. Both partners are hurt, distrustful, and distant, and neither can describe what they feel. Often, when a couple is in this state, they simply blame one another.

More often than not, when we begin therapeutic work, our emotional vocabulary is weak or nonexistent. One of the first tasks of a therapist is to help people learn and name what they are feeling.

We learn the physical landscape of our bodies because we need to be able to communicate our needs. This is one of the first lessons that babies learn: where are your eyes? Where are your lips? Point to your elbow. Point to your chin. We are delighted when Baby begins to know where her nose is, but this information is far more important than an infant's game. As children become verbal, parents rely on shared language to communicate with their child regarding his or her needs.

"Mommy, my tummy aches."

"Daddy, I cut my knee."

"Mommy, my arm is burning."

"Daddy, my neck itches."

When the pain is acknowledged and understood, the

remedy is administered. Children feel safe and loved when their physical pain is attended to. We learn many words for the various parts of the body, and we need them. If a parent doesn't know that their child's head is hurting and not their stomach, they won't know where to start.

We have many words to describe our physical pain: itching, stinging, throbbing, aching, burning, shooting, nagging, acute, dull, and so on. All of these words communicate specific information about the pain so that we get the care we need. As adults, we must learn to care for ourselves appropriately based on what we are feeling to the best of our ability. We will treat a bee sting differently than we will treat a throbbing headache. All of these words give expression and specification to our physical experience so that we can attend to ourselves and our loved ones appropriately.

But what about our inner inexperience – the realm of emotional pain and pleasure? How do we get the attention, care, comfort, and help we need when we have no words for our emotions?

Adults who seek therapy are generally unhappy when they begin the journey of inner work, and an important beginning task is to learn how to describe their feelings. A decent therapist can read the emotional state of a client through facial expression, body language, or intuition. We attend to the emotions present to the best of our ability, but a client will not grow or mature if they do not learn themselves. (And sometimes even the best therapists get it wrong!) In the beginning stages of therapy, the therapist is assisting the client with language for their inner experience.

"You seem sad today."

"You look like you have a lot on your mind."

"I sense your excitement; tell me about it."

"Based on what you've just told me, I imagine you might be feeling afraid."

Eventually, the self-awareness, thus the responsibility, shifts from the therapist to the client, and the session might begin with the client reporting their experience:

"I feel so ashamed."

"I'm filled with fear."

"I feel really content."

"I have a new feeling of hope."

Ultimately, our feelings are our responsibility and learning what we feel is part of being an emotionally healthy adult. Therapy, in many ways, is a circling back to childhood and learning as adults what we did not learn as children, and emotional awareness is a step that cannot be skipped. Just as someone who sees a doctor needs language to describe their physical experience, we need language to describe our emotional experience whether we're in a therapist's office or at the breakfast table with our partner. If we don't know what we feel emotionally, we will be unable to care for ourselves emotionally, express our needs, or effectively attend to others in emotional pain. This is the primary source of disconnection in relationship because emotions comprise the language of connection.

Think of emotions as the dashboard lights on a vehicle. We can't drive around knowing each and every detail of what's going on under the hood, so we rely on the dashboard to tell us if something needs our attention. When the tire pressure symbol lights up, we know we need air. When the engine light comes on, we know that something's is off with the engine. The symbol directs our attention to the part of the car that isn't functioning well. Likewise, our emotions "light up" in different scenarios to inform us about our inner world and how to attend to it.

Ignoring dashboard lights is not a good idea. Neither is ignoring emotions.

We are socialized to express some emotions with more ease than others. Women are generally allowed a broader range of emotional expression than men but not much. Most of us give ourselves permission to feel happy and content with short periods of more unpleasant emotions, like sadness or anger, but it's expected that those will be brief, and we'll return to contentment as soon as possible. This is an unrealistic expectation and has contributed to broken relationships and depressed and anxious people. Emotions are normal, and they will pass, but they must be felt. Instead of feeling safe to express and process our emotions like human beings, we suppress and consolidate them. This leads to an unhealthy emotional habit I call **bundling**.

Bundling is what we do with our emotions instead of expressing them individually and specifically. A man might feel disappointment, fear, worry, and sadness over a son who's not performing well in school, but instead of knowing these emotional states and attending to them appropriately, he'll "bundle" them as anger and go too hard on his son. A woman might feel a combination of anger, disgust, distance, and boredom in her marriage, and instead of parsing these emotions out and dealing with them appropriately, she'll "bundle" them as sadness. In order to avoid bundling and to mature into emotionally developed adults, we must learn to identify and express what we feel with skill and clarity.

THE SEVEN CORE EMOTIONS

When we pick up a new tool, we start with the basics. There are hundreds maybe thousands of words in the

English language to describe our emotional state, but there are seven core emotions from which the rest grow, like branches off a tree.

The seven core emotions are:
1. Anger
2. Sorrow
3. Gladness
4. Fear
5. Embarrassment
6. Hurt
7. Loneliness

---

1. ANGER

Anger is experienced on a spectrum from slight irritation, annoyance, feeling peeved, or vexed to feeling irate, livid, furious, or enraged. This emotional state is experienced in the body as muscle tension, clenching, an increase in body temperature and blood flow to the face. We may feel hot. It's an energetic emotion, and the impulse is generally to spring into action to diffuse it. We describe anger as "seeing red." It's strong, fast, and powerful. Because of this, anger is often the emotion we are experiencing when we respond quickly, without thought. It's uncomfortable, and because of this our goal is generally to diffuse it. Instead of waiting it out, which is an appropriate response to anger, we attempt to dispel it. This leads to a lot of hurt.

There are two kinds of anger: **clean anger** and **protective anger**.

Clean anger alerts us that a boundary has been crossed. It is a natural response to the experience of having our rights violated in some way. This can be as common as the right to be heard or as powerful as the right to protect our own bodies, as is the case in sexual abuse and physical assault. Clean anger signals that an injustice has occurred and is therefore healthy and functional. Without it, we would not be able to protect our rights and personal space.

Protective anger, on the other hand, is a form of bundling. Protective anger serves as a smoke screen for more vulnerable emotions like hurt, fear, sadness, abandonment, or jealousy. Instead of naming the underlying emotion, we show anger. This protects us, but it does not address the real emotions underneath. There is little to no connection possible with protective anger. We aren't getting to the truth of ourselves. Protective Anger may cause great harm to a relationship because the expression of the anger is often aggressive, and the recipient of this aggression does not know what is really going on. Protective anger is therefore confusing. Our partner responds to the aggression, but the underlying emotions go unaddressed, unheard, and disconnection persists.

NOTE: Anger is NOT necessarily dangerous and should not be confused or conflated with unhealthy aggression (not all aggression is unhealthy). Anger is a natural, functional response to injustice or violation. Healthy aggression is using force to protect or achieve. Unhealthy aggression is using force to exert control. Anger is simply an emotion that passes through us, albeit strong and potent. What we *do* with anger is a matter of maturity.

Because of its potency in the body, anger is one of the most difficult emotions to control in the moment.

2. SORROW

The spectrum ranges from bummed out, disappointed, and sad to grieving, mourning, despondent, or despairing. The emotional state of sadness is experienced in the body as a slowness, heaviness, and lethargy. Our energy is as low as our mood. We describe ourselves as feeling "blue." We feel like we are dragging ourselves forward. We cry. We feel as though a great weight has settled onto our shoulders. We often have a feeling of internal coldness.

The function of sadness is to inform us that we have lost something of value. Whether it is a house we have treasured and must sell or a beloved we have lost to death, sadness is how our heart honors what it loves. The process of walking through loss and the resulting sorrow is called **grief.** To ignore our sadness is to rob ourselves of a normal, healthy, albeit difficult human process of letting go. It is the slow and painful passage into the future in the wake of a loss. Grieving is how we come to terms with our losses, and it cannot be skipped or rushed. Small losses (your vacation was canceled) mean small grief. Big losses (death, divorce, job loss) mean big grief.

3. GLADNESS

The spectrum of gladness ranges from tickled, delighted, and happy to ecstatic, blissful, and euphoric. Gladness is experienced as a feeling of lightness, openness, expansiveness, safety, warmth, unity, and peace. We describe gladness as "walking on sunshine," having "a spring in our step," and being "on top of the world" because there is a sense of largeness and lightness experienced in gladness that we don't experience in other emotional states. We may use words like "heartwarming" or "sweet" to convey the inner sensation of warmth and delight. We say we want to "throw our arms around the world" to convey the sense of unity.

The function of gladness is to let us know our needs have been met or the goal of our efforts has been realized. It is the emotion that signals us to repeat the actions that met our needs. For example, after a workout, we feel a sense of pride and lightness. We do it again because we associate a pleasant feeling with the accomplishment. Our loved one surprises us with our favorite meal for dinner. Our gladness is an expression of gratitude and pleasure, and our loved one notices and shares our joy.

4. FEAR

Fear exists on a spectrum that ranges from mild concern, worry, apprehension, and trepidation to shock, horror, fright, and terror. This emotional state is experienced by a tightening of the neck and shoulders, the pupils dilate to allow more light, a shot of adrenaline, and an impulse to fight, flee, or freeze. We cannot think well in a state of fear, rather we are reacting as quickly as possible to move ourselves to safety. If we respond to fear in "fight" mode, we will attempt to overpower that which is threatening us. If we respond in "flight" mode, we attempt to distance ourselves as quickly as possible from the threat. And if we react in "freeze" mode, we do not make a move that might exacerbate the threat; we will likely submit.

The function of fear is to alert us to real or perceived threat. This is very important! Feeling fear does not mean something is actually threatening our safety. Sometimes a current situation *reminds* us in our body of a formally threatening situation, and we react in the present as if we are still in the past. (This is called a trigger and forms the basis of Post-Traumatic Stress Disorder or PTSD.) Sometimes we misread a situation, and we feel fear, but there is no threat. Ex: I see a figure crouched down in the corner of my bedroom at night. In terror, I switch on the bedside lamp. It's just my backpack. The fear was real; the threat was not. For this reason, when we feel fear, we must face our perceptions. As far as emotions go, fear is essential. Without it, we would not protect ourselves from existential threats. We would have been eaten by the lions long ago.

5. EMBARRASSMENT

The spectrum of embarrassment ranges from feeling self-conscious, sheepish, red-faced, and awkward to ashamed, mortified, and humiliated. This emotion feels hot, intense, and urgent. The body instinctively wants to cover private and vulnerable areas. We cross our arms in front of our chests, we cross our legs, we want to become smaller, small enough to hide. Blood flow increases to the face, and we are flushed or we blush. There is a sense of vulnerability we may experience as danger. We may feel a collapsing in our chest, and it can feel crushing, like an implosion. We may feel like stone, unable to move. Our eyes might become downcast as a means of avoiding.

The function of embarrassment is to alert us that we have been exposed in a way that does not feel safe. We all have parts of ourselves that we share with others and other parts that we tend to cover and hide. Embarrassment is forced exposure. If we are exposed in front of someone who reacts with judgment or disgust, embarrassment can compound into feeling mortified or ashamed. If we experience embarrassment in front of someone who is compassionate and understanding, we experience safety and connection. The human tendency to hide is where the rubber meets the road in relationship. Embarrassment occurs when vulnerable parts meet with the fear of rejection. For this reason, this emotion is one of the most vulnerable and therefore protected frequently with anger.

6. HURT

The spectrum of hurt ranges from feeling forgotten, disregarded, and unseen to sucker-punched, betrayed, and devastated. Hurt is experienced as a blow to the core. We might feel the emotional equivalent of being struck or kicked. We generally feel hurt in the abdomen, around the area of the solar plexus. It's a strong, pointed feeling. Anger is a common mask for hurt because admitting we have been hurt is very vulnerable. Feeling hurt is feeling a blow where we wanted a gentle touch.

Even though the physical body is strong and resilient, it can be cut, broken, and bruised. Likewise, the heart – the seat of emotion – is also vulnerable to being hurt through lack of consideration, forgetfulness, disregard, and meanness. Hurt is the emotional experience that informs us that our personhood has been unacknowledged or disrespected. We innately expect to be treated with respect, kindness, and consideration. Hurt is generated when these expectations are unmet. It is the emotion that actually reflects our worth. When we have moderate to healthy self-worth, we will notice when our value is ignored or dismissed. If we have low self-worth, we may not even know we have a right to be treated with kindness and respect, and it is difficult for us to actually register hurt.

7. LONELINESS

The spectrum of loneliness ranges from listless, bored, and wistful to longing, tormented, and desperate. Loneliness is experienced in the body as a feeling of emptiness. It is as if the ties that bind us to others are hanging by threads or severed. We may feel cold, dull, uncreative, uninspired, restless, and anxious. The physical experience is similar to sorrow. Both convey the sense that something we want is absent. Loneliness can be a chronic feeling of separation and disconnection. We may settle into it and grow numb and distant. We can become desperate and panicked.

Loneliness signals that we need connection. Humans are the most emotionally complex of all animal species on the planet. Our systems of socialization are equally complex. Loneliness is the emotion that signals that one or more of those systems needs attention. We might need to focus on our connection to ourselves, our family relationships, our social circle, or our intimate friends and/or lover.

These are the seven core emotions. The best way to identify what we are feeling is to learn how these emotions feel in the body. Like all tools, it will take time for us to master our emotional experience. We move from nonspecific declarations of discomfort into accurate descriptions of our inner world, able to bring others close and ask for what we need. "I feel upset" becomes "I'm aware of feeling some shame." We can then hear others' emotional experiences with less discomfort. The days of feeling ashamed because we are afraid will end. The days of suppressing our most outrageous joy for fear of looking a fool will disappear. We will become mature adults, aware of how we feel, able to use our emotions to connect and reconnect with one another. Our first step is to name them by knowing how they feel.

THOUGHTS ARE NOT FEELINGS

A thought is an idea or opinion. Thoughts originate in the brain and are an outcome of learning, thinking, and processing.

A feeling, on the other hand, is our body's way of communicating information about how we are responding to our environment. We feel excited at a theme park. We feel sad at a funeral. We feel dread at an exam. We feel hope watching a sunrise. Feelings happen in the body. The brain processes and names them (joy, anger, fear, etc.), but the body feels them and communicates that sense to the brain.

Distinguishing thoughts from feelings is important because intellectual connection is very different than emotional connection in relationship. Thoughts and feelings are two very different human processes, and their conflation leads to relational discord.

Why?

Because thoughts and feelings require very different responses. Often, when confronted with feelings, we respond with thoughts. We answer the heart with the head, and the result is disconnection. Sometimes we are trying to describe what we feel, but without an emotional vocabulary, we wind up sharing thoughts, and we don't receive the care and comfort we need.

In my office, I ask my clients what they feel frequently, and in early stages of therapy, they will often answer with thoughts.

"What do you feel when your partner calls you to complain in the middle of your day?"

"I think it's unfair. I'm in the middle of my day."

"That's a thought. What do you feel?*"*

85

"I feel like she should know that I can't do anything about what she's telling me."

"That's another thought, and it's a fair one, but what do you feel?"

"I don't know."

"I'm wondering if you feel helpless to do anything about it."

"Yes! That's what I'm feeling! I feel helpless, and I hate feeling that!"

Now we have somewhere to go. We can explore the feeling of helplessness and the appropriate response to it. As long as we express thoughts instead of our authentic feelings, we are in the sparring match of Who Makes the Most Sense. This leads to conflict upon conflict. When we move into a place of sharing the emotions inside of us, there is no reason for conflict. No one can argue with what we feel. It's happening inside the body. It's not up for debate. It requires a different response. We might argue that our partner has no right to feel what they're feeling, and we'll address that in a later chapter (Chapter 4 Validation), but the fact is: we feel what we feel. It's not up for argument, and we don't have to prove it. We need to attend to it instead. In the above scenario, a disclosure of feeling helpless will draw a very different response than the accusation or demand that we not be interrupted in the middle of our day.

Thoughts are functions of the brain, and they are useful for discovering, learning, assimilating, and functioning in the world. When our relationships are difficult, we may use them to keep us safe behind a wall of intellect. We don't have to feel as vulnerable expressing our thoughts as we do expressing our emotions. Emotions reveal the desires of our hearts, our pain, and our pleasure. These are deeply intimate, relational parts of us. If someone disagrees with us, it's very different than someone not caring about how we *feel*. We all want to feel safe, loved, connected, and known. Without shared emotions, this is impossible. The emotional parts of us are the places where we feel a sense of oneness with each other. We are all sharing this strange and wonderful experience of being alive, and emotions are what we all have in common. This connection is what we long for in relationship. When we share our thoughts in place of our feelings, we move to a shallower place of connection which is intellectual comprehension and/or assent. This is indeed a place of connection, but it is not as deep as emotional connection. The first part of emotional connection is being able to name what we feel, and to do that, we must be able to distinguish between a thought and a feeling.

"STOP YOUR CRYING!"

How our parents interacted with our emotions during childhood will significantly affect how we experience and handle emotions now.

Children are born as infants with a full range of emotions. They feel everything from bliss to satisfaction to fear to anger without any filter or editing process in place. They simply feel and express.

Before children are verbal, parents generally (with few exceptions of tragic infant abuse) accept their emotions because the child lacks words at this stage of development. Parents are understanding, comforting, and tolerant of the emotional swings of an infant because the child has no other means of communication. Facial expressions, body movements, and sounds are their language, and the attuned parent can read these with spectacular accuracy and meet their baby's needs on a consistent enough basis for the child to feel safe and known.

When children begin speaking, their emotional expressions become more pointed and their actions more potent. An infant flailing in a car seat is far less destructive than a four-year-old overturning an end table. As the expression of emotion becomes more intense, the tendency of the parents to suppress the child's emotions follows suit. Parents move from snuggling and cuddling a distraught infant to commanding that a four-year-old stop crying!

By the time children are ready to begin school, they know which emotions they can express and which will get them into trouble. If they are raised in an emotionally suppressed environment, the troublesome emotions – meaning the ones that trouble the caregivers most – have gone underground, deep into the subconscious, and are generally inaccessible without professional assistance. What the child *will* do, however, is act those emotions out.

Parents will send signals of approval and connection to the child who expresses joy, cheer, contentment, and gratitude. They gather the child in their arms, stroke the hair, kiss the cheeks, smiling with the mouth and eyes, enjoying closeness and intimacy. Conversely, when the child is angry, confused, sad, ashamed, or hurt, the parent may communicate their disapproval with facial expressions of dislike, physical distance, coldness, silence, and a sharper tone. Thus, the child learns that some emotions are acceptable and some are not.

The problem is: children need to feel all of their feelings as every feeling is communicating something about the self. And once the child can feel and name the feeling, they need to learn to express their feelings appropriately. We want to raise children who can say, "Mom, I'm feeling lonely. Can I invite Peter over to play?" rather than throwing a fit. We want an adolescent who can respond as to why they're downcast, "I feel ashamed. I didn't do well on my history exam," rather than lighting up a joint. What we often see instead are children and adolescents who are moody, withdrawn, angry, or overly compliant. "How obedient little Suzy is!" we exclaim. Perhaps. Or perhaps Suzy learned early on that if she is anything other than compliant, she experiences emotional withdrawal from a parent.

I recall a night I taught a class on emotional health. An elderly woman approached me after the talk with a worried expression on her face.

"Vanessa, I need your help with my granddaughter. She's so *angry.*"

"What is she so angry about?" I prompted, eager to offer help.

"I don't know, she's just so angry," she emphasized, the worried expression never leaving her face, her eyes searching mine for answers.

"Well, has anyone asked her why she's so angry?"

Silence.

"No, I don't guess we have."

We are so afraid of our own emotions that we fear emotions in others. We don't allow anger in ourselves because our parents didn't allow anger in us, and now we cannot accept or engage it skillfully in anyone else. We couldn't admit we were afraid, so we don't ever allow ourselves to feel it, we just try to control everything.

We must go back and do the work. How was anger handled in our family of origin? Sadness? Gladness? Fear? Shame or embarrassment? Hurt? Loneliness? With these answers, we will begin to understand what we suppress, what we express, and why.

Teaching children that only certain emotions are acceptable is like teaching them that they can only experience certain types of physical pain and only at a certain intensity. "Charlie, you're not allowed to have a stomach ache." "Maya, you're not allowed to tell me when your head hurts." This is insane, but we do it with emotions! Physical pain? Tell me. Emotional pain? You're fine.

We may have heard the following as children:

"Don't cry. You have nothing to cry about." (rejecting sorrow)

"If you're going to be angry, you can go sit in your room!" (rejecting anger)

"You're not afraid; you're just nervous. Don't be afraid. Be strong." (rejecting fear)

"Why are you acting like such a baby? Stop sulking!" (rejecting hurt)

All of these responses communicate that certain emotions are not okay. It is as though children ought to be perennially chipper, content, grateful, hopeful, and resourceful. This is not a parenting book, and there are many that deal effectively with shepherding children through their stages of emotional development, but we've all been here. We can all point to emotions that were shut down. The inconvenient problem is that suppressed emotions don't go away. They simply fester. The good news is: it's never too late to learn.

EMOTIONAL EXPRESSION IN ACTION

We need to feel it, name it, express it, and attend to it. The right mindset about emotions is this: they are ALL okay.

Yes, even disgust or the feeling of hatred. No one wants to hear their partner express these emotions in relationship to them, but if they are present, they should be heard. All emotions are healthy and productive bits of relational information. The first step of emotional expression is to notice what we are feeling in our bodies. We notice the ups and downs of our moods, the tension and release we experience in a day. The body is where we begin to be emotionally aware. Think of the body as the road map of your emotional life.

The next step is to learn to name your emotions (a non-exhaustive list of emotions can be found in Appendix B). While some clients refer to the list of emotions I keep in my office as the "cheat sheet," there is no cheating taking place! Cheating is a cowardly short cut. On the contrary, naming our emotions is hard and requires great courage, especially when we have been raised to suppress them and experience strong feelings of shame when we let them show. We are learning a new language, and we need help. We use the list until we integrate these words into our personal lexicon.

Here is a basic list of the seven core emotions and appropriate responses.

ANGER

- If Clean Anger, set a boundary.
- If Protective Anger, get to the real feeling. Deal with that.

SORROW

- Cry, grieve, ask for comfort and consolation.

GLADNESS

- Identify the cause and repeat.

FEAR

- Identify if it is real or perceived.
- If real, get yourself to safety.
- If perceived, reassure yourself or get reassurance.

EMBARASSMENT (AND SHAME)

- Reveal your thoughts, deeds, and secrets to a safe person.

HURT

- Describe the events that hurt you.
- If the person responsible for the action(s) that hurt you responds with understanding and care, continue on.
- If they do not, revisit the conversation or implement boundaries.

LONELINESS

- Reach out, connect, plan something fun, talk.

Emotions need a safe place to be felt, named, expressed, and attended to. This does not mean we will drown our relationships in a flood of emotional outpouring, but it does mean that *we need a safe place to talk about them.* Couples who accept the significance of emotions will experience a much deeper connection. In order to create the safety necessary for emotional disclosures to take place, we practice non-reaction. We use the tool of Listening while our partner practices Emotional Expression. We do not interrupt, negate, or argue. Their emotions are real for them, and we'd rather know than not know. To ignore emotions – ours or anyone else's – is denial. Instead of denial, we allow and listen. Emotions are not a threat or a statement of failure. They are simply the expression of experiences we are having inwardly. Therefore, we meet emotional disclosures with acceptance and curiosity.

• • •

I remember the day Scott walked into my office, plopped down on the sofa like it was his own living room, and smiled.

"How are you feeling today, Scott?"

"Well, I'm a little tired physically, but emotionally I feel hopeful. Now that I think about it, I also feel a little resentful of my boss, but that's easy. I have a meeting with him tomorrow, and we'll talk about the issues then."

"It's been a while since you've had an anger outburst, hasn't it?"

Scott stopped and considered what I'd just observed out loud.

"Yeah," he said with astonishment. "I guess it has. I don't even feel angry anymore. Not much, anyway. I feel pressure more than anger. I used to feel the pressure and get mad as a way of punishing everyone around me for what they needed and wanted from me. Now, I just feel it and talk about it. No one is cornering me into a role, I do that myself. And when I do, Patrick has been really comforting. He reminds me that I'm allowed to be human!" he said with a laugh.

I marveled. The boy who was trapped in the role of the "hero" as a child, only allowing strength and protection, had matured into a man with the emotional range of a healthy, self-aware adult. He knows his own heart, can feel what's happening inside, and can communicate without shame.

The tool of Emotional Expression had become a skill.

TOOL TIPS:
EMOTIONAL
EXPRESSION

- When we do not know what we feel, we react instead of respond.
- Knowing our emotional state and being competent to name our feelings is part of being an emotionally healthy adult.
- The Seven Core Emotions are: Anger, Sorrow, Gladness, Fear, Embarrassment, Hurt, and Loneliness.
- Bundling is grouping complex emotions into one feeling instead of expressing how we feel specifically.
- We must separate thoughts from feelings. We lose connection when we respond to the heart from the head.
- We learn to edit our emotions in childhood. This must be undone if we are to become emotionally healthy adults.

- Knowing what we feel allows us to ask for what we need.

QUESTIONS
FOR
DISCUSSION

1. Which emotions were "allowed" in my home growing up? Which were suppressed?

2. What did my parents teach me about my emotions? What did they say explicitly? What was implicit, or implied?

3. What beliefs do I have about expressing my feelings? Do I consider it weak? Strong? Necessary? Unnecessary? Easy? Difficult?

4. Which emotions are hardest for me to express in a healthy way?

5. How often do I check in with how I'm feeling? With whom do I feel safe to share my feelings?

CHAPTER 4

Validation

Shana was visibly upset. She arrived for her therapy appointment on the brink of tears, and the door had barely shut behind us when the flood erupted.

"I'm so tired of this!" she lamented.

We had been working on her ability to express herself emotionally. Raised by an alcoholic mother and a workaholic step-father, emotions weren't respected or even acknowledged in her childhood home. She was expected to do her chores, make good grades, and essentially not pose a problem. When Shana began therapy, she was unaware of her feelings and therefore unable to express herself in words. Through slow and steady work, she began to notice her feelings and learned which word went with which feeling. The skill of emotional expression was beginning to take shape as her heart found its voice again. The problem was: her husband wasn't listening.

Kyle was a successful salesman who was constantly on the go. If there was a committee, he chaired it. If there was a softball league, he was the captain. He shined in whatever he did, and without saying so explicitly, he expected Shana to work just as hard. This was a familiar expectation for her. Work, work, work. Feelings? No time for feelings.

Too much to do. She'd left a beloved career in nursing to raise their two young children full-time. As the demands of motherhood took their toll, Shana identified feelings of loneliness and longing in her heart. Being a stay-at-home mom wasn't as fulfilling as she'd hoped. She missed being part of a dynamic community of professionals. When Kyle expressed exhaustion and satisfaction at the end of a hard day's work, Shana affirmed him. When Shana expressed a similar exhaustion and a desire for more adult interaction, Kyle dismissed her.

"What happens when you tell Kyle what you feel?" I asked.

"He goes deadpan. I can't tell if it's because he doesn't understand how long and hard my days are or because he just doesn't care."

"How do you feel when he goes deadpan?"

"Abandoned. Like I'm in this – this journey of motherhood – alone. He doesn't get it."

"What would it be like if he did get it? What would that do for you?"

"I'd feel like I had a partner in the work. Even though he works at an office and I 'work' at home, I'd feel like he was in it with me."

I asked Shana how she felt about having Kyle come in for one of our sessions. I felt I needed to meet him and hear his perspective to understand her predicament more completely. Shana agreed, and Kyle joined our next session. As he entered the room, I could feel his apprehension and also his warmth. I liked him immediately. As we discussed Shana's feelings about their marriage, I began to see what she meant. Kyle spoke easily about what a devoted mother she was, but when she described how hard her days were, he went cold.

Our fourth tool is Validation.

• • •

CAN EMOTIONS BE VALID?

To validate something means to declare it to be true, reasonable, or sound.

In academic fields of study like history or science, to validate an object, finding, or theory means to prove its accuracy through empirical evidence. For example, an archeologist might validate that an artifact discovered on a dig is indeed an item from antiquity through a rigorous process of studying anthropological evidence and material testing. Once the object is validated to be of a specific culture and time period, its value is assigned. We might be looking at a fragment of bone from a horse who died in battle during the Peloponnesian War, or it's the bone of a wild dog who died last year on this hill. A research scientist validates a theory through the scientific method of experimental testing. Once the experiments have been run, the data gathered and analyzed, the theory is either proven to be valid or invalid. This element bonds to that element in these conditions or it doesn't. In the world of science and facts, validation is a matter of proving authenticity and value through detailed examination. There is an objectivity to the process that keeps emotions at bay. It's either true or it's not. And if it's true, it can be proven.

In the realm of relationships, validation follows the same principles, process, and outcome, but the "facts" are different. Rather than objective, empirical evidence, the elements we are examining are subjective human experiences. To validate an idea or theory empirically, we must find evidence that proves the idea or theory is true, therefore valid. To validate another person, we must learn their perspective, story, and personality well enough so that their emotional reactions *make sense*. These personal "facts" present the evidence necessary to be able to truthfully say, "What you're feeling is valid."

Same process, different "facts."

Validating another person's emotional experience does not mean we condone their behavior. We may perceive our partner's behaviors to be healthy (productive in fostering and maintaining connection) or unhealthy (destructive and hindering connection). We may judge another's actions as mature (informed by wisdom, self-reflection, self-control) or immature (selfish, unaware, reactive). Validation does not mean we share the same perspective. Our lens is not our partner's lens. It doesn't mean we agree or disagree, declaring their position as either right or wrong. Emotions are neither right nor wrong, and using that categorical classification doesn't work because emotions are wholly subjective. It doesn't mean they win and we lose.

Validation simply means this: given their perspective, personality, and history, what another person is feeling makes sense.

Validation often occurs naturally when there is shared experience. For example, new mothers who are nursing infants and missing out on precious hours of sleep receive genuine (and necessary!) validation from other mothers. The looks, gestures, and words that communicate "I get it" are priceless to the new mother. It is not a stretch for another mother to do this. The shared experience creates a bond of understanding. That bond is a cord of connection.

Validation also occurs naturally when there are shared personality traits. An introverted parent may have a very compassionate and understanding view of a shy child. In this case, when the child struggles to make friends or feel that he is a part of a group, the introverted parent might find it easy to say, "I get it. Me too." This relaxes the child and communicates a message that says, "We are alike. You are not alone."

We naturally validate what we have experienced and know within ourselves. However, the *skill* of validation involves the ability to genuinely validate that which we have never experienced. To do this, we must become like scientists – curious about our partners, asking questions, driven to understand.

INVALIDATION

What happens when there is no shared experience or personality trait? What happens when another person's emotions make no sense to us whatsoever? What happens when we cannot conceive of why another person would do or say or feel (fill in the blank)?

Often, when we are confronted with behaviors or emotional states we do not understand, we form judgments to fill in the gaps of understanding. In general, humans do not tolerate uncertainty well. It raises our anxiety, and we would rather know than not know. When our partner does something we think we would never do or expresses something we think we would never feel, we don't like the confusion. We may exclaim, "That makes no sense!" We may form judgments about them to bridge the gap between what we know and what we are experiencing. This is mostly about reducing our own anxiety. Judgment takes us on the opposite path of understanding, and validation is a disappearing ship on the horizon. Forming judgments will take a relationship from love to hate faster than anything else. Judgment replaces intimate understanding of another with distrust and contempt.

So we have a choice. Our partner does something or reacts emotionally in a way we just don't get...

"I would NEVER do that," we say out loud or to ourselves.

"Why are you being so emotional?" we throw at our partner.

And the kingpin of invalidation: *"You're overreacting! It's not a big deal!"*

What we are actually revealing is that we do not know and/or understand our partner. We are saying, "You are not like me, I therefore don't understand you, and I don't know what to do with it." Do we then rush to form judgments, just to fill in the lack of knowledge and quell our anxiety?

"You're unreasonable."

"You're dramatic."

"You're irrational."

"You're cold."

Or can we get the information we lack? We need to seek and acquire the information. And how might we do this? We ask. Like scientists in search of evidence, we ask. Instead of filling in the gap between who we are and who our partner is with judgment or exasperated confusion, *ask a question.*

"Hey, I can see you're really upset. What just happened? What are you feeling?"

"This seems to be a bigger deal to you than it is to me. Can you tell me what makes this very important to you?"

We assume a judgmental, hence invalidating, position

when we tell another person that they have no right or reason to feel what they are feeling, that their emotions are unfounded. This is at the very core of invalidation and a narcissistic viewpoint. We are assuming everyone ought to think and process as we do. We launch into detailed sermons on why their perspective is wrong or irrational, and all we accomplish is deepening the divide. Invalidation is an unhealthy, destructive way to reduce our own unpleasant emotional state. Rather than learning about another, we rely on our own assumptions and judgments to fill in the gaps, and sadly we are often wrong. We miss out on the complexity, beauty, and richness of another person when we invalidate them. We may feel intellectually superior, but relationally we are immature.

YOUR ISSUES ARE NOT THE ISSUE

Conflict is simply the process of approaching the same issue from differing perspectives. How we do this determines how satisfying and connected our relationships are. Often in working with couples, I see people who are battling the same issues as everyone else: raising children, finances, future plans, sex, communication styles, and so on. Satisfied couples have the same struggles as unsatisfied couples. What I see in couples who are generally satisfied with their relationships is that the way they approach conflict is different. Instead of attacking, they learn. Instead of invalidating, they listen to understand. So the issues are not the issue. The issues of life are common. The real issue is how the challenges are being handled in the relationship, and without the tool of validation, we are incapable of learning who another person truly is.

Without validating we may attempt to shame, criticize, or control another person into being someone we can understand through our small, limited lens. We may avoid our differences and move into denial, denying the feelings that arise within us and our partner because we lack the tools to navigate the waves of emotion. We may shut down and stonewall our partner, a passive-aggressive way of expressing discontentment, disappointment, or hurt. We may form judgments that kill our respect and desire for the other. We may corner our partner until they agree with us. We will not grow in compassion or understanding, remaining rigid and narrow in our tiny zone of comfort.

Validation is not just about giving our loved one a moment of understanding; validation reflects the reality of our differences. We are, in fact, different people with different perspectives and life experiences. That richness is reality, and we can learn to love it in our relationships. We don't have to agree with one another to understand one another. We don't have to approve to accept. We must, however, be able to say, "I get it."

BUILD BRIDGES, NOT WALLS

No one reaches adulthood able to give and receive love perfectly. We all favor certain expressions of love over others. This is at the heart of the concept of "love languages." Because of our histories, lessons, and personalities, we each express and receive love in unique ways. Sometimes those expressions of love are a home run. She absolutely loves peonies, and you happen to bring peonies to her door on the first date. Goal! He grew up enjoying family time in front of a cozy fireplace, and the first time you cook him dinner, you light a fire. His body is flooded with warmth and openness. Score!

We have relational strengths that we bring to the table of relationship, and we have limitations. For example, your spouse never felt heard as a child, and you have a gift for listening deeply and parsing out meaning. Home run! Your partner grew up in a cold house where little affection was shared. You are warm and affectionate. Touchdown! These natural expressions meet the need, and we feel we have found our other half.

But what happens when there is a gap between what we need and what our partner is giving? What happens when the expression of love we are most comfortable giving is not the expression of love our partner wants? We feel close when we are talking deeply and connecting through vulnerable conversation; our partner is less comfortable with that kind of self-expression. Maybe we prefer to connect through shared outdoor activity, but our partner likes to take it easy on weekends.

Validation is the bridge.

We all have limitations in how we love. No one offers complete love, every day. If we discount and diminish what our partners offer or ask of us, we create relational wounds. Simply because they are not expressing love as we do does not mean their expressions of love and connection are without value. They are simply different. Validation is how we honor the differences.

"Why do we have to talk about our feelings? You're too emotional."

Nope. Let's try that again.

"Honey, I can see how important emotional conversations are for you. It makes sense. You feel so connected to me after a good, deep talk. Obviously, it's not something I do often outside of our relationship, but I want you to know that I get it when you ask for that."

Or...

"Why do we have to be doing something active all the time? Can't we just relax at home?"

Let's have a redo.

"Sweetheart, I see why outdoor activity is important to you. So many of your family memories were centered around fun activities outside. I get it. Let's find our own rhythm. I'm open to it. I probably won't be as active outdoors as your family was, but we can find our own speed. I know this is important to you."

These responses *validate* the relational preferences of the other person without discounting their uniqueness. We need to accept that we all have relational preferences and limitations that create a gap in connection. We cannot give our partners everything they need, every time they need it. And no one can meet our every need. But we can validate their needs and offerings. Every time.

Validation is how we show emotional respect. We show intellectual respect to others by disagreeing without insult. Perhaps we are even curious about their thoughts because we respect their intellect and want to learn. We know this to be a person of sound mind, so we trust that if they think it, perhaps there is merit. We do not have to agree with them, but we do not need to discredit or dismiss them either. Likewise, we show respect for others' feelings and needs by accepting emotional differences without disparaging or dismissing one another. Validation is the tool that allows us to remain connected in relationship even when our needs and emotional states are different. Remember that validation is not agreement. It is simply a way of acknowledging that given who another person is and all the experiences they've had, their emotions make sense.

"I get why you're hurt," even when we believe the

same thing wouldn't hurt us. Different wounds, different triggers.

"I understand why you feel lonely right now," even though we just spent the day together. Different internal experience of connection.

"I get why you're feeling disconnected," even though we just had sex. Different connection between sex and closeness.

"I get why that made you angry," even though the same thing likely would not anger us. Different sensitivity.

Emotional respect. We connect differently. We need different things to feel and remain connected. Validation is the tool that bridges the gap.

SELF-VALIDATION

Saturday Night Live used to feature a segment called "Deep Thoughts by Jack Handy." Every thought or reflection was so obvious that speaking it was unnecessary, hence the joke was that these thoughts weren't deep at all. One went like this:

To me, clowns aren't funny. In fact, they're kinda scary.

I've wondered where this started, and I think it goes back to the time I went to the circus and a clown killed my Dad.

We laugh at the absurdism, and yet this is a great example of self-validation. We all experience emotions every day, both strong and weak responses to what is happening in our environment. When we are able to understanding our feelings and behaviors though the lens of our story, we begin to understand *why* we feel what we feel, *why* we do what we do. When we understand our emotions this way, this is called self-validation.

Often, we beat ourselves up unnecessarily for feeling what we feel.

"Why am I so nervous?"

"Why am I so insecure?"

"Why am I always afraid?"

"Why am I mad all the time?"

Clients often ask these questions in therapy. It's understandable to seek professional help when we can't make sense of our inner world. We can feel both confusion and shame around our difficult emotions, and we enlist a counselor in sorting it all out. When my clients ask these types of "why" questions about themselves, I'll often respond with, "I don't know. Why do you feel afraid all the time?" This encourages them to connect their story with their present emotional state. Our emotions arise from somewhere, and the ability to connect the past with the present in informed compassion is the act of self-validation.

Our emotions make sense! There is either a present situation stimulating the emotional state, or there is a previous situation stimulating the emotional state. Both deserve attention and care. It is a powerful and transformational moment when people begin to connect their hearts with their personal stories and see that their emotions and behaviors make sense. Emotionally mature adults can differentiate when their past is being triggered versus discomfort in the present, but whatever we are feeling, it's valid. *Something* is coming up through our emotional system, and we need to pay attention to it.

Through loving, patient, curious inquiry, we can learn ourselves and our loved ones. We can see and acknowledge what they are feeling, why they are feeling it, and then say with sincerity:

I get it. That makes sense.

"YOU'RE TOO MUCH!"

We have learned that as infants, we came into the world with a full range of emotions. This is natural and healthy. As we mature into adulthood, we work to know ourselves and express our emotions appropriately, but the range need not shrink for maturation to occur. Indeed, an edited emotional life is a sign of emotional immaturity and a lack of development. It generally points to unresolved shame and fear. Mature people don't feel less, they react less. Emotionally mature adults can feel all of their feelings and act on them appropriately if necessary.

In order to nurture emotional development, parents must validate their children's emotional states. Children need to hear regularly that their emotions are okay, that they make sense, and how to productively handle what's happening inside them. Families in which there is little to no validation are families where there is little to no compassion. To validate a child is not to excuse them or their behavior, but it is to see them as a human being with an inner life.

Let's look at an example: when an adolescent grows upset because they cannot attend a social gathering due to a family obligation, parents can be quick to minimize the importance of the teen's desire, thus *invalidating* their emotions and position. From the perspective of adulthood, we know there are going to be a multitude of opportunities for social gatherings, and we might think the teen's emotions are irrational.

"Get over it. It's one party."

"Why are you so upset? We are your family."

"You're acting like this is the end of the world."

And the champion of invalidating remarks: *"You're making too big of an issue out of this."*

All of these responses deride the teenager's perspective. From the lens of adolescence, a time when social development picks up to full speed and social acceptance feels like life or death, the young person's reaction is totally rational — for *them*. To them, this is as important as it feels. A teen does not have the perspective of adulthood. How could they? To validate the youngster is to say, "I know this is a big deal for you. Of course it is. I get it. Your social life is important to you, and it should be. However, on this occasion, your family needs to come before your friends, but I do see how upset you are, and it makes sense."

We do not need to agree or disagree. This young person is neither "right" nor "wrong" in wanting to skip the family's event to go to the lake with their new crush. We are simply saying that given their perspective, personality, and life experience, their emotional reaction makes sense. Therefore, in their world, it is *valid*.

Parents who invalidate children have forgotten what it is like to be a child. A child's world is small. Their community is first their family, then their school, then work, and so on. Their landscape is their home for the most formative years of life. When children react strongly to events in their small worlds, it is because that is their world. When parents tell their children that they are blowing things out of proportion or that they are overreacting, they have forgotten: this little world is all they have.

This is like telling a grown man with a family, "For Pete's sake! You're only losing your job, get over it!" We would never do this or even think this. We respond with compassion, concern, and if our friend or partner is deeply upset, we understand. When children miss recess, can't go to birthday parties, or lose their favorite toy we say, "Don't get bent out of shape! You'll have plenty of recesses, birthday parties, and toys." We know this from our adult perspective, but the child does not. The first and appropriate response is, "Of course you're upset. I get it." There is plenty of time to reach the mind with reason and perspective once the heart has been soothed. Validation is the balm of raw emotions. We go through the heart to reach the head.

Let's ask ourselves: *did I experience validation as a child?* Perhaps some of our emotions were validated and some were not. The emotions that were validated are likely the emotions we allow in our adult lives. Were we forced to defend ourselves when we felt feelings our parents couldn't understand? If so, perhaps we are still doing this today. And when others tell us how they feel about us, perhaps we launch into defensiveness even more. We aren't allowed to feel what we feel, and neither are they. Many parent/child conflicts are born from a lack of simple validation.

VALIDATION IN ACTION

Let's go back to fact finding. Remember that scientists don't quit until the outcome makes sense. They not only want to know how a thing works, but *why* it works the way it works. We need this same spirit of curiosity and thirst for discovery if we are going to be partners who can validate one another. Let's look at the facts we are working with in human relationships.

FACT #1: FEELINGS ARE REAL

Feelings are bodily responses to environmental stimuli. When we experience joy, we want to laugh, dance, or celebrate. When we experience fear, we want to move quickly into a place of safety. The stimulus inspires the emotional response, and the emotional response, felt in the body, inspires action. It does not matter if the stimulus is true or not for the emotions to take place.

For example, a woman believes her family has forgotten her birthday. Not a mention of it in the weeks leading up. With every passing day, she feels more and more despondent. She begins to tell herself, "These ungrateful people! After all I do for them, not one of them has even thought of my birthday." On the night of her birthday, she walks into a house full of her friends and loved ones. The surprise party delights her and reverses the despondent feelings, but as they were happening – even though not based in reality – they were real to her. She *felt* them.

In the realm of relationships, all emotions are valid in that if we are feeling them, they are real. This is the first step in validating another person. We must accept that what they are feeling is real inside them. We are not yet at the point of gathering information or addressing perceptions, we are simply stating, "You feel _____, and that is real for you." To deny another person's emotional experience is ridiculous. If it is happening in the body, it is real. The reasons why have not yet become known or identified as true or not. The emotional response is a matter of bodily experience, and that is not up for debate. To *invalidate* emotions is to deny another's bodily experience. This is like someone stating that they have a stomach ache, and their partner responds with, "No, you don't." This is inane.

In order for the bonds of connection to bind and

hold, the emotions we feel must be acknowledged before our perspectives enter the picture. Why? Because these emotions are parts of us. To deny their existence is to deny experiences that are present and real in our bodies. What is right and true is not yet important.

The first step of validation is to acknowledge what another person is feeling. We can do this in a number of ways:

"You're afraid. I hear you. I think we are seeing things differently, but we'll talk about that later. Come here, let me give you a hug."

"I know you're hurt. I think there's been a misunderstanding here, but before we get to that, I want to acknowledge that I see you're hurt, and from your lens it makes sense."

"You're angry. I see that. Why don't you take some space, and we can talk about it whenever you feel ready?"

All of these responses acknowledge another's emotional state without losing our sense of reason and logic. We'll get to the head; we need to start with the heart. This essential step of validation in relationship cannot be skipped! We are used to feeling our feelings unconsciously and reacting unconsciously. In other words, we are not used to having our feelings reflected back to us in real time, and yet since our feelings are an integral part of us, to have our feelings reflected back to us is to feel known and seen.

We must stop rushing to prove something as true or not true from our own perspective. Acknowledge what another person is feeling *first*.

"Honey, I feel hurt because you couldn't keep our date night."

"Well, I don't know what you want me to do! I couldn't step away from work!"

Let's try again.

"Honey, I feel hurt because you couldn't keep our date night."

"I get that, Babe."

It's that simple!

Why do we need this step? What's so important about acknowledging, thus validating, emotions first before we move forward with differing perspectives?

The first reason is that we need to know what emotional state another person is in so we can respond accordingly. Different emotions require different responses. Anger generally requires space then boundaries. Fear requires reassurance. Hurt requires softness and sensitivity. Embarrassment requires acceptance. If we don't stop long enough to acknowledge and validate the emotional state of someone else, we may offer a misguided response and the result is deeper disconnection. We may convince someone that their emotional response was irrational, but we are no closer together, no more connected. This is winning the battle and losing the war.

The second reason is simple and obvious: *the emotions are real for the other person.* Whatever perception or misperception may be taking place, the emotions are real. So we acknowledge what is real because we need to live in reality for our lives to make sense, and emotions, founded or unfounded, are real. *Acknowledge them.*

We need not worry. There will be plenty of time to clarify perceptions. First, we validate the emotional experience, then we move to perception.

The third reason arises out of emotional intelligence:

we cannot get to the head without going through the heart. If we want to reach the mind, validate the heart first. If we want angry acquiescence or vehement resistance, go ahead and force your perspective without validating first. Eventually someone will cave or walk away, both without connection. If our goal is connection, validate first. This creates a bond of shared emotional safety that sets us up for intellectual reasoning later.

FACT #2: ALL EMOTIONS ARE RATIONAL

In the realm of the heart, *all emotions are rational.* Yes, you just read that correctly. All emotions are rational! Not all responses are appropriate to the given situation, but all emotions are rational. By rational we mean that our emotions emanate from real events that have taken place in our lives. Whether the emotion is a response to the present or the past, it's coming from a lived experience. It's connected to needs that have been met or not met. Simply because we don't know the source of the emotional reaction does not mean there is no source. If a man was criticized harshly by his father during his childhood and responds defensively when he receives constructive criticism as an adult, we may experience his strong reaction and say, "Gosh! You're being irrational, Bob! Calm down!" And indeed, his *response* in the moment may not be appropriate for the situation, but his emotions are *rational* given his story.

We must differentiate between situation and story.

Our situation is our present. Situations can be calm, frantic, confusing, or enjoyable. Our story is our past, our lived experience. And our pasts can be edifying, wounding, nourishing, or traumatizing. Very often, our situations trigger our story. The second step of validation involves discovering if the emotions present are because of the situation or the story. Either way, they're coming from somewhere; they're rational.

First, we acknowledge what another person is feeling because they are, in fact, feeling it. We acknowledge emotional reality.

Second, we engage in information gathering. We need to learn why our partner or loved one is feeling what they are feeling. Is it the present situation? Is it connected to their earlier story? Perhaps it's both. Remember that either way, the emotions are real, so whether or not we understand them we can still accept and validate that they are feeling what they are feeling, but the *why* is going to bring us into a deeper place of connection with one another. The why is going to foster understanding. Understanding fosters knowledge, and to be known in relationship – to have a robust knowledge of the other – is part of intimacy. Validation is therefore an essential tool of intimacy and relational satisfaction. Just because another person's feelings or reactions don't make sense to us does not mean that their feelings and reactions don't make sense at all! If things don't make sense to scientists, they keep digging and asking questions, searching for more information. Likewise, if feelings and reactions don't make sense to us, we keep digging! We don't, however, have the right to tell our partners that their emotions are overreactions. We haven't lived their story. We don't get to make that pronouncement.

Here are some examples of ways we can get to the truth inside another person:

"Your reaction seems to be pretty intense for the situation we are in. I'm wondering if this is about what is happening right now or something that has happened in the past..."

"I see that you're angry, but I cannot see why. Can

you explain to me why you're so mad?"

"I know you're scared, but I'm not sure why. Can you share that with me?"

In order to validate, we do not need to know why another person is feeling what they are feeling. We can remember Fact #1: Emotions are Real, and we can simply reflect back what we see without judgment. If we want a closer bond, we remember Fact #2: All Emotions are Rational, and we learn the why behind the feelings. How we ask is important. We cannot go about learning the why by demanding or demeaning what another person is feeling, simply because we don't understand it.

"Why are you so mad?"

"Why are you afraid? Don't you have any self-confidence?"

"What are you so upset about?"

These are indeed "why" questions, but they convey the opposite of validation. They are invalidating and communicate that another person's feelings are irrational. And they are not. They are connected to the situation or the larger story, and we need to learn which. Once we learn why our partner is feeling what they are feeling, it becomes effortless to say the six magical words of validation:

I get it. That makes sense.

Then we can clear up any perceptions. Validate first. Validating words convey understanding and respect. These words emerge from love. They say, "I see you, and I understand you." They say, "I get you." Isn't that what we all desire? To be understood for who we are? We accept responsibility for how we engage our relationships, how we listen to one another, how we express our own emotional states, and next how we accept the truth of another person's emotional state – both the what *and* the why – by validating each other.

This creates safety, and safety breeds intimacy. This is what we want.

• • •

Shana and Kyle both grew from the process.

Kyle never realized that a life largely comprised of chores and domestic toil was a daily reminder of a lonely and unattached childhood for Shana. Shana didn't know that Kyle's mother used the tasks of motherhood as a tool to exert control through guilt. Shana associated being home alone with children and caring for them all day with the dreadful pain of childhood loneliness. Kyle associated normal expressions of maternal exhaustion with feeling manipulated. Their situation was a normal one for parents of small children, but their stories helped them find compassion, patience, and support for one another.

In the end, they got one another. It made sense.

TOOL TIPS:
VALIDATION

- Validation means given another person's perspective, personality, and history, what they are feeling makes sense. (It has nothing to do with intellectual agreement.)
- We naturally validate what we have experienced.
- When validating another person becomes difficult, we can be quick to form judgments.
- When we cannot see how or why our partner is feeling what they are feeling, we ask.
- Validation is how we bridge the gaps between us - by honoring our differences.
- Validation is an essential first step in soothing raw emotions. We cannot reach the mind until we connect with the heart.
- The six magical words of validation are: I get it. That makes sense.

QUESTIONS
FOR
DISCUSSION

1. How did my parents validate or invalidate my feelings as a child?

2. What do I do when I don't understand why my partner is doing or feeling what they are doing or feeling? Are my actions bringing us to a place of greater connection? If not, what would be more productive?

3. How understood do I feel in my current relationship(s)? Who does a good job of validating my feelings? Who doesn't?

4. What do I do when I feel misunderstood or invalidated? Is this healthy or unhealthy? (In other words, does your behavior lead to being understood or does the problem persist?) What can I do differently so that I feel understood?

5. Can I see how validation is distinct from agreement?

CHAPTER 5

Gratitude

Karen didn't know if she wanted in or out.

Her marriage to Glen had been unhappy far more often than it was satisfying. As the years went by and the bad progressively outweighed the good, Karen wondered how long she could stand the pain of distance and loneliness. The birth of their daughter hadn't brought them any closer together, as she'd hoped. Her presence simply gave them more reasons to busy themselves apart from one another and further entrenched the disconnection. Karen was desperate. Something had to change.

She had grown up in a family where she was frequently criticized. Her harsh and punitive military father expected all of his children to "pull their weight," and Karen felt more valued for what she did than for who she was. After every chore, there was a fearful waiting period between its completion and her father's unforgiving examination. Karen was used to finding fault in herself before it was found in her. If she could stay ahead of the curve, anticipate the criticism, and do things perfectly, she stayed in her father's good graces. A critical eye towards herself and her siblings kept them all safe and increased their chances of acceptance from their dad. To give herself grace was to invite punishment. All the years of self-criticism and constant self-checking had made Karen a successful IT professional. No one ever worried that Karen's coding would be anything beneath flawless. She could easily catch mistakes that slipped past others, but that same critical eye was wreaking havoc on her personal life. "Hard to please," "impossibly high standards," and "high and mighty" were terms Karen frequently heard and overheard about herself. Glen had simply given up. His best wasn't good enough, and it was no use trying in vain.

Karen expressed her exasperation through anger. She was bundling the loneliness, exhaustion, and tension she felt in the only emotion that kept her feeling safe. It erupted out of her in cold contempt for Glen.

"He's useless! I can't rely on him to do anything right."

"Sounds like you feel as though Glen is failing you. Tell me about how he does this."

I readied myself for stories of laziness, carelessness, and absentmindedness. From Karen's description, Glen sounded like a hopeless cause. Karen recounted one episode after another in which she felt that Glen wasn't "pulling his weight." She described her morning routine and complained that he was woefully out of sync with her. It seemed that Glen never had the right words to say at the right time. Their nights were just as disappointing as their mornings, and she went to bed, night after night, feeling disconnected and alone.

The only trouble was, when Karen described Glen's behavior and contributions, I didn't see anything wrong with them per se. He didn't sound out of touch, lazy, careless, or absentminded. He just sounded different than her. Not wanting to invalidate her experience, I acknowledged that from her perspective, Glen wasn't satisfying her practical, emotional, and relational needs. I also wondered aloud if

Glen did anything right.

"Well, he's great with Stella."

"How is he great with Stella?" I prompted.

"He plays with her. I mean… " she smiled an intimate, inward smile as she reflected on her husband's love for their daughter, "he adores her. And she knows it. Their connection is really something to behold."

"Is there more?" I was curious now.

"He's good with my parents. My father is so critical and negative, but around Glen… I don't know… he softens. Glen brings out the best in people."

"Do you ever tell him this?"

The room was quiet.

"No. It never occurred to me. I mean, I see how great Glen is, but in the craziness of our lives, with work and raising Stella and every other obligation we have, it slips my mind."

"What do you feel about Glen as you talk about his finer points?"

"It's funny… I miss him."

Our fifth tool is Gratitude.

• • •

A GRATEFUL STATE

Gratitude is both an experience and a skill. As an experience, sometimes we are awash with it. Someone exceeds our expectations, surprises us with their care, or steps in at the hour of our need. We feel the warm rush of human connection. The goodness of another has broken through our mundane, difficult world, and the feeling of gratitude is like grasping a strong hand stretched out to us, free of obligation or pressure. Gratitude is the response of a heart that has been seen and met in its need.

The skill of gratitude is something different. Gratitude, as a skill, cuts through disappointment, anger, and expectations and sees the good in another. Like all skills, we get better at it with practice, and this simple tool has the power to change a relationship every day and forever. Gratitude is the skill we develop and the tool we use when criticism rears its ugly head. When we feel let down and frustrated with our partner's behavior, we pull out the tool of gratitude from our relational toolbox, no matter what the situation. Why? Because gratitude is *always* appropriate. Even when relationships are ending, we can be grateful for what they brought us and taught us. When relationships are in full swing, we can be grateful for who and what people are. And when relationships are hurting and weakened, gratitude is the cord that can bind us together again.

As with all tools and the new skills that must accompany them, gratitude is difficult when it is not emotionally inspired. Feeling grateful requires no effort. Choosing to be grateful requires self-will and self-control. We do not let our critical thoughts lead us like blindfolded horses. No, we lead our thoughts. We choose to see the good instead of the disappointing. There is *always* some good at hand. The skill of gratitude involves a decision and eventually a honed ability to mentally set aside our demands, wishes, expectations, and others' perceived faults in order to focus instead on where they are succeeding, trying, changing, and growing. There is always good to discover. With patience and practice, we can mine these gems more and more easily.

The mental process associated with gratitude is that of noticing. We notice and make a mental note. The relational process is speaking – we say what we see. A grateful heart is a beautiful thing, but spoken words of gratitude are healers, both for the recipient and the speaker. This is a way of living. Rather than discontentedly focusing on how we suffer, we focus instead on the gifts we are witness to, the beauty of another from which we benefit. Gratitude is the language of noticed and expressed goodness.

We do not only notice and vocalize when our loved ones do good, we must notice and vocalize when they are *trying*.

Change is difficult. Don't believe me? Try changing yourself. When our partners, lovers, children, friends, parents, and other relations make or take a step – no matter how small – we notice and encourage them with expressions of gratitude. Every attempt at growth deserves a grateful response.

> *"I see you trying to stay in this conversation right now. In the past, you have shut down when things get tense, and I see you trying. I want you to know how grateful I am. You're doing it. You're breaking the habit. I see it."*
>
> *"I see that you cleaned the garage. Thank you."*
>
> *"I notice that you are making more of an effort to help me with the housework. I'm grateful. Even your smallest efforts mean a lot to me and go a long way."*

The state of mind we can easily inhabit is one of high standards and equally high criticism. These "high standards" we demand are usually a reflection of our own strengths! We assume others ought to have the same strengths as we do. We follow this expectation with rigid rules and cutting critiques. If our partners don't do as we do and think as we think, we assume they are less than us rather than *different* than us. We mask our fear of the unknown with criticisms, and instead of growing gratitude, we cultivate contempt. We can err on the side of "that's simply not good enough" or we can err on the side of "you're trying, and your effort speaks volumes. I see you trying. I'm grateful." Change and growth sometimes happen swiftly, but most of the time, change is a slow, gradual process. If we want our loved ones to remain rigidly stuck in behaviors we hate, criticize them. Wouldn't we rather see trust and connection blossom? Then notice and speak up about every small step.

Gratitude flows from uncertainty. In a world of constant change where not everything promised can be counted on, gratitude is the experience and expression of relief from the unpleasantness life sometimes brings us. We feel alone, but a warm phone call conveys the opposite. We feel overworked, but a helping hand relieves the hardship. We feel undeserving, but a generous gesture affirms our worth. Gratitude flows partly from an element of surprise. We do not know what's coming, so when it is pleasant we are thankful.

Being on the lookout for goodness is a way of living, a state of mind.

WE DON'T UNDERSTAND ITS POWER

Gratitude transforms the focus of our minds and therefore the emotions we feel. There is much psychological debate over whether thoughts drive feelings or feelings drive thoughts, but suffice it to say they are indelibly connected. While we can't always control how we feel, we can control our thoughts. We have control over what we fixate on and what kinds of thoughts dominate our mental landscape.

Gratitude can transform a gloomy day into a joyful one. It can transport an angry, sullen heart into a space of soft openness. It enables the one who has been hurt to make peace. It inspires the one who has grown bored and restless to reengage. It reimagines and recasts our beloved from a dark adversary to a shining light once again. Gratitude does all this and more! By changing the thoughts of our minds, we change the chemical experience of our bodies. We can literally change ourselves and our outlook by choosing to see what we are thankful for rather than what we despise, resent, dislike, and resist.

Gratitude softens hearts faster than apologies. An apology is a complex offering, and we'll take a closer look in Chapter 11, but gratitude holds a power that an apology never will. An apology comes from seeing ourself and the pain we've caused. It is an outward demonstration of self-reflection and self-knowledge (when it is sincere). A statement of gratitude, on the other hand, is an acknowledgment of good in another. To apologize, we need to see ourselves. To show gratitude, we need to see another. We turn our attention, our eyes, our thoughts, and our hearts to the other, and the expression is one that says, "I see you, and *you are good.*"

This has the power to transform us. We tend to become what we hear about ourselves. People who are constantly told "you can't do it" have a tougher time believing in themselves than people who hear frequent messages of encouragement and affirmation. Gratitude is a gentle or powerful rush of oxygen to a fire. It feeds the flames of the best of us. Criticism will function like cold water on those flames. Gratitude can bring it back to life.

An expression of gratitude for even the smallest good deed will water the seed that is trying to take root. Some of us are simply stingy with our gratitude. If it's not done "right," "perfectly," "completely," or up to our standards, we won't give a shred of our heartful thanks to another. We wait for others to live up to what we expect, and when that happens... then we'll show gratitude.

No.

Show it now. Show it today. See the good, however small. Speak it. We all need to hear it, and our partner is no different. If we see one courageous step in the right direction, we stoke that fire with every grateful word we can find. Then we watch it burst into life.

INGRATITUDE

We fail to show gratitude for four main reasons:

- **Forgetfulness**
- **Blindness**
- **Resistance**
- **Entitlement**

Forgetfulness is usually the outcome of a life that is overbooked. The human mind can only hold so much information and activity day to day. We need spaces of silence, solitude, and reflection to function at our best, but when any or all of these three go lacking for extended periods of time, life starts to blend and bleed, one day into another, into an endless race of busy-going-nowhere. We forget which day it is, birthdays, important events, and we forget to show appreciation and gratitude. Acts of love, goodness, thoughtfulness, and generosity may be happening all around us, but all we can see is a to-do list we simply must complete.

When we forget to communicate gratitude, we strain the relationships in our lives. Relationships are a dance of seeing, reflecting, and connecting with one another.

Gratitude functions as the pause between the dance numbers. No one can keep up the dance without stopping. We need a pause, a break, to look at one another and say, "This is fun!" Without that pause, that moment of recognition, the dance loses its meaning. We feel no warmth. Not because it isn't there, but because we haven't paused long enough to notice it. The first person who misses out when gratitude is absent is the receiver. We've all heard the phrase: "stop and smell the roses." What does that mean if not to stop and appreciate what is right before us? The scent of the rose is always available; it's up to us to bend our head and breathe it in. Gratitude is a wonderful and effective way to hit pause on the rush of life and come back into the present moment.

Blindness is the inability to see. It can be congenital or the outcome of an accident or disease. Relational blindness can occur the same way. Some of us weren't raised in households where our goodness was seen and appreciated. Some of us come from family environments where we not only didn't receive positive feedback on our strengths and gifts, we were unseen or criticized instead. We are used to working without encouragement or thanks. In this way, we were "born blind." We do not perceive our own goodness, and therefore we can be blind to it in others. We don't give ourselves any grace, we withhold it from others, and this makes it difficult for us to see their goodness and show gratitude. Some of us have learned ingratitude as a result of trauma or harm done to our hearts. At some point in our lives, we naturally bubbled up with the spontaneous delight in others' gifts and beauty, but we've learned not to show it. We've learned that good things are yanked away, so why bother? We have tragically been conditioned to believe that vulnerability leads to pain, so we keep our thankfulness close to the vest. This is ingratitude as a disease. We were healthy. Ingratitude crept up on us.

To become grateful, we need to simply open the eyes of our hearts and begin to *see* again. As a means of developing this powerful mindset and skill, some keep a gratitude journal. They list three things, at the end of the day, for which they feel genuine gratitude. Some do this in the morning, as a way of setting their mindset for the day. All these techniques work! The practice is painful when we are accustomed to finding fault instead. We may feel like we are losing control and dropping our standards when we express gratitude instead of dissatisfaction. But how in control of one another are we anyway? Criticism fosters fear and shame. Gratitude endows another with power, energy, joy, and purpose. We get to choose how we want to influence one another. By opening our eyes to see what is already there, we give our loved one the experience of being seen.

Do not pretend gratitude. Nothing is hollower and more useless than empty compliments, also called flattery. *Really look.* It's there. The goodness, effort, and beauty we desperately want to experience in love is there. Blindness means we can't see, but that doesn't mean the world is blank. To be blind to the good in another person means the problem is with our eyes, not the other person. When you see goodness in your partner, share it.

> *"I see you getting up earlier to work out. I'm proud of you and grateful that you're taking care of your body."*

> *"I loved the gift you gave me. It showed me that in the midst of your busy life, you take the time to find something special for me. I feel special to you. Thank you."*

Let it be true. Let it be honest. Let it be heard.

Resistance is the choice to willfully refuse and reject another's goodness. We prioritize power over connection;

we choose a win over a kiss. Resistance occurs when we are living in such deep anger that spite has become a wall around us. We simply *will not* express gratitude. We lie to ourselves and our partners by effectively saying, "I don't see anything good in you to appreciate." This is a choice to be blind. It is a choice to not see. This is a function of the will, not a forgotten gesture or a failure to see. This is a choice that means we will not bless another because we have been hurt. Maybe it was our partner or someone from our past, but whatever the cause, we resist gratitude because we won't give up our anger. It is our armor. We have believed the lie that we are safer behind anger than in the power of love. Gratitude, as an action that conveys appreciation of another's goodness, is the ultimate disarmament. To hold contempt over another is an attempt to hold power over them. We are the judges. We are the moral superiority. We are in the right. It's awfully high and mighty up there in our ivory tower. It's also very lonely.

Entitlement can occur when we are unaware of or unexperienced with suffering. The hardship of suffering and survival creates a lived experience of how bad things can get, and we are therefore more apt to notice when things are good. In the absence of suffering, we assume that ease is the norm, and we fail to show gratitude. We expect, we receive, and we take.

Entitlement can grow when we take our partner's gifts and strengths for granted and fail to express our thankfulness for what they do.

"Are you saying I should thank my husband every time he takes out the trash?"

Well, would it kill you?

"Why should I have to express gratitude for things my wife should be doing anyway?"

You can choose not to. But if you'd like to create an atmosphere of joy and warmth in your home, maybe rethink the entitlement.

Entitlement by its very nature assumes. It takes for granted. It expects. Relationships are not about assumptions. They are about choices. We choose to love, and that choice deserves appreciation and therefore expressions of gratitude.

We are prone to habitual behaviors. Why not foster a habit of expressed gratitude instead of silence or constant criticism? We're going to have habits one way or the other. Our habits are our choice. Gratitude is a happier, more productive, more connective habit than criticism or entitlement.

"WHAT DO YOU SAY?"

Children are natural givers. They find a precious flower and hand it to Mom. They find a neat rock and can't wait to share it with Dad. They give cuddles and kisses generously and freely. For most of us, our "gifts" were perceived and received as charming tokens of innocence and affection. A picture we colored and gifted to Mom was acknowledged with a squeeze and an exuberant "Thank you!" A Christmas ornament made of popsicle sticks earned us a hug and a kiss from Aunt Martha. Our parents and loved ones showed gratitude when we expressed our love for them in tangible ways – through gifts and tokens. This is indeed healthier than parents not expressing gratitude, and some of us grew up in that kind of cold environment, but the gift, the token isn't the whole story.

If we had distant parents and experienced little to no gratitude from one or both, we may have grown up with a sense of despondence. We may have had a hopeless attitude of "what's the point? If I give and nobody notices or appreciates, why give at all?" If we keep trying and giving and aren't receiving any thanks, acknowledgment, or connection in return, it dampens our enthusiasm to keep putting forth the effort. Effort and energy must be met with acknowledgment and appreciation at least some of the time. Often is better than seldom. Newton's Third Law of Motion states that for every action, there is an equal and opposite reaction. Relationally speaking, this holds true. When children give and it is noticed and appreciated, the giving continues and increases. When children give and their gifts go unseen, their energy does not fall off. It is diverted elsewhere – to friends, to themselves in isolation, to school, to romantic relationships, to video games, and so on. It is drained from the relationship and poured out some place else. This can show us quite a bit about the importance and purpose of gratitude. It connects the giver and the receiver. Children who do not receive thanks and therefore do not feel seen divest their energy to other receptacles. To be thanked is to be seen, and we needed this as children. Everyone needs it now.

Some of our parents were absent-minded and/or distracted. The worries and responsibilities of adulthood – money, providing, schooling, relationships – kept them sorely disengaged from their children. They were present enough to be a fixture in the room, but their heart was not attuned or available. Children who grow up with absent-minded or un-present parents often form patterns of withdrawal or enact strong emotional displays for attention. These extremes do not foster secure relationships between parents and children, and the patterns are almost always repeated in adult relationships. Gratitude – spoken words that say, "I see you, and you are good" – is a powerful tool for bringing parents back into the room and into the moment with their children.

Some of our parents were rigid in their authority, and in this world view, parents do not thank children. These parents will not offer gratitude because children are simply doing what is expected of them. They do not praise a job well-done because they are comparing their children's relative ease with their hardship growing up. "No one thanked me. Why should I thank you?" The problem with this perspective is twofold. First: the past is not the standard; it is simply the past. If it was healthy, repeat it. If it was unhealthy, do not repeat it; transform it. But we cannot nostalgically remain fixed on past behavioral patterns if those patterns did not serve us or our relationships. Second: becoming emotionally alive and expressive is vital here. If we cannot feel the pain from our past, we will cause the same harm to our children. Denial allows trauma to be passed down through family systems. We need to feel in order to heal. That which we feel and heal is not passed down to the next generation.

Some parents are critical. They find fault much more readily than goodness. If our parents were critical and our lives were examined under their lens of negativity, this becomes how we see ourselves and others. We are highly self-critical, and we do not tolerate normal human weakness well. We were not appreciated; we were found to be inadequate, time and again. And so we do not thank. We see everyone around us as not measuring up. The healing process here begins with the self: we grow in our appreciation of ourselves. We practice noticing and expressing when we do well, the steps we are taking, the growth we are accomplishing. This naturally, organically shifts our perspective on those around us. As we can see ourselves and proclaim, "I am good!" we can see others and proclaim the same truth.

However our parents showed gratitude for us or failed to show it, the real gift must be acknowledged. The gift of a child is not a card, an ornament, drawings, or crafts. The gift is not behavior, obedience, or any other action.

The gift of a child *is* the child.

When we were children, were our actions and gifts highlighted or the heart behind them? How often were we seen? Not what we did, made, built, or gave... but us. Did our parents communicate that they could see our hearts – our caring, thoughtfulness, creativity, kindness, selflessness, or compassion?

If they could not and did not, we must begin this now. The wounds of childhood are felt and healed in adulthood, bringing us into mental and emotional maturity. It is time to notice ourselves and give ourselves the appreciation we need. We can then do that for our children.

GRATITUDE IN ACTION

Some of us shrink from the language of gratitude because it is vulnerable. Gratitude reveals the softer, needier places within us. We are sick in bed with the flu, and a friend delivers soup and crackers. Our genuine expression of thanks is due to our human weakness and need. If we were strong, capable, and healthy all the time, there would have been no need for the visit and the charity. We don't like to feel or be perceived as weak and needy, so some of us have a difficult time acknowledging inwardly and verbally when someone meets us at the level of our need. To show gratitude is to be aware of the places in our lives where we simply receive, and receiving is far more vulnerable than giving.

Some of us don't express gratitude because we simply

don't make or take the time to notice or say it aloud. It's not worth our effort, and our lives are one continuous cycle of doing and working and worrying and criticizing and judging and perhaps enjoying someone or something, only to run on the same hamster wheel day after day.

Honing the skill of gratitude necessitates that we stop long enough to notice what is happening around us. We cannot find the words if we do not find the time. Relationships require investments of time and energy. Gratitude is another way of saying, "I see you. I see your goodness, it enriches my life, and I'm so grateful. You are worth the time it takes to see and say this."

Sometimes a look is enough to convey gratitude. We have all watched someone open a personal and specific birthday card at a gathering and give the writer of the card the "look." The look says, "Gosh, you know me." Words are important, but communication is what we are after. We need to communicate our gratitude – with words, looks, a thank you note, or an embrace. When you feel it, express it. This is glue in relationship.

• • •

Karen had never explored or processed the effects of her father's criticism on her. She had numbed the feelings of humiliation, disconnection, and shame. Once those feelings entered her consciousness, she immediately became aware of another set of feelings: the yearning she had always felt for her father's approval and appreciation. She felt the pain of both the constant criticism and the unmet desire, and it changed her. She realized she'd been doing the same thing to Glen, and if she didn't change some things quickly, she'd inflict the same pain on their little girl.

"If Dad had just said, 'Good job, Karen. Thanks, Honey,' it would have changed everything. I would have wanted to do so much more! And I would have offered more of myself with joy instead of fear. I know how that feels. I don't want Glen or our baby to feel that way. I'm far more grateful than I show."

Karen learned that in offering herself grace, noticing her own good work, she was much more able to notice, note, and speak to Glen's efforts and strengths. Her image of him as a useless dolt was beginning to transform into a respectful relationship with a man she deeply admires for being exactly who he is. In conflict, she uses gratitude to balance her perspective when critical thoughts take the lead. She can speak her mind, heart, and needs with appreciation for what he is doing, and more importantly, who he is.

TOOL TIPS:
GRATITUDE

- Gratitude is both an experience and a skill.
- Gratitude is always appropriate. There is always goodness to acknowledge.
- Gratitude can be expressed for perceived acts and qualities of goodness – both great and small.
- We are ungrateful because we are forgetful, blind, resistant, or entitled.
- In relationship, effort and energy must be met with acknowledgment and appreciation.
- Gratitude connects the giver and the receiver.
- Gratitude must be expressed to work its magic.

QUESTIONS
FOR
DISCUSSION

1. Would I describe myself as a grateful person? Am I more inclined to criticize or thank? Why do I think this is so?

2. When did I receive my parent's gratitude or words of thanks as a child? What behaviors were appreciated by Dad? By Mom?

3. When and why do I experience difficulty expressing my gratitude for what another person has done or who another person is in my life?

4. How do I feel receiving others' gratitude?

5. How do I feel giving others' my sincere gratitude?

CHAPTER 6

Compassion

Justin and Monica met at a 12-step recovery meeting. Monica had been attending her usual Tuesday night Alcoholics Anonymous meeting when Justin landed in the empty seat next to her. After five minutes had passed, Justin leaned over and asked, "Is this Adult Children of Alcoholics?"

"No, this is AA," Monica informed him. "ACOA meets next door."

Justin thanked her, scooped up his bag, and headed next door to a different 12-step recovery group for adults who grew up in alcoholic and dysfunctional families. After the meeting, they both emerged from their respective rooms and found one another in the lobby. Eye contact, a smile, and a conversation brought the chemistry between them to life.

They came to therapy five months into what they described as a tumultuous, rocky dating relationship. Monica complained that Justin made too many demands of her. His constant need for attention, affection, sex, and activity was draining her, and he didn't seem to be able to hear the word "no." Justin complained that Monica was cold, aloof, and emotionally unavailable to him. Their energy was aggressive, conflictive, and sometimes downright abusive. I surmised quickly that I would need to separate them in order to make any therapeutic gains otherwise our sessions would disintegrate into arguments, and I'd be in the role of referee. I made arrangements to see Monica on Monday and Justin on Thursday of the following week.

Monica was born into a longstanding family history of functional and dysfunctional alcoholics. Strong and frequent drink was part of the fabric of her Russian-Irish heritage, and by the time she was nineteen, she was a full-blown alcoholic herself. During her childhood, being driven in a car by a drunk adult, being left alone for hours and sometimes all day, and family screaming matches were normal. Monica's formative years involved surviving dangerous situations in which her safety and security were threatened due to her parents' inebriation. As an only child, Monica found solace in her room, alone, a safe distance away from the chaos downstairs.

Justin also came from a line of alcoholics on his father's side. His mother's line was generations of preachers and missionaries, and religiosity ran as strongly in the veins of that family system as alcohol did on his father's side. Justin described his childhood as one long sermon, the title of which was "Be Perfect or Else." Shame was the language spoken at home. Be perfect or Dad will find you when he's drunk with a belt in his hand. Be perfect or Mom will condemn you for being "just like dad." A handsome boy from childhood to adulthood, Justin found a sense of safety and acceptance in attention from women. As a boy, they found him irresistibly adorable. As a man, they simply found him irresistible.

Monica grew up in an environment of fear and shame. Justin grew up in an environment of fear and shame. And neither of them knew it.

After meeting with them individually for several weeks, I suggested we resume a joint configuration and see where things were. As soon as they sat on the sofa, habit took over, and the fighting resumed.

"Nope! Hang on, Folks," I cut them off strongly. "We're not going to do this."

They looked at me dumbfounded, waiting for further explanation.

"This is what you do at home. It's not productive for you to do the same thing here, while you're paying me by the hour, so we're going to try something different. Turn your bodies so that you're facing one another. Look into each other's eyes and breathe. You're going to spend the rest of today's session telling stories, your stories."

Monica bravely volunteered to go first. She started slowly, tentatively, not knowing what to include or exclude, but eventually the narrative spilled out of her. I watched Justin's expression and energy switch from anger and defensiveness to curiosity to horror and then to sorrow as Monica described her childhood. Justin paused for a moment after Monica finished, taking it all in.

"Okay, Justin. Your turn."

Justin began. Tears rolled down his cheeks as he described the physical abuse he endured from his father and the spiritual and emotional abuse he endured from a mother who was clinging to religion with the same white knuckled grip with which his father clung to a bottle. Monica listened with a respectful, solemn stillness.

When Justin finished, silence as thick as smoke filled the room. Monica, generally more stoic than Justin, was reaching for a tissue to wipe her eyes, now wet with tears, when I gently asked, "How was this for you?"

More silence.

"I had no idea... what you went through... I didn't know," Justin whispered.

"I didn't either," Monica returned.

What needed to happen over the course of therapy never had a chance if we didn't start here.

Our sixth tool is Compassion.

• • •

PAIN MATTERS

Compassion is a stirring inside of us to move toward and help another who is in pain. The feeling may be described as a softening, a warmth, a focus on another accompanied by an energy to act. We look upon the person or being who is in pain, and everything else we were thinking or noticing shrinks to nothing as their pain becomes the sole focus of our attention. We immediately and intuitively inventory our resources: what can I offer this person in need? Without consciously choosing the thought, we immediately assess how much money we have in our wallet for the homeless woman on the corner. Without consciously choosing the action, we reach for a tissue to hand to the crying man on the park bench. Even if we do not act on the compassion we feel, many of us are simply aware of the stirring within us. All this movement toward another, emotionally and energetically, is the result of a phenomenon we call compassion. For most of us, it is automatic and unchosen. It simply occurs when we are moved by another's pain.

When we feel compassion, we are moved by the suffering of another because we are generally not suffering in the same way at the same time. There is space inside us to notice and hold pain because we are not in the same pain. The homeless woman on the corner may not feel a stirring to move toward and help another homeless woman. They're in the same boat. The brokenhearted man three park benches down may not have it in him to help the man who is crying alone. Those who suffer are usually helped by the strong, capable, and ready, not the exhausted, used, abused, broken, and weary. The space necessary to feel compassion may be present, but the energy required to act with compassion is generally held by those who are not presently suffering in the same way.

Feelings of compassion have motivated some of the most benevolent and compelling stories in human history. Mother Teresa's compassion for the children of Calcutta led her to start a ministry that lives on past her death. Her compassion became a way of life. Nonprofits, agencies, and ministries crop up all over the world because those who are capable feel moved to offer what they have to alleviate the suffering of others. The one who lives in the first world is compelled to bring clean water to those in the third and begins a nonprofit to dig wells. The one who has food is moved to provide for those who hunger. The loving couple with resources to share adopts. The stories are as beautiful as they are plentiful.

We are especially moved when we see those in pain reaching out to help others in pain, moved by others' pain in a way that eclipses their own. The poor help the poor; the suffering help those who suffer. We refer to a "well of compassion" when the capacity to notice and attend to others in pain is as deep and seemingly bottomless as a well.

Compassion requires a sort of forgetfulness. In order to feel and act out of compassion, we must momentarily forget what we suffer and focus on the needs of another.

Compassion is the stirring within us that says, "pain

matters." Life isn't easy, and losing our innocence is a painful rite of passage. We are all born with the assumption that our needs will be met in the world as they were in the womb – effortlessly and continuously. As we discover that this is not the case and that we must learn to tolerate pain and loss, we need to readjust our expectations so we don't incur the constant agony of disappointment. Why is compassion so important to us? Because people generally don't enjoy pain, and we expend a lot of energy and spend a lot of money trying to eradicate it or at least escape it. Humans have articulated advanced spiritual and philosophical systems of thought and rituals to transcend our pain. In every religious worldview, the promise of heaven, afterlife, or transcendence is a world where there are "no more tears," where pain has ceased. We deeply desire a world, a reality, an existence that is pain-free, but we know we cannot have it in this life. So how do we live in a world where pain is inevitable?

We attempt to reduce or eliminate it for ourselves and one another, and the impetus to do this is compassion. Compassion means hope for relief. It means that when another person sees our pain and is moved by it, it increases our chances that they'll do something about it.

COMPASSION IS A CHOICE

The feeling of compassion is automatic and involuntary. We do not choose it. The skill, unlike the feeling, involves choice. Compassion as a skill means we have the ability, through repetition and practice, to consciously move our focus away from our own pain and onto the pain of others. It means that when there is conflict and strife in our relationships, we are willing and able to effectively say, "I see that we are both suffering right now, but I am creating space inside me to hear your pain and act toward alleviating it." This is what enables us to truly listen when we want to be heard. This is what enables us to validate another when we feel unseen and misunderstood. This is what allows us to hit pause on our own anger and hurt when we realize we too have hurt another.

If both partners in relationship insist on their own pain taking priority, no resolution or repair is possible. We will both stay rooted in our own woundedness and never reach toward one another to bridge the gap. This is like driving by a starving man when we have a carload of groceries and saying, "Well, I'm going to be hungry too. I can't afford to give him anything." We have a name for this person: Ebenezer Scrooge. We may judge Scrooge harshly, but we are Scrooges in our relationships! We withhold our love, attention, and care when our partner is clearly suffering. We withhold our compassion, because we are also in pain. We refuse to listen, validate, and console because we have been wounded. Scrooge blamed the poor for their situation and failed to see the injustices of the system of which he himself was a part. Likewise, we blame our partner for their faults instead of seeing how we have participated in creating the relationship system in which we find ourselves! Superiority and self-interest replace compassion in a heartbeat.

To have compassion for our partners is to notice their pain and move to alleviate it. Do we only do this when we are pain-free? When their pain was not caused by us? When they have caused us no pain whatsoever? If we are waiting for the perfect conditions in order for compassion to arise, it never will. All humans are flawed. Perhaps we move toward the crestfallen man on the park bench with openhearted compassion until we realize he's wracked with remorse; he's cheated on his partner. "Well then, he doesn't deserve my compassion! He chose this pain!" We yank back our hearts and our resources in cold judgment.

Scrooge.

Perhaps we join an agency that travels to the third world to provide clean drinking water for the poor, and when we arrive at the village, we discover that the villagers condone and practice child marriage. We turn on our heels, gather up our supplies, board the plane, and off we go to find people more deserving of our goodness!

Scrooge.

The man needs compassion. The villagers need compassion. And both deserve it. So do we.

The discipline of practicing an action over and over, regardless of feelings, is the very essence of skill development. The skill of compassion means we have trained our minds to view ourselves and others with attention to their pain. It means we can find the place in us that cares, and a soft, compassionate heart soon follows. It means we do not judge the reason for the pain; we simply attend to it. To stand in judgment of our partners as to whether or not they are worthy of compassion is to embody Ebenezer Scrooge. It is to turn off our hearts toward others and see ourselves as superior. To offer compassion does not mean we agree with another's behavior, nor does it mean that we are eliminating the consequences of said behavior. Compassion is not condoning. It simply means we are responding to pain with the emotional and physical resources we have.

We might find it necessary to address unhealthy, hurtful, or harmful behavior at a later time, but the moment of suffering is the moment of care. It is difficult to learn lessons when we are in pain. We must first move out of the pain, and then the space opens for learning. Compassion says, "Your pain matters." And it does. The source, the conditions, and the reasons matter too, but they matter later. In the moment, we attend to one another in pain, despite our own. This is a skill.

POLYANNA AND
LITTLE ORPHAN ANNIE

In order to understand our own tendencies toward giving, withholding, and receiving compassion, it's useful to reflect on how our parents showed or failed to show us compassion as children.

All parents want to give their children a "happy childhood," but we know that this is impossible. No child is happy all day, every day. To be born is to face life itself, and life involves pain. We cannot escape it if we are alive on the earth. Without the perspective that years of life give us, pain in childhood is especially scary. Children don't know when or how their pain will end. Compassion from adults gives children hope: relief from pain is possible.

In order to alleviate children's pain, some parents will simply deny it. "You're ok!" they cheerfully declare, when the child is crying. "Shake if off!" they call out, when the child limps toward the sidelines of the soccer field. "There are plenty of fish in the sea," they remind the heartbroken teen. With the best of intentions, parents shove their children past pain into a "positive" mindset. We never had a moment of connection, embrace, or consoling. We just "adjusted our attitudes" and got "back in the game." This is the Polyanna approach. *Polyanna* was first a novel then a major motion picture released in 1960. It tells the story of an orphaned girl who turns the tide of an entire town with her relentlessly cheerful attitude. While this was a charming depiction of childlike innocence and resilience, it is not an effective or realistic parenting strategy. If we were raised by people who constantly taught us to "look on the bright side" without hearing our hearts first, we were raised to be Polyannas – constantly cheerful, never discouraged. But denying pain doesn't reduce it; it suppresses it. Compassion, on the other hand, involves attunement. Parents need to attune to children, hear and see their pain, acknowledge it, then help with perspective and resilience. If we didn't receive this kind of attuned compassion, we may struggle with giving it to ourselves and others.

If our parents witnessed our pain and did not show concern or care, we may have grown up with a deep sense of hopelessness within. This kind of adult callousness toward children was depicted perfectly in the classic film, *Annie*. The overseer of the orphanage, Mrs. Hannigan, watches with a combination of glee and disgust as the filthy, little orphaned girls race around the orphanage, slaving away at one chore after another, singing about their "Hard Knock Life." The film portrays the orphans in a charming and playful light, and we all know how the story ends. Daddy Warbucks, a Scrooge who finds his heart, rescues Annie from the mean Mrs. Hannigan, and everyone is redeemed into one, big, happy family. But the reality for children who do not receive compassion – whether orphaned or not – is quite different.

Children lack the maturity, intellect, resources, and agency to effectively address and transform their own pain. They need adults to see, notice, and take action. Without adults in their lives who move to help the child's pain, children are left to languish on their own. Most parents will not allow their child to suffer physically, but a great many parents will allow their children to suffer in excruciating emotional pain. Too many parents fail to give daily compassion while children are on the exhilarating and painful ride of simply growing up. This is a form of emotional neglect.

In cases of parental abuse, we experienced pain in

the form of harm *caused* by parents who did nothing to reduce it or make amends for it. And it continues without reprieve. When parents treat children without regard for the tenderness and sensitivity of their young hearts, frightening and forcing them into submission, and then do nothing to address the hurt and shame they cause, children grow up confused as to what is acceptable and unacceptable treatment.

On the contrary, if we received compassion as children, we had parents who saw our pain – regardless of the cause – and *cared*. The acknowledgement of our pain, demonstrated by the compassion we received, set a standard in our hearts: we deserve kindness, protection, and concern. The message of compassion to a young child's heart is: you deserve love. Parents will hurt their children from time to time, but in order to heal the relationship, amends must be made because the parent feels compassion for the hurt the child feels. When parents make amends, it sends three important messages to the child: (1) my behavior was not kind or loving, (2) your hurt matters, and (3) you *deserve* kindness and respect. This is the core of compassion.

Some pain is productive for children, like the pain children feel when parents institute healthy boundaries for the child's wellbeing. This pain need not be removed as it is functioning in a productive way for the child. Mom tells Ashley that bedtime is in five minutes. Ashley begins to cry and protest. She does not want to go to bed. Mom holds the boundary, reiterating that Ashley has five more minutes, but gathers the crying child in her arms and consoles her through the tearful protest. Ashley's bedtime boundary remained intact, but she was not alienated for disliking it. In fact, her tears moved her mother's heart toward compassion, and she was comforted in her distress. When she went to bed, she was in a state of safe connection with her mother, not distant aloneness. We must face pain, but we need not do it alone.

Some of us had to not only face the pains and disappointments of life but had to do so without loving parents softening the blows of reality. We grew up tough, able to withstand vast amounts of pain. We had to. No one was noticing or softening the blows, and the result was we hardened our hearts out of pure survival. A heart that feels pain and is not seen or comforted will simply harden in order to not feel anymore. The emotions are there, but they are buried. The desire for comfort is there, but it is buried. We grow so accustomed to a world without compassionate love that we deny even needing it. By the time we are teenagers, we are calloused souls.

COMPASSION IN ACTION

Compassion is a stirring within, not a function of the intellect. This is involuntary when we witness the suffering of others from a place of comfort and ease. We drive by someone standing on the side of the road in the pouring rain with a flat tire, and from the comfort of our warm, dry vehicle, we pull over to help. We didn't cause the flat tire, but we can do something about it.

Perhaps we have suffered a similar struggle as a person expressing their pain. We listen to our friend recount their work woes, and we recall our own struggles to keep the money coming in. We have not caused their struggle, and perhaps we don't yet know why our friend is struggling in their job, but we share their pain. We offer encouragement.

Compassion informs care. We see misery, we express concern which connects us to the one who suffers, we may ascertain what might be lacking, and if we have the resources to help we move into action. Compassion is what happens between seeing and acting.

Compassion in intimate, romantic relationships can be far more complex.

Sometimes the pain we witness in our partner is brought on by external factors. A job is lost, a parent dies, a friend betrays, or a possibility extinguishes. These are painful experiences, and it is easy to find the compassion within our hearts because the source of the pain is not connected to us. We comfort and encourage from our "well of compassion," and if compassion comes naturally to us, our well is deep for the task. We are innocent as to the cause of the pain; we simply get to respond to it.

But sometimes and even often, the pain is caused by factors *within* the relationship. Our relationships are an intricate web of actions and responses, and what hurts and needs attention is different for everyone. Many of our failures to love one another fall by the wayside and can be overlooked and forgiven. Sometimes, however, our failures and our partners' failures to love well are pronounced. They hurt acutely, and they need compassion and care. Our actions may cause others pain, and their actions cause us pain. In both cases, we have a choice: we can grow in compassion or we can be a Scrooge.

When we have acted in unkind, unloving, or ego-driven ways, the onus is on us to do the repair work. It's our responsibility (Chapter 1). The actions committed against us do not matter...yet. If we have acted outside of our values and caused another pain, we must take responsibility to repair the relational wound. There will and should be time to address the wounds committed against us, but our partner's willingness to do this is outside the boundaries of what we can control. Our path is our responsibility, and this is where our power is. This means that we offer compassion, even when we have also been wronged, *because it is right.*

"But he hurt me!" Offer compassion.

"But she's cold!" Offer compassion.

Friends, we must stop being five-year-olds on the playground of life who pull the ponytails and kick the shins of those who pulled and kicked us first. Two wrongs don't make a right, remember? If we have caused harm, we repair it, and we do this, in part, by offering compassion. To grow in this is to mature into adults.

Offering compassion when we have caused pain is, by default, an admission of wrongdoing, and some of us have a very difficult time with this. We cannot sit in the presence of pain we've caused, so in order to avoid admitting that we've done anything wrong, we withhold our compassion so we can effectively avoid seeing our fault. "If I act like I haven't hurt you, I haven't hurt you" is how this way of thinking goes. We make a joke, we "lighten the mood," or we busy ourselves with "serving" to avoid the difficult truth. We become defensive, trying to trick ourselves and our partners into the perception that we've done nothing wrong. We need to learn to say, "I've hurt you with my behavior, and I'm sorry. I can see I've caused you pain. Please tell me what I can do to alleviate the pain I've caused." We hear the voices in our heads that scream, "Are you kidding me?! He doesn't deserve this!" "Look at all she's done to me, and I'm the one offering compassion?!" Yes, you are. Because if our relationships stand any chance of healing and becoming safe and connected, we must develop the skill of compassion, even when we've been wronged too.

This is what it looks like to take responsibility and offer compassion when we have caused pain:
- We see the pain (we've caused).

- We stop what we're doing.
- We acknowledge it.
- We allow our hearts to be moved by the suffering of another.
- We address it: *"How can I reduce this pain?"*

Often what's needed is simply an authentic apology. Perhaps we need to sit and listen for a few minutes while our loved one processes the pain they are carrying because of our unloving actions against them. Feeling heard is incredibly healing on its own. Perhaps we need to offer reassurance that the harm will not happen again and again. We cannot promise perfection, but we can absolutely demonstrate awareness, concern, and the intention to grow. We do what we can to heal the wound we have caused, and we hold the wounds committed against us on the back burner *for the moment.* Our own pain, entitlements, wounds, and rights are distant right now. We are "forgetting" ourselves in a loving way. We take a deep breath, and we focus on our partner. The more we do this, the easier it gets.

We breathe and refocus.

When we have been wronged, compassion is different. Instead of engaging the pain of the one we have hurt, we engage their brokenness and when present, their remorse. Both of these must be engaged with compassion.

"Wait a minute! I'm the one who's been wronged here! Aren't I the one who's supposed to be receiving compassion now? When's it my turn?"!"

And so we find another place within us that is five-years-old on the playground of life...

Friends, it is *always* our turn to offer compassion. We cannot control the compassion offered to us nor can we demand it. Compassion doesn't work that way. It is a stirring within the heart of the person who offers it. In all situations, we can only control the compassion emanating from one entity: ourselves.

Every voice in our head will scream at us,

"No way! This person will never reciprocate this compassion, and I'll be all alone! I will be taken advantage of! He wronged me! She doesn't deserve my compassion!"

When our loved one admits their wrongs, we offer compassion because the humility and self-awareness necessary to do this are difficult virtues to hold and enact. We need not cause more suffering by beating the dead horse or withholding our forgiveness. We feel compassion for the discomfort of the person who is admitting fault. It's difficult. We notice it. Our hearts are moved.

When our loved ones cannot admit their wrongs, we offer compassion because it is lonely and fearful to live in a body that cannot hold and acknowledge its own brokenness. If we have been clear about the wrong committed against us, and our loved one cannot acknowledge the wrong or even validate our emotions (validation is a step toward admitting), we offer compassion because it is painful to live this way. Relationships are shallow, even dead-end experiences when we cannot admit our wrongs. We do not grow, and our relationships do not grow either. This is sad, painful, and deserving of compassion.

Both of these scenarios are difficult but not impossible. It is possible to offer compassion to the person we have hurt. It is possible to offer compassion to the one who has hurt us. It requires conscious attention, practice, patience, and time – just like any other skill.

Offering compassion does not mean we must stay engaged or committed in relationships. We can choose to move on from friendships and dating partners, even spouses,

if compassion is consistently absent. If a relationship is of an intimate nature but lacks compassion, it is destined to be unsatisfying at best, wounding at worst. This skill meets a deep need in all of us, and that need is: *we need to know and feel that our pain matters and that those close to us care enough to act.*

• • •

Justin and Monica had their work cut out for them. They had both developed so many unhealthy survival skills to sustain emotionally damaging childhood environments that they needed to essentially rewrite the script of how they communicated as adults. In many ways they were starting from scratch.

Their new, compassionate views of one another were the foundation for the process. When it was hard, taxing, stressing, and seemed impossible, they would remember the pain they'd both endured, and they were able to see the unhealthy behaviors in the other through eyes of compassion, not judgment and blame.

"I still get mad at her," Justin confessed. "She withdraws when we argue and leaves me alone in the living room by myself. But then I think about *why* she does that. I keep thinking about that little girl, alone and scared in her room, and I go knock on the door."

"And I come out!" Monica exclaimed with a laugh. "I need to remember that attention feels like love to you. When I withhold warmth, you don't feel loved by me, even though I do still love you but need space."

Their dialogue had changed. They had moved from accusation to awareness. Coping with one another's behaviors and differences was going to be a challenge, but if this relationship was ever going to move out of surviving to thriving, compassion was a nonnegotiable.

TOOL TIPS:
COMPASSION

- Compassion is a stirring inside of us to move toward and help another who is in pain.
- Compassion is how we survive in a world in which pain is inevitable.
- Compassion means we forget our own pain and attend to the pain of another, regardless of who caused it.
- The moment of suffering is the moment of compassion. We can address the complexity of the situation later.
- When we fail to receive compassion, our hearts grow hard. Compassion is how hearts are softened.
- We offer compassion in relationships, even when our partner has hurt us too. This is adult maturity and humility.
- We cannot control the compassion we receive, only the compassion we give.

QUESTIONS
FOR
DISCUSSION

1. How was pain handled in my family? Physical pain? (cuts, scrapes, bruises, medical issues, etc.) Emotional pain? (loneliness, boredom, hurt feelings, alienation, etc.)

2. Did I feel pain (worry, fear, anxiety, shame, premature responsibility, abuse, etc.) that no one saw? How did I handle it? How has this affected how I interact with my pain and others'?

3. What did I learn about how to attend to other people in emotional pain?

4. What do I want from others when I am in emotional pain?

5. When is it easiest for me to offer others compassion? When is it most difficult for me?

CHAPTER 7

Boundaries

Beverly was a rock star. She'd graduated high school and college a year before her peers due to the combination of her intellectual aptitude, her self-confidence, and her ambition. These three qualities rocketed her ahead. She thrived in whatever she endeavored. When I met her, Beverly was at a comfortable and financially successful point in her career. A divorcee, Beverly had a thriving circle of friends, a close relationship with her sister, and the freedom and financial position to truly enjoy being single.

Most people liked or at least enjoyed Beverly. Her outgoing personality coupled with an endearing, self-deprecating sense of humor took the edges off what would otherwise have been a rather intimidating presence. Standing at nearly six feet with model-like features, Beverly commanded attention. I noticed in our first session how easy it was for her to connect with me and communicate her thoughts.

Her primary reason for seeking therapy: she had trouble setting boundaries.

I found myself in disbelief. How could this dynamic, confident, accomplished woman have any trouble whatsoever expressing her boundaries to others?

"I get lightheaded whenever I have to confront someone," she explained. "I find myself diluting my words, weakening my position, or flat out capitulating. Then I just beat myself up. And I can't have a healthy relationship because I can't seem to talk about what I want and don't want, so I wind up settling because I can't walk away. I hate disappointing people. I'm afraid to hurt others, and I've wasted a lot of time…"

For a woman who used time on her side – to learn, grow, and advance herself – this was indeed a painful problem for Beverly.

I needed to learn her history. Her strong and capable personality didn't match her current struggle. Something was amiss. Some part of her, the part that could say "no," had been damaged.

"Beverly, when you were a child, how did your parents respond when you told them 'no'?"

She grew introspective and pensive, even appearing confused. Her eyes narrowed as she turned her gaze out the window for several moments, allowing the answer to arise from within her. Then she turned back toward me.

"I couldn't." She said it simply, quietly, and then said nothing more.

"What do you mean you couldn't?" I probed deeper.

"We weren't allowed, my sister and I. Mom and Dad were always right. Even when they were flat out wrong, they never apologized. They didn't believe parents should apologize to children. And their opinions were gospel truth, so I didn't really bother speaking up. The couple of times I did, I was shot down. I learned to shut up."

"So you had an impulse to say 'no' at one time," I reflected back to her, "and the word you just used is very important: you 'learned' to shut up. Is that right?" Beverly nodded. "In your most intimate relationships, you learned to shut down and shut up. And that's still going on now."

"Yes," Beverly said looking straight into my eyes, catching on to where I was going. I could feel her hopefulness. "The closer I get to someone, the harder it is for me to be honest."

"Well, that makes sense. Our relationships with our parents set the imprint for the relationships we'll have with intimate partners later in life. This is where we learn how to build intimacy or avoid it, and in your most intimate relationships as a child, with mom and dad, you learned to shut up. You didn't shut up naturally. You had to learn. You had thoughts, feelings, preferences, and a voice you learned to silence."

"Yes," she said with a hard edge of anger in her tone.

"Well, now you're going to *unlearn* how to shut down and shut up. You're going to learn to speak up and show up. It'll take some time, but you can learn."

Our seventh tool is Boundaries.

• • •

FROM THE INSIDE OUT

Boundaries originate inside us. We experience signals (in the form of emotions) that communicate comfort or discomfort, pleasure or pain, safety or danger. The verbalization of these preferences and needs is called setting or stating a boundary. Since they originate inside the body, feeling our feelings (Chapter 3) and being aware of our bodies is essential if we are going to be people who can set effective boundaries. When our bodies become tense, we pay attention. When our bodies relax and open, we pay attention. When we experience anger, we pay attention.

When we feel excitement and curiosity, we pay attention. We allow our whole being into our awareness, not just our thoughts which are only one part of us. Emotional awareness is the first step of setting boundaries.

Before we understand boundaries, we must understand commonality and difference. Imagine how humans would be perceived by aliens visiting us from another planet. They'd likely observe us as one race of people who do many of the same things. They would notice that we all experience common emotions, we communicate with one another in various languages, with facial expressions and sometimes our hands and arms. We go to work; we live in families and communities. We come and go, quite busy in our lives, and we only live so long.

The closer we zoom in, the more differences emerge. Some of us prefer the city life, some a more rural setting. Some of us get up early; some stay up late. Some of us love lively music; some enjoy silence. Some live in the colder regions of the planet; some love the heat. An even closer view shows even more difference. Some of us laugh more than others, and we laugh at different things. Some of us grew up in one place and moved somewhere else. Some of us stayed in our hometowns. The differences are endless! The closer we zoom in, the more different we are.

And yet… we are all still members of the human race.

Boundaries in relationships are how we remain connected in our humanity and distinct in our individuality. The closer the relationship, the more distinction.

"But wait! Aren't we supposed to be like our partners? Aren't we supposed to have a lot in common?"

We already do. And we are also quite distinct. The healthiest relationships don't require sameness. In a healthy, intimate relationship, differences are celebrated, not feared.

We accept individuality as a fact of life, not something to be altered, and that individuality is preserved and protected by our boundaries.

Let's get a better understanding of what boundaries are.

Imagine yourself walking along a path wide enough for just yourself, winding through a stunning wilderness. There are fields, mountains, valleys, flowers, waterfalls, and life all around you. Everywhere you look, there is beauty, adventure, and infinite landscape. Off in the distance, you can see a rain shower on the plains while the sun sets in a rainbow painted sky before you. As you look around you, the beauty stretches on forever in harmony and diversity. This path is you, internally. This is who you are inside: vast, beautiful, diverse, serene, rugged, filled with staggering mountain summit heights and deep, dark valley lows.

As long as you stay on your path, you have access to everything you see. Sometimes your path winds through the desert, and you meet with danger and despair. Sometimes the path winds through sandy beaches and warm ocean breezes, and your world is filled with ease and fulfillment, but no matter where it winds, it is *your* path, and as long as you stay on it, you stay true to who you are and who you are becoming.

Our boundaries are what keep us on our path. Everyone's path shares similar features: adventure, despair, fulfillment, joy, creation, beauty, wonder, boredom, and fascination, but our paths wind through different landscapes at differing speeds at different times of our lives. This is both the connection we feel with one another and the loneliness. We feel connected when our paths seem to align; we have a companion on the journey! Then we feel painfully disconnected when we perceive that we are walking alone; no one is close by. Two people create a child together. They share the paths of parenthood, but they do not parent in identical ways or even share all of the same opinions on what parenting should be. Their uniqueness informs their unique relationships with their children, and so even though there are many similarities and shared experiences, they are each still walking the path of their lives on their own, sharing stories and connection along the way.

Relationship does not mean walking the same path. It means choosing to share the journey. We tend to believe that love and marriage are a joining of two paths into one broader path. This is not the case. Love and marriage mean that we have chosen a partner to lend us company, support, humor, and help along the way, but if we believe that two paths merge into one, we will lose ourselves. We may perceive that our partner doesn't love us because he or she isn't jumping off their path and onto ours, and we may feel angry and desperate. Maybe we grow to resent them for being distant, separate, and "other." Or perhaps we find ourselves in relationship where another person is overly dependent, too close to us while we are walking our path, needing more than we can rightly give, and then reacting when we don't welcome them onto our path. We say, "That's your path; this is mine," and they feel abandoned. Or we say, "Please come a little closer to me for this part of the journey," and they cannot and will not reach out to take our hand while we walk through our pain.

This is why we need boundaries. We have to know where our limits are. Boundaries, emanating from inside us, tell us when to reach out and draw something or someone toward us and when to push back and restrain someone or something from us. The path is ours. Boundaries keep us on it.

In relationship, we tend to seek out similarity because it is familiar. After all, we've been living alone in our own skin for all the years and days and seconds of our lives, so when we think we've found someone else who "gets us," we believe we won't feel alone anymore! This is the myth of "falling in love." We see the other person as the perfect counterpart! What we are actually seeing is a reflection of the parts of ourselves we desperately need and want to see. We are seeing ourselves through their eyes, and we "love" what we see. Friends, we are merely falling in love with ourselves as seen by the other! "He thinks I'm beautiful, so I feel beautiful!" "She thinks I'm brilliant, and so I am!" I feel so good about myself when I'm with this person = I feel and see parts of me I already had but this person seemingly brings them out. Therefore, I feel alive! Therefore, it must be love! You were beautiful and brilliant in the first place. And when this mystical fantasy wears off and we begin to see the other person as they truly are, the person who was there all along, we say the "honeymoon is over." Then, and only then, can we begin to truly love. What we loved before, *who* we loved before, is a person who brought out of us what we longed to see and know of ourselves. But the stunning beauty of the other is there when the honeymoon wears off, ready to be seen and loved in their magnificent uniqueness.

Boundaries, therefore, are an essential part of love. The sooner we can get to the reality of "I am me and you are you," the faster we can really know love and give love. When we "fall" in love, our boundaries fall too. It's as if we and our partner are merged into one. "We're so alike!" we perceive. We even promise these things to one another in wedding vows! We are making promises we cannot keep. We will never be "one."

But we can be *unified*.

Unity is not conformity. Unity is choosing to bond in commonality instead of standing apart in our differences.

It occurs when the reasons for commonality are more important than those which separates us. But in order to have unity, there must be diversity first. Conformity is oppressive and soul-stealing. Unity is transcendent and bonding. Boundaries are part of what informs our diversity so that we can choose unity, so that we can choose love. Unity is a paradox because it arises from diversity. The greater the diversity, if it is allowed and honored, the greater the experience of unity and transcendent love we can have. If we cannot tolerate separateness and distinction, we cannot know love and we cannot unify.

Boundaries arise from conscious awareness. We become increasingly aware of how we are different from one another by listening to our internal emotional experience. We pay attention when our bodies say, "I don't like that," "that's not me," "I don't agree," "I want something different," "that doesn't feel good to me," and so on. External or expressed boundaries are simply the vocalization of these internal messages.

WHAT THEY ARE
AND WHAT THEY'RE NOT

1. **A boundary is not a punishment.** We don't withhold our love, affection, connection, or withdraw from loved ones in hurt and call that a boundary. A boundary is an expressed statement of preference and/or limitation, not a retaliation.

   "Do we have to go to the Johnson's tonight?"

   "We promised them we would..."

   "Peter drinks too much! I don't want to be in his house..."

   "What am I supposed to tell them?"

"If you don't care that I'm uncomfortable, fine! I'm not going anywhere with you."

Let's try again.

"I don't want to go to the Johnson's tonight. Peter drinks heavily, and I feel uncomfortable when I'm there. I think I need a break from this friendship to sort this out and figure out my next steps. I'd love it if you'd stay home with me and watch a movie, but I'm not going to go."

The boundary arose from within. He noticed his feelings of discomfort and chose to disconnect from the evening's activities in order to give himself time and space to choose his next steps. He does not tell his partner what to do or punish her for being in her own lane. He simply states his emotional experience, his plan to take care of himself, and invites his partner into that space.

2. **A boundary is not a threat or a negotiating tool.** We do not use boundaries to control others, instilling fear where there can and should be freedom.

"You've worked late four out of five nights this week."

"Yeah, I know. I'm sorry. I just have so much going on."

"Well, I'm tired of fixing dinner and waiting until you come home. If you want to eat, come home on time!"

Let's try again.

"I notice that you're working late more often. You must be tired, and I'm thankful for the long hours you're putting in to contribute to our bottom line. I'm also noticing some irritation inside me. I'm taking the time to prepare our meals, but they are cold by the time we sit down to eat. I'd love it if you could

move some things around so that you can eat with the family, but if that's not possible, I'm going to go ahead and serve dinner without you. We can heat up your dish when you get home."

This approach does not use threats as a negotiating tool. It respects the autonomy of each member of the relationship and opens up a space for choice. She can choose to come home or keep working late, but the consequence will be missed meals. The choice is hers to make.

3. A boundary is not a limitation dictated to others, informing them of what they can and cannot do.

"You haven't done a thing all day! You're so lazy!"

"You can't talk to me like that!"

Let's try again.

"I hear that you're upset with how I've spent my day. I'm willing to take a look at it and make some adjustments, but when you call me names, I feel hurt and insulted. I feel the need to self-protect from your words. If you want to talk to me about what you're feeling, I'm open to listening. However, if you are going to call me names, I'm going to leave the conversation until we can talk about this respectfully and productively."

Unkind language and abusive words are never, ever acceptable, but in reality, our partners can speak to us any way they like. They have that right. We, however, don't have to be present for hurtful language that we do not want to hear. That is *our* right. It is not our right to tell another person how they can act, but it is our right to choose whether or not we engage or disengage. This leaves both partners equally accountable with their autonomy intact, and the person receiving the boundary has a choice. They can lose connection by remaining in a reactive state, or they can choose to communicate with more gentleness.

"YOU'RE YOUR MOTHER'S SPITTING IMAGE!"

Children develop and are born in a state of experiential oneness with mother. Even though their DNA is distinct from hers, the nature of gestation is that the two persons share one home. When children are infants, their dependency on their mothers is both bonding and exhausting. Mothers frequently express conflicting desire of wanting their children to remain small but simultaneously urging them to the next developmental marker. *Once they're weaned... once they're potty-trained and out of diapers... once I get them in school... once they have their driver's license...* It's a dance of holding on, letting go, pushing forward, and grieving as they grow.

At the earliest stages of infancy, when child and mother are merged as one in the child's mind and body, it is normal for the child to enter a state of abject panic when mom is not present. It is as if the child is losing their world. When children begin to advance into the awareness of their autonomy, famously studied by John Bowlby and articulated in attachment theory, it is normal for children to become more at ease when mother is absent. They develop what mental health professionals call "object permanence." This means that when mom is absent, child believes that mom will eventually return. Just because mom is not in the room does not mean that mom has vanished forever. When children enter the next stage of attachment and begin to assert their will, our experience with boundaries and boundary setting begins in earnest.

If parents do not allow their children to have their voice by stifling them when they disagree with or challenge them, children may grow into adults with difficulty setting personal boundaries. If we have this difficulty as adults, it is likely that our voices and boundaries were not heard or honored as children. Parents may unknowingly sabotage boundaries in several ways.

One way is called enmeshment. This is when a parent and child form an unnaturally and unhealthily close bond. It's *too* close. There is no room for boundaries and distance in the relationship which are markers of healthy, autonomous people. When a parent enmeshes with a child, the parent is meeting their emotional needs through the child rather than the other way around. The parent is in effect leaning on the child for a sense of security, purpose, or companionship. The result of this unnatural and unhealthy configuration is that the child cannot voice their "no" to their parent without experiencing fear. Saying "no" may hurt the parent and disconnect the relationship, and no child will risk this. Children need freedom and safety to test and try their voice on their parents and trust that their differences will be met with wisdom, security, and respect. When a parent is relying on a child for their own emotional needs, their objectivity is at best skewed, at worst nonexistent. When letting a child take one step away means loneliness and despair, the parent will keep the child tethered through one means or another. They will often use guilt or emotional withdrawal. Children who experience enmeshment may become adults who suppress their voice because they fear being rejected. *If I couldn't have my voice with Dad, I can't have it with anyone.* Conversely, the child may grow into an adult who equates intimacy with feeling suffocated and may avoid intimacy in adulthood for fear of losing themselves. *If Mom needed every bit of me, you will too.*

If parents withdraw from their children in hurt or anger when the child voices his/her individual thoughts, feelings, and needs, this emotional withdrawal feels like abandonment to a child, **and there is nothing more terrifying for a child than abandonment.** Children will do *anything* to avoid parental abandonment as their very survival depends on their relationship to their parents. Children will form survival behaviors like people-pleasing and lying to avoid the emotional withdrawal of their parents. They will abandon themselves by ignoring their thoughts and feelings if those thoughts and feelings contradict mom and dad. They will choose this before they will risk feeling abandoned. Adults who people-please and fear setting boundaries have likely experienced the emotional withdrawal of parents when their thoughts, feelings, or needs were in conflict with mom or dad's.

Authoritarian parenting cripples the development of healthy boundaries as well. This parenting style is characterized by parents who assume that by virtue of their role and position as the parent, the "authority," they are always in the right. This style of parenting is common in highly religious or dogmatic households. When children agree with parents, children are allowed their voice. When children disagree with parents, simply because they happen to be in the position of lesser authority, they are by default wrong and should be silenced by dismissal or overpowering. These parents identify strongly with their egos, and any disagreement is viewed as a threat to their position. Resistance in children is met with punishment and emotional hostility. These parents exploit their authority, and the children are disempowered. If children experience authoritarian parenting, they can grow into adults who struggle with intense fear of punishment and anger should they assert their voices.

The common denominator is allowing differences

and learning to have relationship with differences *intact*. Boundaries are an assertion of differences. When parents discover places of difference or disconnection in children, the work is to honor those differences, even learn from them. Parents who insist that their children be in lock step with them are insecure and raise insecure children.

On the contrary, if parents listen to their children – validating, reasoning, guiding and allowing natural consequences for poor choices when appropriate – children grow up to become adults who can tolerate the similarities and differences inherent in relationship. How our authority figures responded to our individuality when we were children will play a large role in how easy or difficult it is for us to set boundaries as adults.

In truth, we are *not* our parent's "spitting image." We are *us*, wholly unique and worthy of individual respect and curiosity. Acknowledging the boundaries of children sends a message of respect and awareness of their individuality and personhood. We are like our parents in some ways, and we are vastly different in others. This understanding informs a balanced, healthy family system.

BOUNDARIES IN ACTION

Now the rubber meets the road. How do we do this? If setting boundaries is an essential tool in the relationship toolbox, where do we start and how does this become a skill?

1. Describe your emotional state.
Here's a helpful phrase: "I feel _____ when you _____ ."
This casts no blame, instead it describes an emotional reaction we are having. This is about actions

and reactions, stimuli and consequences, and these can be pleasant or unpleasant.

"When you really listen to me, I feel heard and loved."

"When you stare at your phone during dinner, I feel unimportant to you."

"When you stroke my lower back while we watch television, I feel aroused and sexual."

"When you don't return my text messages, I feel forgotten."

All of these expressions are simply statements of what is happening inside us. This is why emotional expression is essential (Chapter 3). Without an awareness of what we are feeling, we have no internal cues as to whether we are on our path or not.

When we set a boundary, we may choose to let our partner know *why*. The unpleasantness or pleasure of the emotion is what is driving the boundary. The more unpleasant, the stronger the boundary.

"I feel hurt and angry when you are consistently late. If you cannot be ready on time, I am going to plan on leaving for outings without you."

"I feel betrayed when you look at pornography. I cannot continue to give myself to you sexually if you are offering your sexual energy to porn."

2. Speak your boundary gently.

Gently. With gentleness. Be gentle. Did I say gently?

Why the emphasis on gentleness?

Boundaries are difficult to say and hear. Again, we want to live in the fantasy that we are one with another.

A boundary is a reminder that we are distinct which can feel painful, so we speak our boundaries gently. Deep down, we sometimes avoid setting boundaries because we fear we'll "hurt" each other, so we either skip over them altogether – too afraid to inflict pain – or we shout, expel, or throw them at each other like a bullet shooting from a gun. Neither is healthy. To stay silent or to verbally assault one another are two extremes. Rather, we learn to set boundaries gently, and we develop the skill.

"When you stay up later than me and then initiate sex after I've already fallen asleep, I feel tired and frustrated that I'm being awakened. I am already asleep. I am more open to sexual connection before 10pm on weeknights. After 10, I'm going to say no. I need sleep."

"When you see me doing chores and stay on the sofa watching television, I feel angry and somewhat abandoned. I can't keep this entire house clean on my own. If you'll help, I know we can finish it quickly together. If you won't help, I'm going to look into hiring a house cleaning service."

Let your tone be gentle.

3. Repeat the boundary calmly, if necessary.

We are creatures of habit. Our partners can't feel precisely what we feel in our bodies, so it's easier for them to forget a boundary than it is for us. We need to have an attitude of patience and pacing when we set a boundary. Be willing to repeat your boundary over the course of two to three weeks until your partner has the opportunity to learn it and integrate it. We rarely learn after the first hearing. We need repetition and practice. This is also true of boundaries.

"Sweetheart, it's after 10pm, and I need sleep. Let's talk in the morning about how and when we can share time together sexually. I love and want you too, but not this late."

"Babe, I'm sure you're engaged in what you're watching, but I need help right now. Will you help me? If this isn't something we can cooperate on, I'll look into hiring a service."

Patient and respectful reminders are essential.

4. If your boundary is not acknowledged, repeat it firmly. Not loudly.

Volume is only helpful if one is hard of hearing. Most of us are not hard of hearing; we are distracted or dismissive. When we need to reinforce our boundaries, we do this with firmness, not loudness. Loudness elevates blood pressure, pulse, and agitation. This is not what is needed. Firmness elicits more attention to what is being shared, and this is what is needed.

"I have made it very clear that if you will not change your tone, I'm not going to remain in the conversation. You are not changing your tone. I am leaving this conversation. I'll be willing to talk to you when you can change your tone."

5. If your boundary is not acknowledged verbally, it might be time for physical distance.

Sometimes what we need and feel is perceived as threatening to our partners. If we have expressed our emotions clearly and set a boundary that seems honoring to our own autonomy and theirs, and there is resistance and push back, there might be a need for a stronger boundary which is physical distance.

"You are following me around our home, screaming at me. I'm leaving for a while. I will be back in two hours."

"You are not honoring my request that you not wake me in the middle of the night. I'm going to sleep in the guest room."

This is how it goes. When boundaries are honored and understood, people paradoxically move closer together. When boundaries are fought and resisted, people must move further apart to remain autonomous. We have the choice: how we set them and how we honor them.

In extreme cases, where boundaries will not be honored, it might mean the end of a relationship.

NEGOTIATING AND STANDING FIRM

Negotiating another's boundaries is a matter of trust and at times necessity, but be careful! Our default position when someone brings a boundary to us should be to honor it. Period. If we want to move the boundary, this is done with open acknowledgement of what we are asking. Honoring the boundaries of those around us conveys respect and builds our relationships with safety and trust. Disregarding boundaries does exactly the opposite.

If we have to renegotiate a boundary, we speak the original agreement first. This demonstrates to our partner that we were listening and that we take our word seriously. This reinforces trust.

"Hey! My friend just showed up! Let's stay a little later."

"I'm exhausted. I'll work on the yard tomorrow."

Let's try again.

"Hey, I know we said we'd leave the party at 10pm, but an old college friend just walked in. How do you feel about staying an extra 20 minutes?"

"Sweetheart, I realize you asked for my help with the yard and I agreed, but I need to start this first thing tomorrow. I'm wiped out today."

When you have set a boundary and someone is asking you to move your boundary, ask yourself: will it cost me my safety? Will it cost me my dignity? If the answer to either of those questions is yes, *do not move your boundary*. You need to feel safe and honored to be in healthy relationship. If the answer is no, ask yourself: can I afford to move this boundary? Can I manage the inconvenience? If the answer to either of these questions is yes, we have a conversation to see where the new boundary might lie.

Negotiate where there is an opportunity for cooperation and growth. Stand firm when your dignity or safety is at risk.

Like everything else, both setting and hearing boundaries is a tool in our relationship toolbox. No relationship can or will be healthy without these tools, and with use, practice, failure, and retries, this can become a life-giving, bonding, unifying skill.

• • •

Beverly accepted the challenge. As she worked through her feelings of rejection, leftover from childhood, she realized that the problem she had in setting boundaries was *fear*. Asserting her distinctness had resulted in emotional abandonment and shame in her family of origin. This part of her needed healing first and relearning second.

"I think my parents were just as afraid as I was. They feared losing me, and they saw my distinctness – my thoughts, opinions, preferences, and lifestyle choices – as a threat to the unity of our family."

As we worked through the difference between unity and conformity, Beverly began to have new hope.

"I want to be with another person but not so much that I lose myself," she reflected.

"When you say, 'lose myself,' what exactly are you losing?" I asked.

Beverly grew quiet and introspective once again. "*My voice*," she whispered as tears filled her eyes. The wounds from the past were healing, and her "no" is now undergirded with self-knowledge and self-respect.

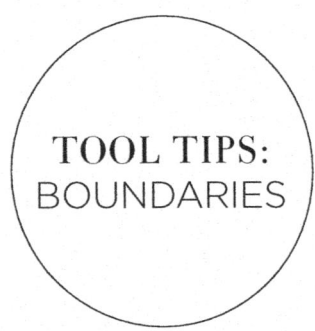

TOOL TIPS:
BOUNDARIES

- Boundaries originate inside us in the form of pleasant or unpleasant emotions.

- Relationship does not mean we are walking the same path; it means we are walking our own path and sharing the journey.

- Boundaries are an essential part of love because they respect our differences.

- Unity is not conformity. Unity means we value what makes us similar more than what separates us. Conformity oppresses us into sameness.

- Boundaries are not punishments, threats, or dictations to others as to what they can or cannot do. They are personal statements of preference or limitation.

- State your boundary clearly and gently. Repeat calmly, if necessary.

- The appropriate response to someone else's boundary is to honor it.

QUESTIONS
FOR
DISCUSSION

1. Do I notice feelings of anger, resentment, or bitterness in any of my relationships? If so, have I addressed where my boundaries are with myself and this person?

2. What physical sensations do I experience in my body that inform me that I need to set a boundary?

3. How comfortable am I setting boundaries? Who do I fear? With whom is it easy? What am I afraid of?

4. Are there places in my current relationship(s) where my boundaries are consistently crossed? What is my plan to address this?

5. When are others' boundaries difficult for me to accept?

CHAPTER 8

Humor

Marta and Noelle had been in a committed relationship for three years by the time they decided to seek help. Both were burgeoning Nashville songwriters and met on the job. Their compatibility flowed as easily as Marta's melodies and Noelle's lyrics. As they spent more time together outside of writing rooms, their connection grew beyond collaborative creativity into a deep friendship then a romantic partnership. We met for an early evening session, after a typical songwriter's day in Nashville comes to a close. After reviewing my practice policies and some light questioning about how they met, I asked the couple about their reasons for seeking counseling.

"How can I help you two?"

Marta turned to Noelle, eyebrows raised. Who would speak first? Noelle shrugged her shoulders, passing the ball, and Marta turned back to face me.

"Whenever we have a disagreement, it turns into a World War," she said straight-faced.

"Yikes. Which World War are you currently on?" I asked, making use of her metaphor.

Her face lit up and the tension broke when she

realized she had a partner in jest. "Oh, about twenty-one!" she laughed. I laughed with her.

When I glanced over at Noelle, I noticed her silence. She watched Marta with a neutral expression, neither amused nor perturbed.

Marta's eyes followed mine toward Noelle. "She's more serious than I am," she said, explaining her partner's behavior. "I'm definitely the joker in the relationship."

"Noelle, what does that make you?" I asked, inviting her to join the conversation.

"I don't know," Noelle said, her tone flat as a board.

"She has a great sense of humor most of the time, except when we get into a disagreement," Marta explained further. Her tone was playful, light. Her expression was unworried and expectant, looking at Noelle as she spoke. Noelle remained neutral, tense, not betraying much. The contrast in their energies was palpable.

"Noelle, how does it go for you when disagreements arise? That's usually why couples seek counseling – to learn better skills for navigating conflict. What would you like to accomplish here?"

Noelle took a deep breath, glancing at the ground, finding the right words. Then she looked up at me and said simply, "I hate fighting." Flat as a board again.

"I think most people would agree with you," I offered, normalizing her opinion. "What do you hate most about it?"

"It's pointless. We don't get anywhere. Marta has her position, and I have mine. We just go around in circles, like dogs chasing our tails, and we never seem to get anywhere."

"So the way you're engaging one another seems like a waste of time, huh?"

"Yes. It is a *complete* waste of time," Noelle emphasized. "And Marta treats everything as a joke. It's impossible to have a real conversation with her when we are in a fight. I love her sense of humor, but there is a time to be more serious and deal with stuff. I never feel like we get there."

"It's because not every issue is the end of the world, Babe!" Marta countered with a laugh, masking her defensiveness with playfulness.

Noelle fell silent once again.

"Marta, what do you do when Noelle gets quiet?"

"She gets louder," Noelle answered for her.

Marta and I broke into simultaneous laughter, amused by Noelle's monotone delivery and excellent timing. But Noelle didn't. It quickly became obvious that she hadn't intended to be funny.

"Well, then speak up, Babe!" Marta prodded playfully, ignoring Noelle's obvious displeasure. Noelle's stone-cold stare spoke volumes.

"Give me an elevator speech about how you witnessed conflict in your families growing up."

Marta smiled as she spoke, "My family fought all the time! We're Cuban, so I think it's part of our culture," she said through laughter. "We didn't take it all that seriously, maybe because it was so frequent. There was a lot of love in our family, but also a lot of passion. Everyone had an opinion; and everyone's opinion *had* to be heard. The only way to be heard was to get louder, so eventually it became a screaming match." Marta described her experience of Cuban culture but also an engrained style of conflict: shout to be heard. While this is an amusing stereotype in sitcoms, it is counterproductive toward developing an emotionally mature relationship.

Noelle spoke next, quietly, "Conflicts didn't happen

in my house. Conflict takes two, and my dad was the only person who was allowed to get angry, so it was mostly a one-man-show." Noelle's voice dripped with contempt and sorrow. "Once he was on the attack and started screaming at us, there was no stopping him. We just sat there. There was nothing else to do except wait for it to end."

Marta's experience of conflict was a hodgepodge of personalities, each one vying for the dominant position. Noelle's was a concentrated berating by one dominant bully: her father. Marta's attempts to lighten their conflicts with humor was a threat to Noelle, for whom conflict meant verbal abuse.

"You know, conflicts will arise in any relationship. How we navigate those conflicts is a significant component of how enjoyable the relationship is. You two have very different experiences with conflict. Marta, in your family, it sounds like conflict was loud and impassioned and even funny at times, and then it was over. Noelle, in your family, it seems like everyone sat in frozen fear *until* it was over."

They agreed.

"Ok, let's work on better conflict resolution skills. Your families of origin will affect how you engage relationally in the present, but we don't have to repeat what didn't work. You need your own style of conflict, one that works for both of you in this relationship. Repeating the past simply because it's familiar isn't always productive. We also need to address the use of humor. A sense of humor is essential in a healthy relationship, but it needs to work *for* your relationship, not against it."

Our eighth tool is Humor.

• • •

THE ROOT OF ALL COMEDY IS PAIN

This quote is attributed to Charlie Chaplin, that master of mischief and naiveté. In the classic, *Modern Times*, Chaplin effectively acted out the child within all of us – innocently and cleverly engaging the "dangerous" and "serious" world of adults and turning its utilitarian assumptions upside down. To Chaplin, everything was a toy, an object to be discovered outside of the presumed knowledge of its assigned use. A dreary day at a factory was simply one elaborate game of chasing objects that could use a tightening with his wrench. He opened our eyes to seeing and engaging our world differently, and we delight in his novel discoveries. Always faster and one step ahead of the "adults" in his movies, Chaplin's brilliance was in his resilience: they never bested him. Innocence and childlike deftness won out, every time. The humor was in the contrast: Chaplin never broke a sweat and proceeded along on his merry way unworried with a wake of chaos and confusion behind him.

When we consider the best comedic entertainers of the last century, we notice that those who make us laugh hardest are those who force us to engage our presumed assumptions with a different lens, therefore showing us who we are in a new light. Lucille Ball taught us that a conveyor belt of chocolate candy was really a buffet. Jerry Seinfeld showed us repeatedly that we are all hilariously enslaved to the mundane. Whether the style of comedy is absurdist or screwball, we find humor only when our assumptions are challenged. If left unchallenged, life is simply predictable, dreary, and somewhat tragic. This is the "pain" at the root of all comedy. The comics among us keep reframing our painful, mundane world by offering a different view.

In relationship, humor works the same way. One

partner perceives sorrow at the funeral; the other can't help but notice that the "fragrant" flowers smell like feet. One partner fumes when the luggage goes missing after a long flight; the other is already playfully listing activities that don't require clothes. Same situation, different lens. We can acknowledge that the following two statements are true:

> Conflict results from seeing the same situation through differing lenses.
>
> Humor results from seeing the same situation through differing lenses.

We can fight about it, or we can laugh about it. Much of that will be determined by the situation at hand and how the partners in the relationship engage the situation.

When a comedy routine involves one entertainer their perspective is the only one we see, but when the act involves two or more, we have interplay. The characters must contrast one another for the routine to work. Most classically, a comedy of two will combine the roles of the "straight man" and the "stooge." The straight man's job is to maintain composure, even somber seriousness, in the face of the stooge's antics and eccentricities. Desi's reasonable expectations stood in stark contrast to Lucy's outlandish schemes in the classic comedy series, *I Love Lucy*. David Spade's deadpan accentuated Chris Farley's absurdity on *Saturday Night Live*. Bea Arthur's portrayal of "Dorothy" struck the perfect monotone to foil Betty White's childlike and naïve "Rose" on NBC's classic, *The Golden Girls*.

The "straight man" is only comedic in the presence of "the stooge." Otherwise, the straight man is just boring. And the "stooge" without the "straight man," endlessly offering joke after joke, antic after antic, is often more exhausting than funny. In relationship, if both partners are comics, conflict will likely float by and life may be enjoyable overall, but the relationship may lack the depth and maturity to effectively engage complexities in ways that resolve issues and bring the couple closer together. There is a lot of laughter and little depth. When painful situations arise, no one is prepared for the intensity required to navigate them. Deeper problems are resisted and/or minimized, not because they are not deeply important but because the partners lack the tools to engage. The couple may be unknowingly colluding in denial. Conversely, if both partners are the "straight man" type, the relationship may be overly serious. These couples discuss politics, social issues, and other serious matters with composed intellect, but they don't laugh much. Their connection is most likely intellectual, and the couple may come across as mature and responsible but rarely fun-loving and carefree. The relationship is overly mature... and boring.

Some couples may contain one of each type. This is not to say that the more serious of the two has no sense of humor nor that the comic can't engage on deeper matters. It is to say that we may tend consistently one way or the other. The "straight man" type will more often than not see obstacles and conflicts as terrible inconveniences or Greek tragedies. They may perceive and address challenges dramatically, seriously, and without much humor at all. If humor is used, it is usually in the form of sarcasm. It's not *really* funny. It's just a mask for pain and anger. "No One is Allowed to Laugh if I'm Not Laughing" is the unspoken rule. Challenges are addressed, but they become sources of dread because the mood of the relationship takes on dark clouds whenever conflict appears. If a partner is the "stooge" in the relationship, there will be a pointed movement away from pain or seriousness. This kind of person frequently uses phrases like "lighten up!" or "it's not the end of the world!" The goal is to release tension. The unspoken rule is "If We Laugh About This, It Will Get Better or Even Go Away." This is a Peter Pan type, an adult child who cannot tolerate sitting still and addressing pain. The conflict does not, in fact, go away. The persons involved simply give up.

Both types, if inflexible, are overbearing.

The healthiest couples contain two individuals who can hold space for both laughter and pain *within themselves* and therefore *within the relationship*. We are not in fixed roles like the "stooge" or the "straight man." In fixed relationship roles, we have no other option but to be that one thing. The straight man can't lighten up because everything will fall apart! And the stooge doesn't have the maturity or the brains to take anything seriously anyway. These are characters, not humans. In healthy relationships, all parts of us are safe to be present, and everyone has a "straight man" and a "stooge" inside.

How do we complement each other? How do we find a balance between laughter and seriousness? How do we make use of humor in ways that augment our connection to one another?

First, we need to understand the function of humor in intimate relationship.

Life is tough. It is filled with beauty and meaning, but the overall task of living is a challenge, for sure. The work of growing up, learning how the world works, learning how we work, and figuring out how to get these two systems – ourselves and the outside world – to function symbiotically is no easy task. Lessons are often learned through failure, and successes are fleeting. Finding meaningful work is hard too. Choosing a career path, gathering the necessary tools, acquiring the requisite education, and seizing on the right opportunities are part of the rigors of a full life.

Then comes the realm of relationships. Humans *need* relationships, but we need relationships that *work*. If we were blessed to grow up in a home where we safe to be authentic, we will have an easier time building adult relationships. However, if we grew up in homes where our true self was unknown or unaccepted, we will have a hell of a time both nurturing our authentic self out of hiding and then creating satisfying attachments with others. We will face heartbreak, humiliation, ecstasy, and loneliness regardless.

Add to all this the impending and inevitable truth that we will all die. We are in a race against the clock of our mortality to find meaning and purpose for our existence. We tolerate the mundane; we seek the exciting. Our spiritual development eases some of this existential pressure, but we all live with the knowledge that we will die, more quickly than we can possibly imagine. The race is on! Live! And live well!

We will know fear.

We will encounter obstacles, road blocks, and dead ends.

We will have too many choices but not the ones we want.

We will fall in love, get disappointed, feel regret, and try again.

Does anyone else need a drink?

What is humor good for?

Laughter.

Humor is the singular human trait that adds levity, joy, and diversion from the work of life. It's the happy pause in the parade of effort. Without it, the weight of living would simply crush us. Humor draws us into moments of pleasurable self-reflection. We see ourselves and the world through someone else's lens, the contrast is made, we marvel at the hilarity or the absurdity of it all, and we *laugh*.

In relationship, humor meets the same need. Healthy

relationships provide much relief from the difficulty of life in the form of belonging, safety, comfort, companionship, soothing, and a flesh-and-blood experience of unconditional love (when present). They are also very difficult when it comes time to find compromise, bypass the ego, resolve conflict, tolerate disappointment, communicate through big emotions, and tolerate a lack of unconditional love.

In other words, it's all beautiful and it's all hard. We need to laugh through it. Laughter creates a release of tension in our bodies and minds. It's a whole-person reset, and it's often free! We may feel just as centered and balanced after a laugh-until-we-cry moment than after a full body massage. Our whole person is engaged, and unlike a professional massage, we create lasting memories with the people with whom we've shared the laughs. In this way, humor and the ensuing laughter enhance our quality of life and its very meaning.

However, humor and even laughter can be healthy and unhealthy in relationship.

TO LAUGH OR NOT TO LAUGH: THAT IS THE QUESTION

Healthy humor balances our perspective. It serves as a reminder to keep the small things of life small. It reminds us that we aren't in control. When we erroneously expect that all the events of our lives will play out exactly as we envision, we are taking life far too seriously and have an unhealthy notion of control. We tend to panic over inconveniences, and conflicts ensue. Having a good sense of humor allows us to keep it all in perspective. How important is it? Is this a crisis? Is it urgent? Is it actually tragic? Most of the time it's not. Sometimes we can just as easily laugh about it as we could stress about it. After all, we are simply collections of atoms, magnetically stuck to a rock, orbiting around a star in the midst of outer space! Some of us are naturally more serious. We tend to engage our lives with a thoughtfulness and conscientiousness that can leave little room for spontaneous laughter. If an injustice or imperfection exists, we must attend to it immediately! Life is no laughing matter! For us, healthy humor is essential for balancing. Humor allows space for joy in the midst of pain, laughter in the midst of grief, and perspective in the midst of self-absorption.

Some of us are quite the opposite. We see life as one long comedy of errors. Every situation can be viewed through a lens of absurdity, and we easily laugh at ourselves and others. We struggle to descend from our elevated moods long enough to actually engage situations that need our mature attention. For us, we need to examine when humor is appropriate and when it's a distraction.

Whatever our personality style, humor is useful to balance our experience of life. We can learn to save the really serious responses for the really serious matters. We discover that laughing at a challenge might give us a new way of seeing it so we can better resolve it.

Unhealthy humor detracts from and minimizes important moments and feelings because they are uncomfortably intense. This is using humor as a defense mechanism rather than a relational skill. Defense mechanisms do not engage us with our pain. Their function is the opposite; we avoid it. Some of us dislike intensity so much that we can't sit in it. Perhaps we have never really explored our own feelings and developed tolerance for emotional pain; perhaps the moment is triggering an unresolved hurt; perhaps we don't have enough information; but for one reason or another, the mood is heavy and we crack a joke to "lighten it up." We effectively insult the feelings and needs of those in the situation with us. Instead of adjusting internally so that we can address the situation appropriately, we attempt to force the situation into something with which we are more comfortable – a laughing matter. We must make a decision to grow up. Life is hard, remember? Sometimes that hardship requires that we engage pain and allow a situation to unfold without diffusing it with laughter. The time for laughing will come, but the mature adult can wait. This type of unhealthy humor is at best annoying and at worst insulting. It is not attuned to what is happening at present. We haven't taken the temperature of a situation or of our partner. We are instead trying to make a moment what we need it to be, and in this way, unhealthy humor can be a form of self-serving control. This type of unhealthy humor blocks emotional processing. The people subjected to the never ending current of jokes from an immature adult are chuckling to be polite, not releasing tension through laughter.

Unhealthy humor can be hurtful. Whereas healthy humor has the power to lift our spirits and grant us perspective and release, unhealthy humor darkens our mood and generates fearful self-consciousness. Unhealthy humor is, among other things, **sarcastic, mocking, self-deprecating**, and/or **crass**.

Sarcasm is a particularly dangerous form of humor if used inappropriately. When used in a healthy way, sarcasm highlights absurdity. However, by and large, sarcasm is inappropriate and a weak mask for unresolved anger. The purpose of sarcasm is to convey mockery or contempt. Rather than discussing our feelings maturely, we use sarcasm to cut down that which bothers us, and the result is callousness and disconnection. Most of the time, sarcasm is at best cutting and at worst damaging and hurtful.

Mocking is similar to sarcasm. Almost everyone can

handle a small amount of ribbing or gentle teasing, however the moment we notice that we are hurting feelings, we must stop. Making a mockery of someone else's feelings, actions, beliefs, or thoughts is not relationally healthy, even if we think we are in the right, even if we believe what we are doing or saying should be taken lightly. Mockery is an attempt to hide our contempt for another behind a veil of humor. It is harmful and carries consequences. The people we tease to the point of mockery will not trust us or connect with us intimately. A good marker is laughter. If the person being teased appears to be authentically laughing and enjoying the joke, we notice. On the contrary, if the subject of the joke is not wholeheartedly laughing and appears to be hurt, we immediately stop. We have gone too far. Insisting that others "get a thicker skin" or "lighten up" is not an option. We do not impose our humor on others; we attune to their hearts. Again, unhealthy humor involves us ignoring or dismissing something that is happening in front of us. Ignoring someone else's hurt feelings for the sake of a joke does not mean they are overly sensitive; it means we are callous.

Self-deprecating humor can be a sign of a healthy, balanced adult. Being able to laugh at our mistakes or eccentricities demonstrates humility and self-awareness. People who cannot laugh at themselves carry an intense amount of personal shame. If we have trouble laughing at ourselves, we must ask ourselves why. Do we assume we won't make mistakes? Do we have an unhealthy fear of others' judgments? Are we perfectionists? However, sometimes self-deprecating humor can cross over into self-humiliation, the purpose of which is to abuse ourselves as we may have been previously abused. This is uncomfortable for an emotionally healthy listener who does not wish to see another human being degraded. If we use self-deprecating humor to the point of self-humiliation, we must ask ourselves why. Am I really a laughing stock? Do I dismiss myself because I believe others will as well? Am I using humor to cover my pain? Am I torturing myself in the hopes that someone will rescue me... from myself?

Crassness is a way of using humor to drag complexity down to the lowest common denominator. We do not understand something, and rather than engaging it with curiosity and humility, we attempt to gain control of it by oversimplifying it. Crassness is generally a sign of immature or incomplete development in the area about which a joke is made, and for this reason cross humor is often utilized to dismantle and degrade the vulnerable complexity of sex. Sexuality is a complicated facet of our humanity. It holds the keys to our most powerful and creative life forces and our most tender vulnerabilities. Sexual development is a mysterious and adventurous process from childhood through adulthood. If we have not been taught and tended on this front with dignity and respect, we arrive into adulthood with the maturity of a child and the sex drive of an adult. Crassness arises as a self-degrading and other-degrading way of wresting that which may cause uncomfortable feelings of vulnerability. Once again, we notice that unhealthy humor is a way of controlling a situation, not reframing it. There is no room for crass humor in mature relationship. Risqué humor is a healthy way to engage the adult field of sexual play, but when the body or the sexual self is degraded, we have gone too far. We must mature.

We can see how humor can lift us up or bring us down. Where we learned to be humorous or humorless is a determining factor of how we use humor now.

LAUGHTER IS THE BEST MEDICINE

In healthy families, humor is a natural, beloved aspect of the family dynamic. It flows as naturally from parents as it does from children. If parents are emotionally mature, they assume the role of teaching their children to use their innate humor appropriately within the family system. The adults will act as both models and referees, demonstrating appropriate humor and setting boundaries when children unknowingly cross the line, redirecting them back toward empathy and conscientiousness. This learned awareness prepares children for life outside the home, where their attempts to bond with peers through humor will largely determine their social success. In this respect, having a healthy sense of humor is no laughing matter. It is an absolute must. As personalities emerge in young children, parents and other adults in their lives can see rather clearly the style of humor toward which the child will most naturally gravitate. The witty, goofy, screwball, dry, and absurdist tendencies emerge early on, and the adults in the children's lives have the important responsibility to help them shape their humor in ways that will enhance their relationships.

Children are born jokesters. Their engagement with the world is fresh and unburdened by adult assumptions, so they find the novel in anything and everything! They surprise and delight us because they are innocent. Their charm is in their not knowing. When they see laughter and joy on adults' faces, their young minds want to repeat the behavior, preferring pleasant emotional interactions to unpleasant or neutral ones. Adult laughter encourages children. Parents and adults therefore must assume responsibility: what we encourage is what will proliferate.

If we were raised in a home where humor was used

appropriately – to draw us out of our self-absorption and into fresh perspective – we will become adults who can do the same. We will understand that humor is best when it's situational, not personal. This means we are laughing at situations, not at each other in ways that are hurtful. We learn that humor doesn't require sacrificing respect or compassion. Healthy humor in a functional family system is robust but not reckless. Laughter may be deep, loud, and long lasting but never at the expense of any member of the family. Healthy humor in a family, just as in adult situations, is attuned to the emotional temperature of the room.

If we experienced unhealthy humor in our family systems, we heard jokes that cut others down, often ourselves. When children are the brunt of their parents' immature humor, they harden their hearts to survive the humiliation and may become adults who are calloused, even abusing others in the same way. They may also seek out relationships where they are again the brunt of the joke.

Here is an area that receives far too little attention: interfamily bullying. We name parental abuse in all of its forms – verbal, emotional, physical, etc. – but we rarely touch on sibling abuse. Instead, we rationalize it with phrases like "boys will be boys" and "sibling rivalry," but in reality, this is a toxic dynamic in a family system. When parents use words to harm children's dignity and cause emotional pain, it is verbal abuse. When siblings use words to harm one another's dignity and cause emotional pain, it is verbal abuse. The harm is inevitable, and it must be addressed. The parent who teases a child to the point of mockery will allow it between siblings. The hurt child will often be instructed to "get a thicker skin." What we are actually saying to the child is, "This home is not emotionally safe for you, and in order to survive it you're going to have to bury your heart." Parents who do not intervene and set boundaries between siblings when the joking goes too far are raising children who will be bullied and/or turn into bullies. The onus is on the parents. Children should not be at the mercy of their siblings; the adults are in charge.

When a child registers hurt on their face, indicated by any neutral, angry, or sad expression that does not look like joy, the parent's job is to notice and stop the joke. When we hear joking that is becoming too harsh, too personal, or too pointed, we check in with the child receiving the joke. Children will deny their true feelings and laugh outwardly when they are crying inside. They need adults who are paying attention. When we hear the joke has gone too far, we redirect the attention of the joking child toward the hurt child, guiding the amends process.

"Honey, look at your brother's face. He's not laughing. Do you see that? This joke has gone too far, and you owe your brother an apology."

"Sweetheart, come here, I need to talk to you. I know everyone is laughing at what you're saying, but I think it's a little too harsh. I want you to change the direction of the conversation."

"Hey bud, I know you're laughing but I'm wondering if on the inside you don't really like what's being said."

We can then teach the child how to set appropriate, self-honoring boundaries. This teaches the child self-respect and teaches the children around him/her to maintain empathy in the midst of humor. Without adults helping children to differentiate between being hurtful teasing and having fun, children can grow into perpetual victims or bullies.

In emotionally dysfunctional families, humor is as much a weapon as anger. It is used to cut down, shame, mock, and silence the unwanted voice. In these families, the parents are as immature and dangerous with humor as are the children, and this lack of maturity creates more adults who make cutting jokes, meant to sting and intimidate. The children tear one another down, and the adults do nothing. When the adults use harsh humor on children, there is no one there to protect them. Mockery of the children takes the place of gentle correction, producing shame. Sarcasm replaces healthy emotional disclosure, reinforcing the suppression of anger. The humor is not safe because no one is in charge. A moment of levity can turn into a soul crushing spray of bullets in a second.

In dysfunctional but less abusive situations, humor stands in the way of processing our experiences. It masks emotions. In this type of family system, the parent is using humor to distract everyone from their unpleasant feelings. Dad's constant joking kept everyone laughing, *but no one felt or processed anything.* We didn't talk about or face our feelings because laugher was filling in the gaps. The family has the emotional maturity of a fourth grader. Denial is the name of the game, and "laughter is the best medicine." This family doesn't place a high value, or any value, on authenticity and emotional connection. The blood bond is expected to carry the family forward, and real bonds of vulnerability-based trust are not developed. This family system is generally a shallow one. There is shared history and commitment but little depth. They seem to be having a grand ole' time while they privately shuttle their children to and from therapists' offices to work with the children's depression and anxiety.

When we know and understand how humor functioned in our family of origin, we will begin to understand how we use humor in our relationships today.

HUMOR IN ACTION

It's time to take an inventory on our use of humor. The first step is to ask ourselves if we are attuned to what is going on in the situation. Will humor be a gift or a distraction at this moment? If someone is in a heightened state of emotional distress or tension, it is best to allow that person their feelings. Emotions pass, and when the intensity has decreased, the time for humor may be present. Strong states of anger, fear, shame, or sorrow must be felt and allowed before the person experiencing them is capable of laughing. Mark Twain famously said, "Comedy is tragedy plus time." We must allow the time to pass before we can enjoy the comedy.

We need to check our style of humor. If we find we are in a habit of sarcasm and mocking, it's time to talk about this. The anger inside us must be processed and allowed. Likely, there are other emotional states under the anger that need to be heard and felt. We often use sarcasm, the mask of anger, as a further mask for embarrassment, shame, and hurt. Sarcastic people do not allow intimacy. The sarcasm serves as a "funny" way of avoiding it, however the connection is missed. We can do better than this. Once we have felt our anger and allowed a more tender place in our hearts to emerge again, we will notice sarcasm in others with sadness. We notice how disconnected they are from their own tender hearts, as we were, and we want more for them.

If we notice that we self-deprecate to the point of self-humiliation, it's time to stop this. Forever. We are worth more. We are not laughing stocks, fools in the parade, or worthy of dismissal and deriding. We are human beings, as worthy of respect as our neighbor. Our mistakes are normal. Our shame must decrease. We practice walking with our head held high. We refuse to allow the abuse of the past to be repeated today. Abuse, neglect, and abandonment in family systems are signs of unhealthy adults, not flawed or unlovable children. We choose not to carry responsibility for what was done to us by treating ourselves like fools. We stop acting like abused children who abuse ourselves as adults and allow others to abuse us. We start to act like respectable people.

If we notice that we cannot laugh at ourselves at all, we talk to a close friend or a counselor. We begin to process our shame and allow ourselves to be as children again, able to fall down in fits of giggles at the silly things we do!

Those of us who have used humor to survive trauma may not understand the depth of our pain. Rather than experiencing the emotions tied to traumatic events, we have used humor to move away from our pain and into a form of denial. Likely, we are very sarcastic and/or mocking people. We must develop respect for our emotions so that we do not trample on our hearts. When life is difficult, we engage it bravely, knowing that painful memories of the past may arise. We do not resort to unhealthy humor to cope. We can do this. We are up to the task of being deeper and emotionally available to ourselves. When we bravely give ourselves this emotional respect, we will then give it and expect it from others.

When there are painful emotions or situations to attend to, humor should only be used when the issues have been heard and processed. It is best used as the period on the end of a sentence. Indeed, laughing at an issue is a sign that it is healing or largely healed. We do not laugh at our open wounds, and humor can be destructive when it is offered in the midst of hurt. However, once the issue has been processed, heard, and the emotional needs resolved, humor is the best way to move forward and hit the reset button on joy. We may need to ask our partners: was that appropriate? Was that out of line? Do I use my humor in ways that bring us closer together or in ways that create distance between us? Humor is relational, so we must become aware of how our humor is functioning in our relationships.

INTIMATELY FUNNY

Humor is a strong bond. Our eyes meet, and we burst out laughing. It's as if we read one another's minds. We see the same situation processed in the same humorous way. When humor is flowing in a healthy way in relationship, it is intimacy through joy. If we are not in a relationship where there is much laughter, we can address it. Is there a feeling of gloom or boredom? Is there a heaviness? Have we lost our spontaneity? Humor need not come solely from cracking jokes. For those who are blessed with clever, witty minds, their partners sit in expectation of the next one-liner. Maybe we are not wordsmiths, and we need not be. Humor is a type of play, and all of us can play at any age.

Humor is found in activities just as frequently as in words, and all of us can find humor in the world around us. We can laugh at a sexual position that didn't go quite as planned. We can paint pictures of one another and laugh at our childlike painting skills. We can write one another silly poetry. We can go to a comedy club. We can make pizza together and make faces with pepperoni. We can make shapes with chocolate chips in pancakes. We can read aloud from funny books. We can enjoy a comedic film. We can go ziplining and laugh the whole way down the line. We *find* humor when we *seek* it. When we open the door to humor in our lives again or for the first time, laughter fills our relationship. We find that we really like this person again. Laughter is a stronger bond than misery.

• • •

Marta and Noelle learned that humor and the lack of it were functioning in self-protection but not connection.

For Marta, humor served as a distraction from her responsibility in conflict. As long as she was laughing through it, she didn't have to face the consequences of her actions as an adult. As the older child in her family system, Marta became aware of how her humor had hurt her younger sister. Instead of listening to and respecting her younger sister's preferences, Marta had mocked her instead. Through conversations with her sister and deeper work, Marta learned where the boundaries were by paying attention to how others reacted to her. Humor was becoming a place of *shared* joy. She was able to engage relationally without having to control the interactions with mockery.

Noelle, on the other hand, had been humorless as a way of protecting herself from attack. As a child she discovered that humor might direct the family's attention toward herself, and that was never a safe place to be. Even when her father's anger was not ignited, humor wasn't safe. An unwelcome joke might have meant a night of verbal abuse. Noelle had simply turned it off. She found enjoyment in her adult life but rarely humor. She learned that Marta's humor was one of the reasons she'd fallen in love with her. As Noelle reconnected with herself as a young child, her natural humor – dry and witty – began to emerge. Banter between the two ensued, and a new layer of their relationship was born.

Ill-timed humor and the lack of it was keeping this relationship stuck in unproductive conflict. In conflict, Noelle would turn into a scared, shut down child, and Marta became a disconnected, dominant child. Both pasts needed to be aired out in the light of day so that the responsible, humorous adults they are could emerge.

Humor, offered appropriately and with care, was a new place of bonding for this couple. Marta led the way, and Noelle helped keep it healthy.

TOOL TIPS:
HUMOR

- Healthy humor means we can both laugh at ourselves and laugh at the journey.
- Laughter is a healthy, essential release of tension and a reset on our perspective.
- Unhealthy humor minimizes the seriousness of a situation, mocks another, hurts, humiliates, or degrades.
- Humor should connect us, not divide us.
- We must be aware of how we are using humor in healthy and unhealthy ways.
- Taking ourselves too seriously is a sign of unhealed shame.
- Shared humor is an intimate bond of joy.

QUESTIONS
FOR
DISCUSSION

1. When do I use humor in my relationships? Is it healthy? Am I sharing joy or distracting from the intensity of an issue? Am I laughing with or at my partner? Are they laughing too?

2. Who was the funnier of my two parents? When was their humor healthy or unhealthy? How did they utilize healthy humor? Unhealthy humor?

3. How did my parents' use of humor, or their lack of humor, make me feel?

4. What was the general tone of my home growing up?

5. What is the tone now? Does any aspect of how I use humor need to be addressed? Among members of my family?

CHAPTER 9

Empathy

Jackson and Lucy were a case of opposites attract.

Jackson came from an intact nuclear family, one of two children, and the beloved "baby boy." He had been raised in an affluent suburb of Atlanta with opportunities for travel and education common to the young and privileged. Lucy's parents divorced when she was eight years old, and her father disappeared. Both of her younger siblings looked to her for stability while their mother succumbed to alcoholism. Her life was constant responsibility. Jackson was handed many opportunities. Lucy had to find them. Jackson's basic trust in humanity was that of a safe, contented child. Lucy's was the distrust of a child who had to function as an adult far too young.

Jackson's primary complaint in the marriage was not feeling respected, Lucy's was not feeling supported. Jackson felt that nothing he did was enough for Lucy to feel content with him. Lucy felt that she was the only adult in the marriage, and Jackson had a lot of growing up to do. Jackson wanted to get outside and enjoy life; Lucy had a difficult time walking away from unchecked boxes on her to-do list.

Their shared ambition drew them to one another. They

both saw a fire in the other's eyes that felt familiar. Jackson was climbing the ladder of success as a music executive on Nashville's Music Row, and Lucy's pediatric practice was a blend of her finest attributes: heartfelt care for children and levelheaded management. At every gathering and cocktail party, they were seen as a "power couple," but in private, their emotional connection was weak and their sex life practically nonexistent.

"I know I can be too hard on him," Lucy admitted. "I just don't think that Jack understands the real world. He completes one task on a list of twenty things to do around the house and feels like he's earned the right to chill out with a beer by the pool. The music industry finishes their day at 4:00 PM, and so does Jack!"

"Jack?" I invited him to chime in.

"She is too hard on me. I've told you a hundred times, Luce, one of these days you're going to wake up and your life will be over, and you'll have checked a lot of boxes but *not lived.*"

"Ugh. I hate when you preach at me."

"Consider it a warning," Jack countered.

I stepped in. What I was observing was an intellectual war that had been going on for a long time. This couple was stuck in the vicious cycle of presenting differing opinions and perspectives and failing to reach agreement. They knew one another's position so well they could recite it, but nothing was budging. Their tactics were on full display: present your position, decimate your opponent's argument, dismiss the conflict. Again and again. Their problem was not disagreement; it was disconnection.

"Lucy, what was required of you on a day-to-day basis as a little girl?"

"I had to wake myself and then my brother and

sister, make our lunches, get us all on school buses, and be home after school to let us back in the house, feed all of us a snack, and get homework started. Mom could usually manage to get dinner together, and I guess I shared bedtime responsibilities with her. That's about it."

"That's about it, huh?" I asked, using sarcasm playfully.

I glanced at Jack who was listening patiently without surprise; he knew all of these details.

"How did all of that daily work make you feel? You were a child yourself."

"I often felt dread. There was never an end to it. I hated weekends because they were too short. Before I knew it, it was Monday, and the drudgery began again. I didn't look forward to anything. Weeks were hard and weekends just meant another week was coming."

"You felt dread. Where do you feel that sense of dread in your body?"

Lucy looked at me with confusion. She had been in therapy previously and had honed an emotional vocabulary, but she couldn't yet *feel* her feelings in her body. Her brain was reading her body's signals, but she wasn't yet feeling her feelings consciously.

"I guess I feel it in my throat. Like I want to swallow, but it's tight…" her voice faded as her words were choked off by pure emotion. Tears streamed down both her cheeks. The pressure of many years of premature responsibility had been trapped in her throat, and we'd just hit a release valve. Her pain was big.

Jack was actively listening now. He'd never seen her *feel* her emotions, only talk about them.

Jack and I were silent while Lucy finally felt the emotion she'd been suppressing. When she'd taken a few deep breaths, I turned to Jack. "Jack, how do you feel on your way home, knowing that Lucy has a list of things for you to do when you cross the threshold?"

Jack was silent. He looked down, finding the courage within himself to share a difficult truth with his wife.

"Dread."

Lucy's eyes met his as the realization set in. *He was feeling what she'd felt.* The conscious awareness of this moved her.

"I don't want anyone to feel that, much less you, Jack."

The conversation moved naturally to processing the feelings the couple were experiencing. They both described when they felt dread and how they'd handled it with one another. Without realizing it, Lucy had imposed the same drudgery on Jack that she'd been carrying. A joyless life of work was her normal, and Jack had been recruited as a partner. His carefree attitude only fueled the fire. Without realizing it himself, Jack allowed Lucy to shoulder much of the burden at home, reliving his childhood role as the Golden Child and Baby Boy.

Jack opened up about the fear that kept him from taking on new tasks. He felt tremendous anxiety when asked to step out of his comfort zone. His fear of failure was masked in a *c'est la vie* attitude while he lounged by the pool with a beer. Lucy could now see what Jack was really doing: hiding in plain sight. She remembered and shared about how she'd hide her report cards from her mother while appearing busy and productive to avoid punishment for struggling grades. Tears *and* laughter flowed freely.

A slow exhale followed by a long moment of silence filled the room.

Lucy and Jack had just given one another a great gift.

Our ninth tool is Empathy.

• • •

THE NATURALS

Some of us are born empaths. Our emotional systems are hardwired in such a way that we cannot stop ourselves from feeling others' emotions. If we are in the presence of any emotion exposed or concealed – whether it is sadness, anger, fear, or shame – we feel it in such a way that it becomes an experience in our own body. This is not a conscious choice. Empaths are both gifted and burdened with the inner experience of others' emotions. The gift is in the potential for deep, meaningful human connection. The burden is in the intrusion. Empaths don't always want or need to feel everyone's emotions around them, but without conscious energy, we will.

Empaths feel sadness when another is in grief. We feel lightness and joy when another celebrates. We feel pain when others are hurt. We feel what is happening in another person, in our own body. It is not an intellectual assessment of another's emotional state, as in "you look sad" or "you are angry." It is a physical experience. Empaths actually struggle to hold the distance necessary to live in healthy autonomy. True empaths feel it before we know it. Without awareness, empaths tend to absorb the emotional state around them.

For the "Naturals," our emotional systems are highly sensitive and wonderfully attuned to others. Natural empaths are effective emotional caregivers. Our innate sense of others' emotional states enables us to meet emotional needs in ways others can't. Others feel understood by natural empaths on a level that goes far beyond mere intellectual understanding. Perhaps we cannot identify or even speak what we feel, but with a true empath, we don't have to. The natural empath not only knows what we feel, but they are actually feeling it *with* us. This is a great gift in relationships.

The challenge for Naturals is to set appropriate internal boundaries so that life is not an emotional roller coaster. For the empath, every relationship is a robust experience of internal richness, however this can become draining and distracting. Natural empaths tend to lose themselves in others, unconsciously targeting their focus on how others are feeling rather than their own experiences and needs. Empaths, without conscious awareness and intentional boundary setting, can run ragged as they feel and feel and feel without a strong, internal compass of their own.

The Naturals also must remember that not everyone has this gift. While empaths place high value on emotions and relationships, others simply don't operate in the world with an empath's level of emotional connectedness. This can create feelings of aloneness and resentment. We might assume that everyone *ought* to be more empathic with the same ease with which we can feel and give empathy to others, but this is simply not the case. Some personalities do not contain this amount of empathy. For example, police officers need to have the internal constitution to uphold the law without bias in the presence of a wide range of emotions in themselves and the people they are apprehending. Judges must be objective, which requires a suspension of subjective, personal emotional biases. Doctors and nurses must administer painful interventions, suspending the natural empathy that would stop them from causing another person pain. Parents must love their children fairly, not pour out love on the child with whom they feel the strongest emotional connection.

Empathy has its place. It is a gift, but like all gifts, not all situations require its use. When empaths are ruled by empathy, we are not thinking rationally. We are "thinking" with our feelings. Whatever we feel, we follow. This is a trap for empaths who are not conscious of their empathy. Without the conscious awareness of feeling another's feelings, we cannot distinguish between our own feelings and another's. We wind up pursuing paths of action that have nothing to do with us and are solely focused on others because we did not consciously become aware of what is happening inside. We felt, and we ran with it. The task for empaths is to internally ask, "Is what I'm feeling mine or yours?" This question steers us away from the trap of caretaking.

To own our empathy is to say, "I have this gift, and I will use it with judiciousness. When it is appropriate, I will focus more on my own feelings than others' because their feelings are their responsibility, not mine to feel, express, and care for. My feelings are my responsibility. When I need or want to connect with you deeply, I can and will. When that is not appropriate, I can hold myself within."

Emotional blocking is a healthy boundary for a natural empath. It balances and protects the empathy.

THE INTENTIONALS

For some of us, empathy comes as naturally as reading hieroglyphics. We are not emotionally attuned, day to day, and it takes a tremendous amount of concentration to become aware of our own feelings, much less another's. We see life as a path of doing and building. We see our relationships through the lens of shared experiences, not necessarily shared feelings. We learn and accumulate new information about the world, not necessarily deeper awareness about ourselves. Perhaps we cast our nets wide, not deep. We don't bother with emotions because they are messy and lead to conflicts. We'd rather feel at peace without pesky emotions taking up space. For those of us who focus on life outside of emotional experience, empathy must become *intentional*.

The Naturals must learn to block. The "Intentionals" must learn to *allow*.

Everyone feels emotions, and it could be argued that maturity, in large part, is simply the awareness of one's own emotional state and the self-control to respond well. However, some of us are born feeling our emotions more strongly than others. Everyone feels emotion, but not everyone feels emotion the same way. For some of us, emotions are experienced as tsunami waves, torrential downpours, hurricane winds, and catastrophic floods. For others of us, emotions are experienced like a warm breeze, a brief shower, a sunny day, a chilly shiver.

Empathy is the great connector. Empathy is what allows us to say, "I may not feel the same feeling the same way you do, but I do *feel* it, and my body remembers what that emotion feels like inside me." This means we act and react differently in our relationships. With the conscious awareness of our own feelings, we are able to imagine what something feels like in another. And when an emotion is painful, rather than receiving this information in an intellectual, emotionally disconnected way, we connect and care because we remember the pain in ourselves.

If we are one of the Intentionals, we must do our work to feel our own feelings first, so that we can remember the experience when our lover or loved one feels one way or another. We must call into our memory what shame feels like when our partner says, "I feel ashamed." This memory stimulates empathy. For the Naturals, empathy happens without thinking. For the Intentionals, empathy is a conscious choice.

Let's look at a physical example. If we have broken an arm, our body can recall the pain associated with the event.

When someone tells us they have broken their own arm, we wince with pain at the memory. If we have had poison ivy, we grimace when someone tells us they are covered with the stuff. This is empathy. We are generally more generous with our empathy when we are processing physical pain or discomfort. We must learn to do this emotionally as well.

Emotions are internal experiences, and empathy is the tool that allows us to share them intimately. Without empathy, the distance between us is great. Sharing sex does not mean talking about it, it means a body-to-body connection. Likewise, sharing emotions does not mean an intellectual conversation about them. It means two people, two bodies, sharing the experience of the emotion together.

For the Intentionals, more effort is needed to feel and foster this connection. We must become more curious about our own emotions and thus more available to others'. We must learn to slow down when emotional connection is needed, remember the feeling, let it come up within us (in other words, *allow* it) and be in that experience with our partner. If we are intentional about empathy, we may never be as natural as true empaths, but we can absolutely reach out with our hearts with the intention to connect. This is impossible if we are cut off from our own emotions.

LIVING AND LOVING ON AUTOPILOT

A pilot flying a plane on autopilot has placed the computer of the aircraft in control, not the conscious mind. When trouble occurs, the pilot must switch off the autopilot setting and take command, thus responsibility, of the aircraft. If the plane is maneuvered and landed safely by the pilot's courage and skill, we call it heroic. Autopilot is not heroic. On autopilot, the plane may coast through the skies to its destination, but the thrill and skill of flying is lost.

When we are living on autopilot, we are allowing our unconscious minds to run the show. If we are predisposed to doing and not feeling, we become emotional vacuums. If we are predisposed to strong emotional states, we become turbulent tornados of emotional upheaval. The goal of mature relationships is to find balance within ourselves first and then demonstrate that through skillful connection. We cannot live in the fantasy that our relationships will run smoothly on autopilot. We need to do some conscious work for our relationships to thrive. Remember: the work of relationships is not work on the other. It is work on the *self*.

For empathy to give everything it can to a relationship, for the best possible use of this relationship tool, both people need to be conscious of their own level of empathy. There is no shame here. While empaths enjoy a state of being connected through emotion, unhealthy empathy can be harmful and destructive to a relationship. If we identify with being an empath, we need to own all that that means and become skilled at blocking. If we notice that we do not identify with the traits of the natural empath, we must become skilled at allowing our emotions and consciously, intentionally connecting with another. Everyone has their gifts.

Empathy becomes an effective and powerful tool, not just a predisposition or lack thereof, when we embrace it with consciousness and self-awareness. This switches off the autopilot setting and puts us in control of the aircraft, which is our human body – the heart, mind, and spirit. As a natural empath, I focus my energy on my own feelings and learn to take care of myself when I am flying the plane. As an intentional empath, I take a break from my thinking brain and stop my work to check into my heart and allow the emotional experience of my partner to have my full attention. Both require focus and love for the other.

When empathy is in our relational toolbox, our relationship now has the power to bond us at the deepest, most vulnerable layers of our being. Dwelling in our true hearts is an extremely vulnerable place to live. Empathy is the relational tool in the toolbox that says, "Not only do I see what you are feeling (compassion), not only do I get what you are feeling (validation), I feel what you are feeling." Empathy.

I see you.

I get you.

I feel you.

You're not alone.

Now we're getting somewhere.

IT'S DEEP

There is now potential for deep connection. We know that seeking relationship is seeking connection on different layers of our being. Shallow relationships involve shallow connections. Perhaps we chat lightly while in line at the grocery. Perhaps we small talk with another couple at a bar. These are relatively shallow connections. We are not likely to feel deeply seen, heard, or loved at this layer of connection. This casual layer of human relationship meets the need for a friendly community.

At the level of intellectual connection, we may find satisfaction in both our intimate relationships and at work. These are generally places where our intellectual needs for stimulation, new ideas, and praise are met. This is where we may feel seen for our intelligence, dedication, competence, and drive. Again, this is not the deepest place of human connection, but these are legitimate needs. We connect in the tasks, mission, accomplishments, and rewards. We celebrate our victories together and learn from our defeats. There is camaraderie, pride, shared energy, and teamwork.

At the level of emotional connection, which involves sharing a more vulnerable layer of our inner world, we seek deeper relationships. This layer is filled with friendships, our romantic partner, and family (when family is emotionally healthy and capable). Recall that emotions are named in the brain but felt in the body, thus emotional connection is a sort of intimate bodily experience with another. We may talk about our emotions easily enough, but real empathy lands us in another realm.

When clients have been traumatized, they may talk about the trauma like they are describing paint colors for the dining room. All of the facts of the story are there, but the emotions are missing. They've been suppressed due to extreme pain. This is dissociation. When I hear their stories and empathize with the emotions I know are present but aren't being voiced, it often makes them uncomfortable. The intellectual layer is so much safer! The resistance will start. "I'm fine. It wasn't a big deal. Whatever. Can we talk about something else now?" Empathy is a mirror. It shows us our hearts on the face of another.

Likewise, talking about our experiences in an intellectual, detached way is more vulnerable than not sharing at all, but when we leave the messiness of emotions out, we are playing it safe. When we start receiving and giving empathy, a new layer of connection opens to us. We form an intellectual *and* an emotional bond, and two bodies feel feelings together. For romantic partners, empathy is emotional sex. I feel what is inside you, in the form of your feelings, and you can feel what is inside me too. This is one of the most intimate forms of human connection outside of the sex act.

We may find empathy uncomfortable for this reason. To empathize is to say that we feel. It is to admit the humanity of our own emotions with another. Some of us would rather stop at compassion, and that's not a bad stopping point, but when empathy is called for, compassion will not suffice. Empathy is the experience of emotional oneness, and some of us are repelled by this. Perhaps we had parents who engulfed us with their "love," and we experience emotional intimacy as suffocation that leaves us gasping for air. Some of us had parents who were terribly uncomfortable with intimacy themselves, and we've never known the beauty and flow of emotional connection. To empathize is to make our emotions known. It is to be seen. If we associate emotions with weakness, we will lack empathy in our lives, and our relationships will suffer in that constraint.

We may choose sex as a substitute for empathy. After all, they have a lot in common. There is a joining in our most vulnerable parts, a sharing of experience, and a flow between us. Without emotional connection, sex can only take us so far. Sex is the physical expression of internal desire, and that allows sex to serve a wide variety of self-expressive purposes. All of those are worthy of awareness and conscious energy. "What am I expressing in the sexual act?" is an important question. However, when we are close to our partners *emotionally* – known, seen, and felt – sex becomes a natural physical expression of the connection we have already known.

THE EMOTIONAL DIET

In order to grow into physically healthy adults, children

have nutritional needs. A variety of vitamins, minerals, proteins, fats, and carbohydrates in a balanced diet will feed and energize their bodies throughout childhood and adolescence. If one nutrient goes missing for too long, sickness can set in. A vitamin deficiency, if left unattended, can lead to chronic malnourishment that affects growth over the long term.

Children also have emotional needs. Let's call it an Emotional Diet. In order to grow into emotionally healthy adults — able to feel, connect, express, and mature — the various elements of the Emotional Diet must be readily and consistently available. These are: acceptance, affection, compassion, expression, patience, gentleness, kindness, validation, play, and *empathy*. (This is not an exhaustive list. The Emotional Diet of children is as long as their physical nutritional needs. These are, however, the crucial elements.) As with a physical diet, the human body can compensate and adjust when one or two nutrients are missing. A low amount of vitamin C for a day or two is no cause for alarm. A prolonged absence of vitamin C can render the physical system susceptible to disease.

Likewise, a child will not be harmed if parents fail to show empathy every now and then, but a chronic deficit will cause longstanding emotional harm. If a child does not receive empathy from their parents, the child becomes detached from their own emotions or overly fixated on them. The result is a dysregulation of the emotional system.

A balanced emotional system is one in which feelings are felt, expressed, validated, processed, and addressed through behavioral or relational adjustments. Some unpleasant feelings can be eliminated with behavioral changes, like prioritizing homework over procrastination. The unpleasant feeling of dread and drudgery are eliminated once the homework is completed. Some feelings must be tolerated, like the disappointment and constrain of keeping curfew when one wants to stay out later. In this case, accepting the boundary parents have set will result in emotional distress, possibly in the form of frustration, but this is part of growing up.

Some parents, instead of offering empathy, seek to remove pain from their children's lives. They want to relieve the child's distress, and instead of allowing and empathizing with the normal and formative pain of life, they "solve" or "fix" uncomfortable situations. For instance, instead of allowing a child to fail a test for which they have not prepared, the parent makes a call to the teacher, requesting an extension. The child never learns self-discipline, and the parent fails to empathize with the normal human experience of failure due to lack of preparation. Instead of working with the child to develop life skills, the child becomes accustomed to not facing consequences and feeling the pain of their decisions. Inevitably the child will become anxious which may present itself as an attitude of entitlement or a demanding disposition. Why? Because internally they know that someday Mommy or Daddy will not be here to solve my problems, *then what will I do?* Anxiety sets in.

Another example is a child who is socially struggling. Instead of working with the child on social skills, the parent changes the child's school or decides to homeschool to reduce the child's anxiety. The child remains unprepared for a social life and their education is interrupted. Again, anxiety will set in. Anxiety is not always a result of situational difficulty but rather situational unpreparedness.

Empathy fills in the gap. Instead of "solving" these problems by eliminating them, we can empathize and say: "I know you're disappointed that you flunked that test. Going to the park with friends was a much more attractive option on Sunday, wasn't it? I get it. I've been there. I've put off what needed to be done for what was more fun, and then I paid for it too." We stay attuned to the child and let the emotion be heard while we empathize. Once the emotional intensity has passed, "Let's work on a schedule together."

Or…

"I know it's hard. I had a lot of difficulty making friends in fifth grade when I changed schools. I felt like an outsider for a year. I get it, Kiddo. I hate rejection too." We gauge the child's emotional state. Have they processed the feeling? When a lightness returns, we set to work on improving their skills and helping to plan activities that will foster friendships. We may share what worked for us too.

Removing the hardship removes the lesson, and the child does not mature. Emotional pain is necessary and inevitable for growth and maturation. Children who grow up with parents who avoid emotions with solutions become adults who try to "fix" their children instead of showing empathy, and the cycle continues. The anxiety only worsens.

Often, empathy is all that is needed. Humans have an inherent social need to be seen and accepted. Empathy is a way of communicating that we see and are with another, and we can do this without words.

Sometimes empathy is absent because the parents' hearts are quite hardened by the time they have children. "I lived through it. So can you," is how this goes. Without empathy, children may suffer more emotional pain than they can actually bear because the parent *cannot feel it*. Here is a physical analogy: a miniscule percentage of children are born with a rare condition called congenital analgesia. They cannot feel physical pain. For these children, the world is constantly dangerous. The harmful actions that most of us avoid – bumping into things, touching hot surfaces, colliding with sharp objects – these children do time and again *because they cannot feel*. Without empathy, a child can develop an emotional form of this disease. Without adult empathy to help them regulate their emotional lives, they are likely to enter into emotionally harmful situations because they are dangerously out of touch with their own feelings.

Empathy serves as an emotional mirror throughout childhood. Before we know ourselves well and can guide and navigate our own way emotionally, we need parents to feel what we are feeling and help us with emotional development. If a parent does not empathize with a child, the child has no reference point for their own feelings. Emotions will be scary or confusing with no end in sight. Children can tolerate an empathic failure periodically, but a chronic lack of empathy does not nurture a child into an emotionally healthy adult.

Adults who failed to receive empathy in childhood may have a difficult time connecting with others. Whether they are natural empaths or they must be intentional about it, the ability to trust that others care about our feelings will be woefully deficient. After all, if our primary caregivers couldn't give us empathy, why would anyone else? The connective bonds and pleasure centers of the brain that light up in the experience of empathy remain dark. And the heart keeps its distance.

EMPATHY IN ACTION

If we are not naturally empathic, empathy occurs most naturally and without conscious energy in the realm of physical pain and pleasure. When others have suffered a physical malady that we can either imagine or have endured ourselves, we naturally meet them in the memory or imagination of the experience. The same phenomenon happens when others describe their pleasure.

> *"I'm having my wisdom teeth pulled."*
>
> *"Ouch! I've been there."*
>
> *"I just had a wonderful massage."*
>
> *"Ahhh... I love that."*

This is empathy. What is being described triggers a physical memory in our own bodies, and we enter into their state with them however briefly by remembering our own experience of the same thing. When people do not offer this basic level of personal connection, we view them as somewhat off and may even feel disturbed by the exchange.

> *"I'm having my wisdom teeth pulled."*
>
> *"Ok."*
>
> *"I just had a wonderful massage."*
>
> *"Oh."*

These would be moments of real confusion at best or hurtful disconnection at worst. We experience interactions like this on a spectrum of feeling off to even heartless. "Something is off with her," we notice. "He has no soul," we think. But we do this emotionally when we fail to empathize with one another! We are off and even soulless when our loved ones pass through emotional experiences and we remain emotionally unaffected or neutral. We must get in touch – with our own hearts, then with theirs.

When someone describes an experience, we try to hear what emotion they are expressing. Then we remember what that emotion feels like inside our own body, and we simply say, "You're feeling sad, aren't you?

I've been there." And we mean it. If we say we get it but we do not remember it, we are intellectually hearing the person, but not truly empathizing. Empathy is a bodily experience of shared emotion. We allow ourselves to be moved by the other's emotional experience. We enter into it.

Empathy is difficult yet essential when we are in conflict. As with all of our tools, the spontaneous feeling is different than the skill. The feeling is automatic. The skill requires focus, conscious choice, and practice.

Conflict is two people viewing the same situation through different eyes. It is a shared journey from connection to perceived disconnection and back to connection again. That's all it is. How we honor and empathize with our partner's perspective is what makes conflict useful or detrimental. When we are in a conflicted moment with our loved one, we lower our voice, we slow and deepen our breathing, we notice our heart rate slowing, and we listen for feelings. We stop the intellectual circles of agreement or disagreement that only result in deeper divides. We develop self-control and we use the tool of Deep Listening (Chapter 2).

Sometimes, we have no idea what another person is feeling. We can't make it out. We are too triggered, or they are intellectualizing their emotions, making it even harder to discern. So we ask.

"I didn't hear you last night. I'm sorry. I want to heal this. What are you feeling?"

"I feel disappointed and forgotten."

"Ah... I get it." (validation) *"I know those feelings."* (empathy)

We learned that we must develop the skill of emotional

expression (Chapter 3) in order to deepen our connection to one another. Empathy will require us to learn and practice self-control and Deep Listening. It is not easy for most of us to offer another person empathy when we are triggered in conflict. Instead of empathizing, we rush into self-protection, defensiveness, accusation, and we do great harm in these states. Empathy is the mature alternative.

When we are in conflict, the temptation is to splinter the unity of our relationships into polarized positions. I think this; you think that. I'm this way; you're that way. These static places of ego will never give us the relationships we desire. We desire connection, and digging our heels into our differences is clearly counterproductive. Instead, we use the tool of empathy to find our common ground. We all feel pleasure and pain. Emotions transcend intellectual differences. We may not agree, but we can recall how painful certain emotions are. And we can say to one another, "We don't agree on this, but I know what you're feeling, and I get it. I feel you right now." Empathy is the road map to common ground. It is the great emotional bond.

• • •

Jack and Lucy were in a habit of intellectualizing their feelings into contested arguments. They could express them, but the bodily awareness of their feelings had been lost long ago. When one or the other talked about their emotional experiences, the response of the other felt flat and lacking. Emotions were expressed as facts that could be argued rather than experiences to acknowledge and share.

By working to restore the conscious experience of their emotions in their bodies, the road opened for them to become connected in a deeper way. They weren't simply hearing about one another's emotional experiences; they were *sharing* them.

Their sexual relationship improved drastically as they

learned to maintain and protect a deeper connection. Instead of talking about emotions "because it's healthy," they began to really feel the power of sharing emotions with one another as a place of intimacy. Sex became a physical expression of a deepening bond.

"I was taught not to feel," Jack surmised. "Our family lived in a bubble. We didn't have any problems, or so we and everyone else thought. We weren't allowed to. We had a reputation to uphold as the 'perfect family.' It was out of place to talk about feelings, and no one empathized because no one was paying attention to pain. I've been creating the same farce here."

"I didn't give you any empathy, Jack," Lucy offered. "I didn't give myself a shred of room to actually feel how exhausted I truly was and am, and I've been driving you like I drive myself. No, like I *drove* myself," she corrected.

Their hope grew as they realized an entirely new realm of connection was opening. Their personal histories seemed opposite one another, but they had every emotion in common.

TOOL TIPS:
EMPATHY

- Empathy is the experience of feeling what another person is feeling.
- People who experience and express empathy easily are the Naturals. People who must make conscious choices to experience and express empathy are the Intentionals.
- Empathy communicates togetherness and is an antidote to loneliness.
- Relationships on autopilot grow stale and dead. We must re-engage regularly.
- Empathy is emotional sex in romantic relationships.
- If we do not know what our partner is feeling, we cannot offer empathy. We must ask.
- Empathy unifies us emotionally and bodily through shared experience.

QUESTIONS
FOR
DISCUSSION

1. Are you a "Natural" or an "Intentional?" How can you tell?

2. Describe a time in your life when you felt another person's empathy. How did you know it was empathy? How did that make you feel?

3. Describe a time in your life when you needed empathy and didn't receive it.

4. How close is too close for you? When does emotional closeness become uncomfortable?

5. What can you do to address the discomfort and move closer to your partner?

CHAPTER 10

Confrontation

Kim and Brody were about to call it quits.

Twelve years of painful, frequent conflicts and almost no resolution had left their marriage as marred as a minefield. Instead of growing in their knowledge and appreciation of one another through the years, they had grown bitter, distant, and resentful.

"We fight all the time. There's almost never a day without a conflict," Kim explained. Brody sat on the other side of the sofa looking physically nauseous.

"What happens when you fight?"

"Oh, we fight about everything. The kids, money, we fight *a lot* about money, his job, his hours…"

I redirected her. "Let's try that again. I'm not asking *why* you fight. I'm asking what happens *when* you fight. How does it go? Do you yell? Curse? Insult? Ignore one another? Describe your style of conflict."

Both grew pensive and quiet. When we are asked to describe in words a pattern or behavior we do repetitively or unconsciously, it brings us to a new level of self-awareness.

"She yells," Brody broke the silence. "She raises her

voice at me, and I don't have any other choice but to yell back. Then no one is listening, everyone is yelling. I've cursed at her, I'll admit that. Then I just shut down. I'm done."

"And when he's done, it's over," Kim finished. "Once Brody has decided he's had enough, there is no going back. I could call, text, plead, beg, or send a carrier pigeon. When he's done, he's done." I noted her use of humor.

"So how do you carry on afterward?" I asked. "There doesn't seem to be much connection, just explosion. Do you ever circle back to one another and talk it out?"

"Not really," Brody shrugged. "If we can't figure it out the first time, there's no use going back, is there?"

I resisted the temptation to explain. If this couple was going to find a path of peace between them, it wasn't going to come from an explanation.

"There's no use because you aren't *willing*, Brody," Kim countered.

"I *am* willing, Kim. But I'm not willing to be screamed at, and neither are the kids!"

"Why are you bringing the kids into this?"

I watched in real time what they did in their home.

"Is this how it usually goes?"

They both stared at me. Their silence was confirmation.

"How did your parents confront one another when there was disagreement in your childhood homes? What did you both observe?"

Brody described a scene that was uncomfortable to hear about much less witness. He described his father as a very quiet man who never participated in arguments. When Brody's mom brought an issue or concern to him, Brody witnessed his father passive-aggressively watching the television while mom's attempts at communication fell on deaf ears. He watched the heartbreak and exasperation on his mother's face as she tried and tried to engage a man who wouldn't reciprocate. Brody resolved to never be like his father, but he hadn't learned any productive communication tools either.

Kim had been raised by a single father. Her mother, an alcoholic, had surrendered custody of her and her older brother when she was just three years old. The only female in the household, Kim felt alone, outside, and even ganged up on at times. Her brother and father shared a special bond around sports and hobbies, and Kim sometimes had to shout to be heard. Her father listened but was often more focused on solving the problem than hearing her heart. It seemed his goal was to get her back to "happy," not learn who she was.

"Brody, how did you feel when you witnessed your mother's frustration with your father?"

"Sad," he offered after a long moment. "I really saw her trying, and there was nothing she could do to open him up."

"And Kim, how did you feel when your dad and brother seemed to be enjoying one another and there was no place for you?"

"Alone. The only way to get them to pay attention to me was to act like a brat."

Brody's eyebrows shot up, and he wisely held his tongue.

"It seems that neither of you witnessed healthy, productive confrontation. What you witnessed left you feeling sad and alone. I wonder if you're recreating those emotional experiences now."

As Kim and Brody began to unpack their childhood patterns and emotional experiences with conflict, they began to see how they had been unconsciously repeating the patterns of their childhoods in their marriage. This insight was the first step toward changing the cycle of how they confronted one another.

Our tenth tool is Confrontation.

• • •

"WE NEED TO TALK"

Confrontation is the tool in our relational toolbox that allows us to address our differences without losing or damaging our connection to one another. It is the tool we use, with ever-increasing skill, that illuminates and nurtures our individual personhood with one another in a safe, productive, constructive way.

To understand confrontation, we need to address what spurs it first. The reason for confrontation, the moment in relationship when we pull this tool out of our toolbox, is conflict.

Conflict is simply two people viewing the same situation from differing lenses. Conflict is not arguing. Conflict is not fighting. Conflict is not blowing up. Conflict is not war. Conflict is not a standoff. Conflict simply occurs when two people look at the same scenario from differing perspectives. And why shouldn't we? We are different, after all. And because of these differences, we will eventually come upon some areas of our relationship where we do not see eye-to-eye. The moment we experience the unpleasant emotions that accompany a difference in perspective, we are now in a conflict. That emotion is generally fear. Even though conflict is most frequently experienced through anger, the core experience is of one of fear: we are afraid of separation from the other.

What if we can't see eye-to-eye?

What if this can't be resolved?

What if we don't agree?

What if I can't trust this person anymore?

What if this is the end?

These are the foundational fears that underlie our difficulty with conflict. We are terrified that our differences will result in the loss of connection, which is why we engaged in relationship in the first place! Of all the threats to connection, conflict looms largest and most frightening. This is why "the worst of us" emerges. We will pull out all the stops to avoid that which we fear the most: being alone.

When we meet and fall in love, we experience a phenomenon of merging. We exclaim to our friends and family, "It's like we're the same person! We have so much in common! We never fight!" This cascade of dopamine is the neurochemical equivalent of getting and feeling high. No wonder we want to be in this person's presence continually! Over time, however, the dopamine wears off (Chapter 1). This is because dopamine is not a result of connection; it is the result of surprise. Once someone becomes regular, predictable, known, and well, not surprising anymore, the dopamine slows down. Our differences emerge. Conflicts may crop up. How we handle these emergent conflicts is what determines the success or failure, the pleasure or pain of our relationships. We can choose to see conflicts as indications that something is wrong, or we can see conflicts as indicative that something is right. In a relationship where two people are authentically themselves, conflicts will appear. This is not a bad thing. We just need the proper tools to navigate our conflicts without losing connection.

This is the normal cycle of an intimate relationship, and it is one we have to accept and understand so that we do not suppose or assume there is anything wrong with *ours* when this phase begins. Anyone can meet and fall in love. Only mature adults with relationship tools and skills can nurture a relationship through conflict into greater connection.

Confrontation is the tool we use to navigate conflict effectively. Without a solid understanding of its function and use, we stand the chance of doing great damage. Words spoken and positions taken in heated moments of conflict have the potential to inflict wounds on a relationship that, in some cases, are nearly impossible to heal. The relationship bleeds out. However, if we know how to confront others with clarity, respect, courage, and curiosity, our conflicts transform from moments of dreaded separateness into respectful individuality. Conflicts that result in separation will lead us down a path of disintegrating connection. Conflicts that result in a respectful individuality lead to increased knowledge of one another and an even deeper unity.

IT'S NORMAL

We experience conflict around common issues: money, children/parenting, work, how and where we spend our time, intimacy, sex, religion, and housework/home life. The areas of conflict are not the problem. I frequently tell couples in counseling: "Your issues are not the issue." What does this mean? We all disagree about the same things! What we fight about is normal. The real issue is *how* we fight. I've rarely met a couple in therapy who has a situation so unique that the topic of their conflict is outside this collection of issues. Mostly, I meet couples who are fighting about normal things in destructive, unproductive ways.

Confrontation isn't easy for some of us, and for others

it's as natural as waking up in the morning. Some of us dread confrontation like a root canal, and others of us shrug our shoulders and say, "What's the big deal?" Wherever we fall on that spectrum, the ability to successfully confront our partners is a non-negotiable. We must learn. Even a little growth is good.

Generally, what inhibits mature confrontation in a partnership is either avoidance or recklessness.

For some of us, confrontation is so scary, uncomfortable, and foreign that we have sophisticated mechanisms for avoiding it. We stuff our feelings, minimize our pain, ignore or discount our needs, or rationalize ourselves out of our emotions. We can become so focused on the emotional state or needs of our partner that our own position drifts out of view. The fear we associate with confrontation may leave us feeling foggy, lightheaded, and confused. The nickname for this personality is a "pushover." We choose the discomfort of not being heard over the discomfort of confronting.

For others of us, confrontation is a way of flexing our muscles, so to speak. We do not fear it; we actually relish the power we feel in it. We use intimidation and reason to our advantage. Our goal is to convince, overpower, or overcome our partner. A successful conflict, for us, is one in which our partner has come around to our way of seeing and doing things, rather than an experience of increased connection. We are reckless with our words and energy, willing to inflict a temporary wound for a long-term advantage. The nickname for this personality is a "bully." And those wounds don't wind up being temporary.

Neither being a pushover nor acting like a bully work in intimate relationship. Healthy confrontation incorporates both courageous self-assertion and invitational curiosity.

"YOU KIDS BETTER KNOCK IT OFF!"

Joy, gratitude, and cheer.

For some parents, this is the full range of emotional expression they encourage in their children. The emotions expressed on a holiday greeting card are the sum total what is allowed in the home.

The obvious concern here is that life is not a holiday and a child, as a fully living, breathing, functioning human being, albeit young, will experience every single emotion known to humankind, over and over again, throughout their childhood. Joy, gratitude, and cheer will be present, as will anger, fear, frustration, shame, embarrassment, withdrawal, loneliness, and the rest. When children experience joy, they feel securely connected to their caregivers and peers, everyone's agenda is lining up, the weather is nice, expectations are met, and the obstacles are few if any. Does this sound familiar? This is also when adults experience joy. However, when the connections break down, agendas are diffuse, the weather uncooperative, disappointments arise, and the obstacles mount up, conflict looms. How adults navigate children through normal conflicts sets the stage for their comfort and skill with confrontation as adults.

For children who are not heard, conflict becomes a burial ground or a proving ground. Depending on the innate personality traits of the child and the example modeled and set by the parents, the child will tend toward avoiding or grandstanding.

For a child more inclined to please, shier, more introverted, or more apprehensive, conflict will mean the burial of their feelings and desires. They will, in order to please their parents, subvert their voice and position in favor of going along to get along. This inevitably leads to a loss of personhood. Those parts of the self that fall outside the range of acceptable emotional responses are buried in the heart and the body. These children will generally not risk self-expression if it means feeling separated from their parents emotionally. They will suffer anxiety rather than speak their mind. The natural, healthy self-assertion of a two- to three-year-old becomes a muffled, agreeable, "pleasant" four-year-old who is in the beginning stages of denial. Adults praise this child for being pleasant; the child is systematically losing their voice.

For more assertive children who are not heard, conflict with parents becomes a proving ground. They are more inclined to fight, argue, engage, and exasperate their parents with unceasing words and emotions that advance their will. They will not rest. Unlike their more submissive peers, assertive children, through personality and modeling, seek to dominate and win. They habituate their anger, using outbursts to forward their agenda. The tender places of trust and vulnerability in their young hearts are shielded behind their dominance.

Whatever the style or combination of styles the child expresses, what is similar in both of these situations is that in the conflict, *the child was not heard*.

Children do not have to have their own way to feel secure. In fact, children who can dominate and overrun their parents through emotional outbursts and inappropriate displays of emotion are insecure children, unsure of who is in charge, and often highly anxious. These children do not know where the boundaries are, and as a result they can be both explosive and excessively clingy. Children also should not have to subjugate themselves to adult agendas all the time. Children need space and time to be young, playful, creative, imaginative, and silly. When children are expected to endure adult agendas and expectations without the ability to have a say, they can become withdrawn, rambunctious, and overly serious. This can begin a slow march toward depression. So the child who always gets their way is anxious, and the child who never gets their way is also anxious.

Where is the balance?

The child must be *heard*. Not obeyed. Not dismissed. *Heard*. The child's reasoning for what they want must be validated for the age and stage of development they are in, and whether the parents decide to meet the child's wishes or set a different course, the child who is heard and valued for their thoughts and feelings is the child who feels loved. This is a child who understands the components of successful conflict and confrontation: listening, validating, understanding, compromising.

Whatever our experience was as children, we learned how to engage conflict and confrontation before our memories took root. Aside from our innate personality styles, we also had conflict and confrontation modeled for us. If we were raised in explosive energy, we may avoid conflict to avoid the explosion, or we may light the fuse because it's familiar to us. Our bodies are accustomed to tension, and we unconsciously recreate it in our adult relationships through avoidance or ignition. This is adult conflict on autopilot.

If our parents were unceasingly pleasant and conflict never occurred in our presence, we may think this is normal, healthy, and possible. It is not. In a relationship where there is no conflict, someone is not showing up. Two human beings are not capable of agreement in all areas of life at all times.

Parents understandably save their conflicts for times when the children are not present. It is a widely held belief that "parents should not fight in front of children." This is true. When children observe their parents fighting – yelling, name calling, resorting to passive aggression or outward aggression – it stresses and may even traumatize them. Children need as much safety and stability as parents can provide, and witnessing the two people who are supposed to provide that very safety and stability lose control is scary for children. If the couples' relationship is not capable of healthy conflict, save those intimate wars for when the kids are not in eyesight or earshot.

However, parents ought not avoid conflict in front of their children. It is safe, healthy, and appropriate for parents to model healthy disagreement and confrontation in in the presence of their kids. (As long as the subject in question is not parenting. In that case, parents should present a united front until agreement can be reached one-on-one.) Children benefit from seeing adults model healthy, respectful disagreement and compromise. Parents can teach children the skill of confrontation through sibling and peer relationships, but nothing is quite as powerful as witnessing parents disagree respectfully, hear one another, and continue on without losing connection.

If we were raised in a home where one of our parents was overpowered by the other, this is what we recreate. We typically choose one role over the other; we are the dominator or the subjugator.

If we were raised in a home where conflict was avoided as a means of keeping a false peace, we seek out a partner who will either trigger our anger as a means of healing from an emotionally vacant childhood or we seek out a partner who can carry on the family legacy of shallow connection and milquetoast agreement.

The seeds for how we experience and engage conflict were sown long ago. Our work now is to become aware. What was healthy? What wasn't healthy? What shall we keep? What shall we discard? What role have we assumed? And how can we use confrontation to deepen and strengthen our connection to our partner?

CONFRONTATION IN ACTION

The first sign that we are in conflict is an emotional shift. We may go from pleased, joyful, hopeful, or neutral to irritated, concerned, afraid, or downright shocked. As we become emotionally knowledgeable, expressive adults (Chapter 3) and increasingly self-aware (Chapter 12), we will notice these shifts within ourselves. They occur, they get our attention, and we notice what is happening in our bodies.

We may express this to our partner immediately. In healthy confrontation, we do this with words not actions. We do not storm off and slam a door in lieu of stating, "I feel angry." We do not compulsively wash the dishes instead of saying, "I feel hurt." We do not strive to make everything and everyone perfect in place of, "I'm feeling ashamed." If we are aware of the shift and not yet aware of what emotion we are feeling, we may say, "I'm aware of feeling something uncomfortable. I'm not sure what it is yet, but I need a minute to process." This is what healthy adults do. This is the first step of confrontation. We notice the shift.

Depending on the size of the emotional reaction, we may need time to find words instead of letting our feelings run the show. Healthy confrontation is deliberate, self-guided, conscious, and intentional. If we are in a state of rage or panic or a shame spiral, we are on autopilot. We must let ourselves feel what we are feeling first and identify it, so that we can bring ourselves to another with care.

The first step of confrontation is noticing and

identifying our feelings. It is wholly within us and upon us to notice our own emotions. Without emotional awareness, confrontation can become unproductive at best, destructive at worst. We notice ourselves because if we don't become aware of our feelings, we will act them out.

In discussing their daughter's soccer practice schedule, Nancy notices that she is doing most of the driving to and from the field. She notices the presence of anger within her.

The second step of confrontation is thinking through our position and our partner's, as we currently understand them. Our emotions have alerted us that we have reached a place of discomfort or disagreement with our partner. We need to do some thinking and assessing before we bring ourselves to another. We consider the following questions:

- What is my position?
- What is my partner's position?
- What is informing mine?
- What is informing theirs?
- Is there any agreement?
- Where is the disagreement?

We stop and ask ourselves if there is agreement because so often *there is*. When we experience unpleasant, disconnecting emotions, we can rush to conclusions. The frightened part of us assumes the worst, "All is lost! We are on opposite sides of this issue!" We might wrongfully assume that there is no common ground. Dramatic, extreme thinking takes over! Because we are emotionally upset, we assume bad intentions. We begin to think that our partner *wants* to hurt or harm us. This is rarely the case. Often, there *is* some agreement. There *is* common ground. Identifying these shared positions forms a solid, securing base from which to explore our disagreements.

Rarely are we entirely split on an issue. Rarely is there outright malice.

When the emotions surrounding a conflict are strong, we will need more time before we can think through it. When the limbic (emotional) system is in full swing, the prefrontal cortex in the brain goes offline. The prefrontal cortex is responsible for processing information, integrating it, forming plans, and executing. Sometimes we need to give our limbic systems time to feel the emotions we feel before the prefrontal cortex can come back online. A good litmus test is: if you cannot think about an issue without getting upset, wait. Eventually the emotions will pass. Addressing conflict in a heightened emotional state is risky. We don't have use or access to our thinking, rational brain.

> *Nancy knows that with both of them working, she doesn't have an easy time being the sole driver for Michelle. She wants more help. She knows that Clark wholeheartedly supports Michelle's interest in soccer, and attending Michelle's games is a joy and priority for the whole family. They both love seeing their daughter flourish athletically and will do whatever they can to give her the resources she needs to succeed. The disagreement seems to be around balancing the transportation for her practice schedule.*

The third step of confrontation is asking. We come to our partner with our emotional awareness, our thoughts, and our questions.

Our position is a reflection of our internal experience. Think of internal experience as our own totally unique personal universe. Our thoughts, feelings, assumptions, experiences, and conclusions are the planets, galaxies, and solar systems that fill our internal world. Much conflict is experienced when we assume that another person's internal world ought to be exactly like ours. How could it be? When we bring our questions to another, it is always with the understanding that they are different than us. Not wrong. *Different*. Their lives have understandably led them to a different viewpoint. We need to validate that (Chapter 4). We cannot come to the table of confrontation in an invalidating stance. We come with the understanding that our partner's position and viewpoint make sense to them for good reason. It is on us to learn it and understand it.

Once we have identified our emotional state, our thoughts, and our questions, we use the tool of Deep Listening (Chapter 2) to allow our partner to inform us of how they think and feel and why. Deep Listening in conflict requires us to set aside our own agenda (or ego) for a moment in order to get the information we need to resolve the dilemma. If our goal in conflict is winning (overpowering, proving our point), we will not listen. If our goal in conflict is resolution and peace, we had better pull up a chair and open our hearts and minds.

"When we discussed Michelle's soccer schedule, I noticed myself feeling angry (emotion). It seems to me that the distribution of transporting her to and from practice is unfairly on me (thinking). I know we are both fully invested in her soccer activities (common ground), so I'm curious about some things... What do you think about her practice schedule? About the distribution of driving? What are your feelings and thoughts on this?"

We come to the table with self-knowledge and curiosity. Here are my thoughts and feelings around this issue. What are yours?

The fourth step of confrontation is listening.

This is how we successfully confront. We:

1. Notice our feelings and name them (as best we can).
2. Think through our position, theirs, common ground, differences.
3. Bring our thoughts and feelings to our partner, asking for theirs as well.
4. Listen.

Solutions are not yet on the table. Finding solutions is about resolving conflict. Confrontation is not resolution. It is the first essential step toward resolution. Without healthy confrontation, resolution is not possible. So much devastating conflict is not actually about the outcome but the process. I've seen couples fight one another about subjects on which they agree! When confrontation is hurtful, the hurt feelings stand in the way of any solutions or resolutions that could be attained. When confrontation is aggressive, agreement is elusive. Conversely, when partners feel heard and understood by one another, they have an easier time finding agreement, compromise, or creative solutions together.

Now let's move toward resolution. Once we have ensured that we have both listened and understood one another's position, we discuss possible solutions to our dilemma. If the solution is not immediately obvious, we can list several options that may work. We weigh the pros and cons of each scenario and agree on a course of action. We try it out. If it works, fantastic. If it doesn't, we try another. We might go back to the first step and work through it once again. Emotional roadblocks become workable challenges.

Notice that the first two steps of healthy confrontation are internal. We notice what we are feeling and we think about our position, possible common ground, and our partner's possible viewpoint. Only then do we move toward our partner, and now with curiosity not accusation.

The second two steps in healthy confrontation are honest, open communication with our partner. We ask and then we listen. Then, after we've learned their position, we brainstorm, test out solution ideas, and agree on a course of action. We must be prepared to compromise! This means we will get a bit of what we want and surrender a bit of what we want. If we are unwilling to surrender any portion of what we desire, we should come out of denial: intimate relationships are not our cup of tea. If, however, we can follow these steps, we can move forward with greater connection.

The most difficult part of confrontation for most of us is the emotional piece. We have a terribly tough time allowing ourselves to feel our feelings. We may be in denial, "Everything is fine." No, it's not. We want to feel in control, "What's the problem? There's no reason for conflict here. The way to proceed is clear." No, it's clear to you. We use volume as a means of dispelling and diffusing our anger. This is not fair to our partner who has to hear our noise. Or we move too quickly in hot emotion instead of thoughtful intention. We are emotional therefore we confront! We are emotional therefore we shut down! No. We slow down. We feel. We think. We ask. We listen. We work on solutions...*together.*

We must be realistic (Chapter 1). Reality means we will reach places in our relationship with one another where disagreements arise. The deeper the emotional connection we have to our own position, the more intense the disagreement will feel. We have a choice: we can ignore these forks in the road and bypass all the intimacy and growth that comes from confrontation; we can explode, insist, and dominate the relationship into a forced state of agreement; or we can engage carefully, slowly, curiously with one another. We might see wisdom in the other we never knew was there. We might learn something about our partner and how they think that informs many other situations. We might give one another a chance to grow, to change, to heal, to adjust.

The origin of the word "resolve" means to reduce to liquid. When we are in painful conflict, we are like ice: hardened, cold, and separate from each other. As we use the tool of Confrontation with ever increasing skill, softening ourselves to the other, hearing, listening, validating, understanding, cooperating… the waters begin to mingle and flow in the same direction once again.

• • •

Kim and Brody fought hard in therapy. Only now, they weren't fighting one another. They were fighting against the patterns and habits engrained since childhood with everything they had.

"This is so hard," Brody lamented in session. "I had no idea how quickly I react. Before I know what I'm doing, I've walked away from her, I'm halfway down the hallway ready to close the bedroom door."

"Then what happens?"

"I stop. I remember how stuck we are, and I know that the only way to get unstuck is to break the pattern. Every time I walk back in the room, I get lightheaded."

"I'm not going to bite your head off, Brody. I want to hear what you have to say. Nothing gets better when we scream or hide."

"Kim, how's it going for you?"

"It's hard for me too!" she let out with a cry in her voice. "I am so used to not being heard that I'm getting louder before I know I'm doing it. I've asked for his help, though. When he hears the volume of my voice rising, he has my permission to point it out."

This is a couple who is serious about the work. Childhood patterns and habituated experiences within the marriage had established a pattern, but their love proved stronger than that. The desire to connect, when shared by both parties, wins out. With the tool of Confrontation in our toolbox, we can walk through the deep, turbulent waters of conflict holding hands.

TOOL TIPS:
CONFRONTATION

- Conflict happens when two people view the same situation through differing lenses.
- Confrontation is the tool we use when we are in conflict, and it does not mean we fight.
- Healthy confrontation allows us to address conflicts without losing connection.
- When we experience unpleasant emotions in our relationship, we express these in words, not actions.
- The steps of Confrontation are: (1) noticing what we feel, (2) thinking about our position, our partner's position (as we see it), and finding common ground, (3) informing our partner of our position and open-mindedly asking for theirs, and (4) listening.
- We do not confront in a heightened emotional state. We allow the emotions to pass first so that we can think.

QUESTIONS
FOR
DISCUSSION

1. What did I witness when my parents were in conflict? What was mom's style? Dad's style? How did this inform my own style of conflict? Describe your conflict style. (Be honest. No shame, remember? We are all learning.)

2. How did I respond as a child when I saw my parents in conflict? What did I feel? How did I handle those feelings? How did I protect myself, engage their conflict, or disengage from their conflict?

3. Which is the hardest step for me in the confrontation process? Why?

4. What do we fight about most often?

5. Where is there room in our process for improvement?

CHAPTER 11

Apologizing and Forgiving

Frank was dynamic and smart. He worked from home as a project manager for an IT firm, and his Type-A personality traits enabled him to successfully manage a team of professionals while serving as president of the board for a nonprofit. He was assertive and even aggressive.

Alice was the more laid back of the two. Her easygoing nature and quick humor were a balancing act to Frank's intensity and drive. Alice worked as a freelance photographer. Highly creative, she was sought out for her artistry and unique perspective. Her role in the home was the anchor. Good-natured and steady, Alice didn't let much ruffle her feathers.

They came to see me because they both felt their connection had grown weak. Sex was infrequent and perfunctory, and life was beginning to feel like Groundhog Day. They had been married for two decades, and in their words, the marriage felt "flat."

"How long have things felt flat?" I wanted to know.

"A long time," Alice jumped in. "I don't remember the last time we belly-laughed together. We haven't had connected, satisfying sex in what feels like forever. We're just going through the routine."

Frank nodded in assent.

The passion in their marriage was in danger of flatlining.

"You've been married twenty years?" I looked up from their intake paperwork. "That's a long time to get to know someone."

"That's a long time to put up with someone," Frank shot back, without a hint of humor.

I glanced at Alice. She was looking down at her feet.

"Alice, what do you want to get out of couples counseling?" I asked, moving past Frank's light insult for the moment.

"I don't know. I guess I just want to learn to be a better wife to Frank - to try my best."

"And what would that look like?" I prodded.

"It would help if she'd do the things she says she's going to do instead of behaving like a child," Frank said matter-of-factly, without looking at her.

"Alice?" I redirected to her.

"I could work on what he said. Sometimes I don't follow through, and I know it drives him nuts."

"Frank, what would you like to accomplish here?"

"I think we need to work on communicating. We just don't communicate well."

Almost one hundred percent of the time, couples seek counseling because they want to "work on communication." The truth is, we are all communicating all the time! A tender, loving comment is communication as is slamming a door. A mature request for help or support is communication as is a manipulative guilt trip. The silent treatment is even a form of communication! Humans in relationship, from infancy to maturity, are always, always communicating with one another. The question is not: are we communicating? The question is: are we communicating in a way that encourages and nurtures connection or in a way that drives us apart in disconnection?

"What do you want to work on concerning your style of communication?" I asked, inviting him to be more specific about himself.

As Frank paused to think about the question, Alice answered for him. "Maybe you could stop communicating like an ass. *That* would be an improvement."

When I work with couples, I lay out, in the beginning of our work together, what is allowed and not allowed in my therapy office, and I have a "no name-calling" policy in place.

"Alice, your language leads me to believe that you feel that Frank's style of communication could use some serious improvement. Can you share what that might look like without using an expletive?"

"No, she's right. I do talk like an ass," Frank chimed in. Sometimes it's easier to agree with an insult than it is to confront it.

"I don't know," Alice thought aloud, "I leave conversations with Frank feeling hurt. Unimportant. Like I don't matter to him at all. I don't know how else to say it: *Frank can be an ass.*" Alice did know how to voice her thoughts and feelings, but she went beyond healthy, useful expression to hurtful language.

I glanced at Frank. No reaction.

"So Frank, you feel disconnected from Alice when she fails to do what she says she's going to do, and Alice, you feel disconnected, hurt, and unimportant when Frank communicates in a way that feels demeaning. Is that right?"

They both nodded, waiting.

"Well, there's certainly room for improvement. I can see that. Let me ask you all a question: do you ever apologize to one another?"

There was a moment of silence, both partners looking at one another with looks of confusion on their faces before Frank asked for further clarification, "What do you mean? I guess... sure... We've both said we're sorry before."

"I mean this: you both have legitimate complaints about how your relationship feels right now. Frank, you want more energy and follow through from Alice. Alice, you want more respect from Frank. These are reasonable requests to make of each other, and they're very common. I'm also hearing you both use words that are hurtful, and there doesn't seem to be any acknowledgment. No one misses a beat. Are you aware of this?"

Another moment of silent processing passed...

"I think that's just how we talk," Frank offered in defense of them both.

"I think it's just a bad habit," Alice added, attempting to minimize the harm.

"I think it is too. And we can work on these issues – follow through and respectful dialogue – but in order for us to re-establish some connection, we need to heal some pre-existing wounds. When we become aware that we have hurt someone, intentionally or unintentionally, it's natural to apologize. Do you ever apologize when your emotions come out in hurtful words?"

"No. I think we just focus on the issue, whatever it is," Frank surmised, minimizing the suggestion.

"That makes sense, but we cannot talk about issues when you are taking jabs at one another. This is like trying to touch another person tenderly with boxing gloves on. You have both become numb. No wonder the marriage feels flat."

Our eleventh tool is Apologizing and Forgiving.

• • •

TO ERR IS HUMAN,
TO APOLOGIZE IS ALSO HUMAN

Apologizing is an essential tool in any human relationship. Relationships between lovers, parents and children, siblings, employers and employees, or any other combination of roles will eventually present a moment for an apology. It is wholly human to err, and it is therefore wholly human to apologize. It is the tool that says to another, "I have hurt you or wronged you in some way, great or small, and that matters." Without apologizing, we essentially say, "When I hurt you, let you down, disappoint you, lie to you, or wrong you in any way, it does not matter." Not many of us would say this explicitly, but if we struggle with apologizing when we have done wrong, this is what we are communicating. This fosters callousness in both parties. The one who has been wronged learns to ignore their pain because it is not acknowledged, they may grow resentful and distant, and the one who does wrong learns to ignore their guilt, humility, and humanity.

Apologies wake us up. We can become so accustomed to our patterns and ways of relating that we are numb to the effects we are having on others. However, the effects are still taking place. A spot on the skin that has lost sensation can still be burned. An apology causes us to stop, consider our actions, consider the effects of our actions, and take responsibility for them. The difficulty we can experience in offering a sincere apology is a good wakeup call. We need to remember that we are human beings,

259

fallible and susceptible to weak moments. Apologies get us uncomfortable, and that's a good thing.

An apology is not a set up for problem solving.

> *"I'm sorry I forgot your birthday. Why didn't you send me a reminder?"*

It is not a form of defensiveness.

> *"I'm sorry I didn't empty the dishwasher, but you forget things too."*

It is not an opportunity to point out another's faults.

> *"I'm sorry, but you're so hyper-sensitive."*

It is not a nebulous response to tension.

> *"I'm sorry you're upset."*

It is not a means of avoiding your fault by playing the victim.

> *"I'm sorry, ok? Now get off my back!"*

It is not a manipulative moment of self-pity.

> *"I'm sorry. I'm just the worst. I don't know why you put up with me."*

It is not a shallow reference to yourself.

> *"I'm sorry. I'm not perfect, ok?!"*

An apology is an acknowledgement that we have failed to treat another human being with dignity, respect, honesty, kindness, and fairness.

That's all it is. It is an acknowledgment of wrong that validates and affirms the personhood of another.

And, like all tools, learning to apologize or avoiding apologies begins in childhood.

I'M SORRY, KIDDO

Children who hear apologies regularly from their parents grow up with a sense that this is a normal, healthy facet of being in relationship with another person. All parents err in relationship with their children. They may become harsh in their anger, they may fail to follow through on a promise, they may be inconsistent, or they may even be caught in a lie. These moments and the multitude of others, when the brokenness of our humanity is experienced by our children in ways that hurt, harm, or confuse them, need apology. Children, although small and young, are human beings worthy of dignity and respect. Children do not deserve different treatment than adults because they are young; they cannot help it. Some parents do not believe children deserve apologies simply because they are in the role of the child. These parents, being in the position of authority, feel they do not need to bend to the level of children. This makes no sense whatsoever and is an abuse of the sacred authority vested in parents. Children who hear apologies grow into adults who can give apologies. Children who are taught to offer their parents and siblings forgiveness become adults who can forgive others. These skills – apologizing and forgiving – do not magically turn on in adulthood. They must be taught and practiced within the family home from the time a baby makes his or her appearance on the earth.

When a parent apologizes to a child, it legitimizes the child's personhood. All people are worthy of dignity, respect, honesty, kindness, and fairness. *All* people. Old, young, rich, poor, native, foreign, disabled, able-bodied, convicted, innocent, Black, White, Brown, Asian, gay, lesbian, straight, transgendered, queer, and any other classification of persons we might consider. When people are young, they are especially vulnerable and impressionable, and are therefore worthy of extra measures of protection and care. While this might seem obvious, it deserves emphasis. Children are often underestimated or discredited by the adults in their lives *because* they are young. We dangerously assume that a mind, because it is a young mind, does not require an apology because it cannot fully fathom the dynamics of an offense. This is almost diametrically incorrect. Children are far *more* sophisticated than most adults because their response systems, most of the time, have not been dulled and numbed by life. They are *more* alive. In other words, while adults may receive apologies with cynicism or disdain, children don't! They receive them with innocence, openness, an ability to forgive, and an easier time reconnecting again because their systems are unencumbered by the complexities of the adult person. In this respect, children are better beneficiaries of apologies than most adults, and we should be watching and learning from *them* how to receive an apology well!

When we apologize to a child if we have wronged them, we are communicating that they are worthy of all the rights listed above – dignity, respect, honesty, kindness, and fairness. When we fail to embody these qualities in our interactions with children, we must apologize. This affirmation of worthiness experienced through our actions develops one of the most powerful and essential traits of a child and then a healthy adult: self-worth. Conversely, if we hurt or harm our children and we do not apologize, we raise children who do not know what they are worth because they have been treated *as if* they have no worth, and their pain, experienced as confusion, hurt, or disappointment, does not matter. These children grow into young adults and older adults who may suffer with feelings of low self-worth for the better part of their lives.

Children learn how to relate by what they see and

experience. This style of learning is called modeling, and it is how children learn most of what they learn inter-personally. This is why parents, in a moment of personal failure, will sometimes say, "Do as I say, not as I do." Why do we say this? Because we know that *children are going to do what we do.* It is how children learn. They imitate and integrate what they see. When parents apologize, children learn how. When parents forgive, children learn how. Because some of us didn't receive apologies as children, we do not know how to offer them today. Because we did not practice forgiveness and did not witness it, we do not know how to forgive today.

For the adult who never saw or felt an apology as a child, the process of taking our own inventory, assessing how we've done wrong, and apologizing is as foreign as flying a helicopter. We do not take our own inventories, we do not think through what wrongs we have done in relationship, and we do not apologize. We simply don't know how.

But we can learn. We *must* learn.

When emotional wounds are inflicted on children – different than the necessary pain of discipline and boundaries – it disrupts the parent/child relationship. The pain of discipline and boundaries flows from love. Our children might not like it, but discipline is loving and nurturing when it is administered with maturity and wisdom. Even though they may not like it, they feel loved in the long run. The emotional wounds we are talking about occur when we fail to love them.

"What are you talking about? I never fail to love my children!"

Yes, you do. We must differentiate between feeling love and showing love. The feelings associated with

263

parent-child love may be constant, but loving actions can be inconsistent. Love is not a feeling or a blood bond. It is a way of interacting with another human being that acknowledges their worth and conveys respect. We use words like kindness, patience, gentleness, thoughtfulness, and generosity to describe love in action, but at the root of all of these attitudes and dispositions is the understanding that we are interacting with another human being. This person before us ought to be treated with the value they deserve.

When we are short tempered, unreliable, inconsistent, cutting, impatient, or generally unkind with our children, we must stop. Perhaps we stop because we realize in our gut that we've done wrong. Perhaps we stop because we empathically sense the hurt or confusion in our child. Perhaps we stop because the tension at home has grown out of control. Whatever the reason, we stop. We kneel down to their level (if necessary). We offer our apology. We can then instruct our children on how to humbly apologize to others without sacrificing their self-esteem.

We would never treat a boss or friend with blatant disrespect or dishonor and expect to get away with it, so why do we feel we can get away with this behavior with a child? Because the accountability structure is different. Another adult might take us on. They might hold us accountable with words or actions. A child, by and large, simply wants to feel safe and close, and they will do anything toward that end. Adults can walk away from relationships with us. Our children cannot. This creates even more vulnerability in the child and more accountability for the adult in the relationship. Our children will let us know they are hurt with words, but if they have not been encouraged to speak forthrightly with the adults in their lives, even when the adults are wrong, they will communicate with facial expression, withdrawal, anger, or distraction. It is therefore on us, the adults, to have the character and integrity to notice their behavior, ask them what happened (if we are not aware of how we have hurt them), and offer our sincere apology. We do not dodge the apology because the child does not mention it. Their bodies don't forget. If we know we have done wrong, we apologize to the child. Period. End of story. This is how the wounds are healed. This is how we teach children to be in healthy relationship.

APOLOGIZING IN ACTION: TAKE A STEP

An apology does not change behavior. It therefore does not solve or resolve issues. We know now that resolution is a process that involves being and feeling heard and allowing new behaviors to arise from a deeper bond. An apology does not do all of that, however it is a step in that direction because it addresses the emotional damage our human errors may have caused. Before we can bridge the gap and connect with our loved one again, sometimes we need to assess and repair the damage we may have done to the bridge. This is when we take out the tool of Apologizing from our toolbox. For this reason, when we apologize, we use the word S.T.E.P. as our guide. Every apology we offer should be Specific, Thoughtful, Empathic, and Personal.

S – SPECIFIC

Apologies that are nebulous and vague do less to heal wounds than apologies that are specific. Being specific means that we are in touch with another person in an intimate, knowing way. It means that the specificity of their needs and personalities matter to us. When we fail another person, we have failed them in a way that feels connected to a specific need in their heart. Even if the hurts and wounds have built up over time and we have a general feeling of malaise in the relationship, if we unpack this, we discover that the wounds were specific at the time of their infliction. So, the apology must be specific as well.

> *"When you were sharing that important story with me, I got distracted and never returned to it. I'm sorry for that."*

T – THOUGHTFUL

Apologies must demonstrate thoughtful self-knowledge and self-awareness. If we are apologizing for how someone else feels, we are essentially communicating that their feelings are somehow wrong. "I'm sorry you're upset" is not an apology. Feelings do not require apologies. Feelings require validation (Chapter 4). We may need to apologize for actions and choices that caused emotional harm, but we do not apologize for the feelings themselves. Remember, apologies are an acknowledgement that we have done wrong. Someone else's emotional experience is not our failure, but it does give us reason to pause and reflect on our actions. A productive apology is the result of thoughtful self-inventory and evaluation.

> *"I've thought about last night's dinner. You said you felt left out. I realize that I was more concerned with how I looked in front of my friends than I was about including you. I apologize. Please forgive me."*

E – EMPATHIC

Emotional wounds cause pain. When we apologize in

dry, numb, callous ways without feeling the discomfort, pain, or even torment of another person, our apologies may check a box, but they have not touched a heart. In this case, they are less powerful than they could be. "I got worked up. Sorry." Well, this is specific, and it does involve ownership and self-accountability, but what's missing is what our words and tone did to the other person. When our actions have caused another pain or sorrow, we must allow ourselves to feel that distress. This imbues an apology with a level of empathy that moves hearts and restores connection.

"I said those careless words in anger, and I do not mean them. I imagine you felt insulted, and it pains me to know that I've hurt you. Please forgive me."

P – PERSONAL

When we offer an apology, we do it in as personal a way as possible. This is the difference between a gift and a gift certificate. A light offense does not require a face-to-face, in-depth conversation. "Oh shoot! I forgot the blueberries! I'm so sorry!" we might say as we unload the groceries. Just as we learned the skills of Light Listening and Deep Listening, we must be able to gauge what type of apology is necessary. The deeper the pain, the more intentional and personal the apology. We don't rush it because of our discomfort with it; we grow instead. We don't use text messaging to address real issues. We don't give the bare minimum so we can defensively claim later, "I said I was sorry!" Rather, we mature into adults who can use the tool of apologizing to restore connection in our relationships. We need to know how to repair what we've broken. We muster up our courage and humility, we stand before our loved one, we take a deep breath, and we deliver.

> *"I need to talk to you. Can we have a couple of minutes, just the two of us (personal)? Last week, I know I let you down. I was busy at work, and I allowed that to take priority over the things we had talked about doing together (specific). You felt hurt that I came late to your parents' anniversary party, and rightfully so. I hate that. I feel terrible about it (empathy). I've thought about it, and I realize I feel worried, really worried, and I haven't brought that to you. We have so many financial obligations this year, and in the attempt to keep all the plates spinning, I think I made some mistakes in my priorities, mistakes that have hurt you (thoughtful). I apologize."*

This is indeed a STEP in healing this relationship. And this is what a true, productive apology looks and sounds like.

Use the STEP method to gauge how you apologize. Are you Specific, Thoughtful, Empathic, and Personal?

An apology is one of the most powerful and vital tools in your relationship toolbox because everyone errs. We apologize when we have done wrong. We do not wait. We do not postpone or procrastinate. We simply admit it. From the heart.

Let's switch our focus to Forgiveness.

TO FORGIVE, DIVINE

When Alexander Pope wrote "To err is Human[e]; to Forgive, Divine," he was rightly giving us a sense of what it takes to truly forgive another human being. When another person has hurt or harmed us, it is normal to feel pain. We are hardwired to love and feel connected when we feel we are being treated with dignity, respect, honesty, kindness, and fairness. When we experience an absence of these things, one or all, we experience pain. We naturally have expectations. We expect others to treat us a certain way, and when they fail to do so, we feel hurt. Now we have something to forgive.

In general, we are far more adept at gauging when another person has failed to match this standard than we are at seeing when we have failed to do it ourselves, but this must be part of our self-evaluative process. We are not responsible for how others treat us. We are responsible for how we treat others. When we are faced with a wrong to forgive, we must remember that we too have wronged others. We too have failed to be dignifying, respectful, honest, kind, and fair. This sense of shared humanity is the first step of forgiveness. We see that we are fallible. We are only human, and everyone is flawed. When we feel hurt, we must consciously recall that we have also been hurtful.

We also need to consciously recall that hurtful behavior is often about another person's story rather than their attitude toward us. This helps us keep wrongs in perspective. Most of the time, it's not as personal as we feel it is. We fear personal rejection and abandonment more than anything else, and when our loved one acts in an unkind way, it reinforces this fear. Rather than seeing their fear-based attempt at self-protection, we feel wronged and hurt. We can recall with compassion (Chapter 6) that they are living from a script that was born out of their story. It is not our fault. We didn't write their story. This compassion fuels forgiveness. Let's briefly address what forgiveness is not before we define it:

- Forgiveness is not intimacy. We can forgive someone and not remain close to them.

- Forgiveness is not a restoration of trust. We can forgive and allow time for trust to be earned again, if possible.
- Forgiveness is not commitment. We can forgive a wrong and leave a relationship.
- Forgiveness does not mean we condone behavior.

Forgiveness simply means we release the anger we feel toward another person who failed to give us the love we deserve.

The purpose of anger is to alert us that a wrong has been committed against us or someone we love, but it is not meant to stay in our hearts forever. That's not its job. It's a flashing sign, a warning. Anger is not a good companion or a productive state of mind. On the contrary, looking at life through a lens of anger skews our vision, distorts reality, and misdirects our choices. Anger that is lodged deeply within us begins to eat us alive. We feel hollow and filled with rage at the same time. Forgiveness is the fruitful and mature outcome of anger and hurt.

When someone offers an earnest, thoughtful apology, forgiveness is easier. We see that they have acknowledged their wrong, they are demonstrating that they understand the harm/pain they have caused, and we can join them in their humanity. We all err.

To forgive, we must do the following:

Identify the wound. What happened and how did it hurt or harm me? Have I been treated in some way(s) that lacked dignity, respect, honesty, kindness, and fairness?

Feel the pain and hurt. We cannot skip this step! The pain is what we are forgiving! Some of us come from religious backgrounds that teach and require forgiveness of others, however if we do not fully engage the pain of what was done to us, we cannot fully forgive the offense.

We cannot heal what we refuse to feel, and forgiveness is an internal and relational form of healing. We cannot let go of what we have never felt.

Allow compassion. Remember that we are all struggling to live this life. We are failing and succeeding. Compassion does not mean we re-engage the relationship in the same way, and we may even need to end the relationship altogether, but we can choose to have compassion on others' broken places nonetheless.

Let go of the anger. Compassion has now entered our hearts, in place of the anger. We can thank anger for doing its job and let it go. We no longer look at this person or speak their name with hatred in us. We can see them as beautiful, broken human beings who deserve... you guessed it... dignity, respect, honesty, kindness, and fairness.

This may take a moment. This may take weeks or months. For the deepest wounds, forgiveness can take *years*, and as long as we are on the path of forgiveness, we are making progress.

Some of us believe that shutting someone out and moving on is forgiveness. It is not. We have not let go of the wrongs; we have let go of the relationship. This is disconnection, not forgiveness. Sometimes letting go of a relationship is the healthiest choice we can make, but we can still forgive the person we have left. A good test of whether or not we have forgiven someone is this: we speak their name. If we can hear their name, and no tension arises in us, we have likely forgiven them. If we notice tension or heat, the forgiveness is not complete.

If we are in relationship and we have not forgiven our partners or loved ones, the relationship can become toxic. All actions are viewed through the lens of hurt and judgment, and our thinking and choices are thus skewed. The relationship is stuck as long as there is a lack of

271

forgiveness.

We move as quickly as we can in both apologizing and forgiving. When we are wrong, we admit it as soon as we recognize it or as soon as someone brings it to our attention, we apologize properly, and move on.

When we receive an apology, we begin the work of forgiveness as soon as we can.

Several factors make forgiveness particularly challenging:

- A refusal to apologize or apologize well
- A pattern of harm (as opposed to a single event)
- A failure to even acknowledge that hurt or harm have been inflicted (common in narcissistic personalities, also known as "gaslighting")

If we are in relationship and one or more of the above factors are present, more often than not, we still need to forgive – for our own wellbeing – but we need to examine if this relationship is toxic to us. All of the above reflect a person who cannot see another's personhood. They are likely functioning out of unresolved wounds, and we are bearing the brunt. We must still forgive to release ourselves from anger, but perhaps we need to release ourselves from the relationship as well.

This is conscious work. This is not auto-pilot. This takes energy, thought, and earnest effort. This is a self-directed movement past our ego. This is mature relationship.

• • •

Frank and Alice both resisted apologizing at first, mostly because it was so foreign to them. We fear what we do not know. But the marriage was too far out on the rocks for much resistance, and both were in desperate need of a new stream of energy. I encouraged the couple to sit down and take a detailed inventory together. Were there unhealed wounds? As it turned out, there were stories that had been repeated during times of conflict for years. These wounds had never been properly addressed or healed. Like a physical wound, they were festering. A marriage is an entity in and of itself, and it has its own story. This was not a record of wrongs to hold over one another; it was a tool for self-reflection. (When working with individuals, I will often have them construct a history of the traumatic events in their lives. This serves many purposes, one of which is to have a visual record of the harms they have suffered. This validates their feelings, offers insight into their patterns, and lays out a pathway for healing. This same technique can work for couples as well.)

Starting with their wedding day and culminating in the present, the couple became aware how many dings, cuts, scrapes, gashes, lacerations, bruises, and wounds their relationship had endured. Apologizing became easier and easier. The earliest wounds were processed with care, using the S.T.E.P. model as a guide, and as they progressed through the timeline, forgiveness took the place of resistance. Like a sailboat picking up speed in a strong wind, the relationship healed quickly. As they both experienced the other's willingness to take responsibility, apologize, and demonstrate care about the hurt they'd caused, they began to trust one another again. As the trust increased, the need to talk about each hurt and harm decreased. They were letting go of the past in the healthiest way.

I witnessed the old phrase "love covers a multitude of sins" in action.

When we don't know how to heal a wound, we disengage. We may act like it never happened by suppressing the hurt we felt or caused, but our bodies tell the real story. We do not deeply trust this person, and we do not feel safe.

273

The tool of apologizing helped Frank and Alice to clean up the past. Their "History of Unhealed Harm" served as a guide for each to see how they used aggression instead of healthy confrontation. Resistance changed to self-accountability. There were discrepancies around certain memories... Who was at fault? Did I really say that? The tool of Validation (Chapter 4) worked wonders as they were empowered to worry less about what happened and focus instead on validating how it felt. Forgiveness reaffirmed their shared humanity and brought them back to compassion for one another. These tools – Apologizing and Forgiving – hold the power over our painful pasts. This is how a wound is healed.

TOOL TIPS:
APOLOGIZING
AND
FORGIVING

- All relationships will require us to apologize and forgive. Both are essential tools and skills for all relationships.
- Apologies serve to wake us up and help us become aware of ourselves and how we are relating to others.
- We do not use apologies as a mask to accuse others or avoid our responsibility.
- A healthy apology is a S.T.E.P. It is Specific, Thoughtful, Empathic, and Personal.
- Forgiveness means we let go of anger and grab hold of compassion and peace.
- We cannot forgive what we have not truly felt.
- Both apologizing and forgiving require that we move past our egos and recognize that we all make mistakes.

QUESTIONS
FOR
DISCUSSION

1. How did you experience apologizing and forgiving in your family of origin? Be specific. When he was wrong, did your father apologize? To others? To you and the other children? When your mother was wrong, did she apologize? To others? To you and the other children?

2. How were conflicts settled between you and your siblings/peers?

3. Is apologizing difficult or natural for you? What about forgiving?

4. Which part of the S.T.E.P. method is most difficult for you?

5. Are there unhealed wounds in your relationship(s) today?

CHAPTER 12

Self-Awareness

Alexa rarely showed vulnerability.

She and her husband had met with their parish priest for marriage counseling, and unable to help them through their difficulties, he'd referred them to me. The couple was already drowning in the tumultuous waters of disconnection. A second marriage for both of them with six kids between them, this time it needed to work. She was desperate but didn't show it.

In an initial therapy session, even if someone has previously been in counseling but is seeing a new therapist for the first time, even if they are experiencing intense pain, the first moments are generally filled with introductions on both sides. People will give themselves a moment to take in the room and settle into the energy of the space. We may share some polite conversation about their day, the paperwork they filled out, and review the practice policies.

Not Alexa.

Her presence filled my office as soon as she entered. At the very moment her feet crossed the threshold, she began to unpack details of her marriage to Brandon, before she had even taken a seat on the sofa!

I took a deep breath, creating space for Alexa's intense energy and strong feelings. Her main complaint, initially, was Brandon's lack of parenting skills with his teenage boys. Then she switched to his failure to give her appropriate gifts. Next, his cooking. About forty minutes into our first session, knowing I only had ten minutes to wrap up as well as review some important practice policies, I asked her an important question.

"What do you want to work on, Alexa? I hear how disappointing this new marriage is for you. Second marriages and blended families are often very difficult to establish. We can work on that together. But for yourself, as an individual, what would you like to accomplish through therapy together?"

Alexa's eyes grew wide. The look of surprise on her face was undeniable.

"Are you asking me what *I'm* doing wrong?" she demanded, stunned.

"No, not necessarily. I'm asking what your goals are. For yourself. Your complaints about Brandon are legitimate, but we can't work on changing him because he's not here. You are. So what would *you* like to accomplish in therapy?"

"I'm just trying to live a normal life!" she exclaimed. "Are you telling me that *I'm* the one who has to change?"

I needed to know how well she knew herself, if at all. A wave of heaviness passed over me as I realized both her self-knowledge and curiosity about herself were severely limited. I could see a lot of criticism, demand, impatience, and contempt in her view of her new husband which led me to imagine her childhood. Did she experience criticism, demand, impatience, and contempt that served as a model for this style of relational functioning? Did she have to become aggressive to be heard? Many scenarios could have resulted in this behavior, but did she know anything about it? Was she aware of her anger when it arose within her? Or was she off to the races without a shred of self-control? Her complaints had merit. Feelings of frustration and hopelessness frequently arise in newly blended families where parenting styles differ, where memories of previous spouses cloud the landscape, where children, attempting to adjust, act out in the absence of mature emotional expression and conflict resolution skills. All of this is difficult and challenging to say the least, but how we engage the difficulties and challenges of our relationships is really where our power is. I wondered: did Alexa understand that her power was in knowing and regulating *herself*?

With just a few minutes left, I dropped the question. I already had an answer: her self-knowledge and self-awareness were practically non-existent.

"I'm not at a place where I can see fault, Alexa. You and Brandon have some legitimate struggles on your plates, struggles that have the potential to create bonds or breakdowns in trust. If you'd like to meet again, we can dive a bit more deeply into what you've been experiencing and how best to address your concerns."

She looked annoyed and a little confused but agreed to meet again. I hadn't given her what she wanted in her session: agreement that Brandon was the cause of the problems.

Alexa began her second therapy session with another litany of Brandon's failings that had occurred in the time between our sessions. I heard her out, validating and empathizing with the frustration she felt, and then suggested a different route.

"When two people get married, they bring their current lives to one another in the marital union, but they also bring their histories into the relationship. The tracks of our lives are pretty well engrained in us by the time we reach adulthood, so I think it would be useful to gain more knowledge about your history. I'd like to know more about your childhood and how you learned to relate with those closest to you."

"I had a great childhood. My parents and I are still really close."

I could feel her defensiveness rising again.

"I'm glad to hear that. Tell me about growing up in your house."

Alexa described a childhood of freedom, play, community, and consistency. Indeed, these are all positive, edifying childhood experiences.

"How did your parents handle emotions?"

"I don't know," she said with annoyance. "We didn't really talk about our feelings. We weren't that kind of family."

"What kind of family?" I asked.

"You know… that kind of mushy, gushy, overly sentimental family," she said with disgust. "My parents raised us to work hard and be independent. Look, I didn't come here to talk about my childhood. I came here to talk about my marriage."

I tried to explain that while those are wonderful values to instill in children, children feel emotion, and therefore need guidance to experience and express their emotions in healthy, relationally productive ways. I added that our childhoods are where we learn how to love and be loved. The emotional patterns engrained in childhood carry over into adulthood, which makes them worth exploring.

"I just don't think we were very emotional children."

"An unemotional child does not exist."

Therapy was going nowhere. Not because Alexa couldn't see herself but because she clearly didn't want to. She had no curiosity about herself, her feelings, her story, or how these things were connected and playing out in her marriage. Instead of an openness to learning what her patterns were, she was rationalizing her own position to protect her ego. Instead of accepting responsibility for her part of the relationship, she was insistent on blaming Brandon while her failure to be an emotionally aware and self-accountable person went unaddressed.

People come to therapy for one reason: they are in pain. Some kind of mental or emotional distress has reached a point of interfering with our day-to-day functioning, and more help is needed. A range of therapeutic interactions can reduce pain: validation, empathy, compassion, processing trauma, laughter, and many more. However, the clients who grow and receive the full benefit from therapy are those who can see and eventually learn to value the most powerful tool of all.

Our twelfth tool is Self-Awareness.

• • •

YOUR CHILDHOOD + YOUR ADULTHOOD = ONE STORY

Often when people start therapy, they are reluctant to see any faults or failures in their parents. To talk about our parents' faults seems disloyal, ungrateful, or perhaps even a betrayal. This way of thinking is a marker of a protracted childhood and adult immaturity. Children see their parents as infallible, and whatever treatment they receive is what children perceive as normal, whether it is loving, healthy, or not. As we become adults, we are able to see our parents as real people, beautiful and broken, and rather than denying our parents' faults, we embrace how our parents loved us successfully, how they failed to show us love, how their good love nourished us, and how their brokenness hurt, harmed, and even traumatized us. Everyone is fallible, and the denial or inability to see our parents' failures is the mental state of a very young child. We need not fixate on the ways they failed us and live as angry victims for all of our lives, but we need to know and own what happened during our childhood and how it felt – pleasant, enjoyable, harmful, and hurtful. Then we need to understand how we adjusted or survived it. Our path from childhood to adulthood is called our story.

The first stage of knowing our story is asking ourselves: what happened in our homes while we were growing up? Have we ever sat down and written our story with pen and paper? In a journal? Typed it out? Have we ever told anyone the stories of our childhood? The good *and* the bad? The funny *and* the humiliating?

Without self-awareness, we tend toward over-generalization.

"I had a happy childhood."

"Nothing really big happened during my childhood."

"My parents were perfect parents."

"Nothing stands out. Just a normal childhood."

All of these statements are akin to reading a novel, and when someone asks us what happens in the novel, we respond with, "Nothing much. It was really happy." There is much more! There are characters, plot twists, striking moments, and significant events. The same is true of our childhoods. Our childhoods begin with people trying to meet their own needs while attempting to meet the inexhaustible and ever-changing needs of children, and that's a messy business. Some needs are met, some needs go unmet. If parents expect to meet every need their children have, they convey this erroneous message in the relationship. They revel in the moments when their capabilities match their children's needs, and they shun or ignore the needs they cannot meet. Children may feel confused. Not knowing any better, they shun their own unmet needs. Children do not have the wisdom or awareness to say, "Mom, I need more empathy from you." "Dad, please be more patient with me." They simply internalize the message sent: I'm alone in my emotions where Mom is concerned. My needs make me annoying to Dad. Children need their parents for survival, so admitting where Mom and Dad fail is an existential threat.

As we grow into adults, we must come into contact with these memories and experiences if we are to become fully mature. Why? Because the needs we may be denying – unmet in childhood – have not gone away. They have merely been suppressed. Our emotions are the trail markers as to which needs went met or unmet. (See Appendix C for a List of Needs.) If our needs are met, we generally feel pleasant emotions. If our needs are unmet, unpleasant emotions are the signs that point the way to relief and growth.

We don't stand a chance of becoming fully mature adults if we do not (1) know what we feel, (2) know what we need, and (3) know how to meet our needs through ourselves and our relationships. All of this starts with knowing our story. This is the first step of self-awareness.

Knowing our story begins with tapping into the emotions in our hearts without judgment. We don't need to feel guilt or shame when we acknowledge our sorrow, anger, or hurt. The emotions we have about our emotions are strong markers of how healthy we are. People who can feel their feelings without self-reproach were either raised in emotionally healthy homes or they've done a good amount of personal work. Most people, however, feel some sort of discomfort – shame, embarrassment, or guilt – about their feelings. This is a sign that our childhood was not a safe place for our feelings. This is part of our story.

Once we've turned on the valves of our emotions and we are allowing them to flow (Chapter 3), we begin to remember how we *felt* in our childhood experiences. We remember that we felt afraid in our first-grade classroom, we felt nervous around Grandma, we felt safe and warm in our bedroom, we felt embarrassed in front of dad, we felt dread going to church, and so on. We begin to deepen and enrich our childhood narrative. "I had a happy childhood" becomes "I had a rich childhood." This is truth. This complexity continues to broaden as we become more and more aware of what we felt in childhood and adolescence.

We are now telling the story of our lives and therefore our hearts. We've moved from a shallow tale of denial-based "happiness" to the fascinating, complex story of a human life. We become aware of the different shades of us. How we were bold sometimes, but shy as well. We remember that we hated feeling embarrassed when called to the chalkboard, and we can remember how that felt in our bodies. Our feelings are coming back, and we are seeing the continuity of this beautiful body/home we've been living in for so long. It has been delivering messages of calm, alarm, connection, and disconnection to us the whole time, and now we are listening. (Our ability to listen to our own heart will drastically shape how we listen to others.) We remember that one day in elementary school when we felt like the king of the world! We walloped the game-winning kick during the recess game of kickball. We recall the shock and shame the first time we ever got a D on a test. We can feel again.

Why are these memories important? Who cares?

First, our ability to be self-aware adults does not have neat, tidy boundaries around our adulthood. Whatever emotions we deny in our childhood experiences, we will deny and avoid as adults. If we didn't express shame as children, we will not express it as adults and we will avoid it in our children. If we did not express sadness as children, for any reason, we avoid it as adults and we discourage its expression in our children. This is true for all emotions. We cannot give what we do not have. If we lack emotional awareness ourselves it is because we were not taught to feel and attend to our emotions as healthy, vital parts of the self, and we will not be able to parent emotionally healthy children. This sets the stage for disconnection from one another and the self. Addictions may ensue. Second, that child – the Little You that you used to be - *mattered*. And he/she matters now. The child we were is still inside us in the form of feelings, memories, and neural pathways (the chemical reactions the brain habituates over years of repetition). We do not progress away from childhood; we progress through it. We did not lose our childhood when we became adults, we internalized and integrated it. Knowing our childhood is knowing ourselves. Our emotions and experiences don't start mattering at a certain age; they have *always* mattered.

The second part of knowing our story is understanding how the events of our childhood affected us. Many people can tell their childhood stories, but they are detached from the effects of their experiences and the behaviors they developed to survive those experiences. I see this frequently when people share stories of horrific abuse or soul-crushing abandonment while they are laughing.

We need to understand how our relationships with our parents have shaped how we engage relationships now.

The Toolbox

If we have any chance of changing unhealthy behavior, the first step is becoming aware of it.

"Not me. I'm an adult. I've left my childhood in the past where it belongs."

Yes, you. We are the adult versions of the children we were. We must set our minds to understand how our childhood environment and experiences shaped the people we have become. This gives us a sense of compassion and continuity for our lives. Instead of berating ourselves for the mistakes we make, we connect our actions with our past hurts and trauma, and we grow in our understanding of how life works, how human beings work, how we work. We begin to see the patterns we created based on the patterns we experienced emotionally. We let go of shame and grasp understanding. There are reasons for why we feel what we feel. There are reasons for how we react. There are reasons for our triggers. There is a reason we circle back to the same types of people, time and again. The more we know our story and become aware of our emotions, the greater capacity we have to make choices instead of reacting as we have done before. If growth is the goal, awareness is more than half the journey.

This is where the relational rubber meets the road. The behaviors we habituated in childhood – healthy or unhealthy – have become our adult ways of relating. This is where we learn what our original toolbox was.

We remember our stories, we tell our stories, we begin to feel, and we begin to understand how our stories shaped who we are. This is the third stage of self-awareness: knowing what specific behaviors we developed and why.

Life happened.

We talk about it.

We allow ourselves to feel the feelings that arise from

our memories.

This is emotional healing.

We recall the joyful moments, and we acknowledge that we survived pain by developing behaviors meant to protect us.

What were they? These behaviors, if we have not become self-aware, are still in play today. Perhaps we escaped to our bedroom when mom and dad fought, and today we notice that we still avoid conflict. We could never earn dad's approval unless we made straight A's, and we notice that we are still working long, late hours in order to be "good enough." Mom grew visibly distressed and felt like a failure when we expressed sadness as a child, and we realize that we are still repressing and silencing our deep sadness because we don't want to be a "burden" on others. Children are brilliantly and frighteningly adaptive. We developed sophisticated and numerous methods of protecting ourselves from pain. These behaviors are now unconsciously engrained and require conscious effort to bring into our awareness. How do we do this?

We ask:

- How did I cope with feeling alone as a child? How am I coping today?
- How did I cope with hurt as a child? How am I coping today?
- How did I cope with rage as a child? How am I coping today?
- How did I cope with shame as a child? How am I coping today?
- How did I cope with feeling overwhelmed as a child? How am I coping today?
- How did I cope with fear as a child? How am I coping today?

And so on. Feeling our emotions brings us to a deeper, more realistic understanding of our lives, our childhoods, and the narrative expands from caricature into real life. We were not children playing characters while we were growing up; we were breathing, feeling, tender beings whose hearts needed love, whose minds needed wholesome stimulation, whose bodies needed appropriate affection and protection, whose spirits needed connection. When we did not receive these things, the needs did not go away. We simply figured out a way to cope with the pain. To understand this is to begin to see how and why we have been living adulthood the way we have been living it. It is the beginning of our relationship with ourselves. It is the beginning to understanding our relationships with others.

This is self-awareness.

WHAT SELF-AWARENESS DOES

Self-awareness allows us to participate in our relationships consciously. This awakens the potential for the depth and intimacy we desire. We are finally connected! Not to someone else yet, to ourselves! We begin to *know* ourselves, and we can finally make ourselves known to another with less shame. Not through happenstance or the forced creation of romantic, artificial experiences but through two human beings sharing the essence of themselves with one another. Living unconsciously is living on auto-pilot: the computer is flying the plane. When we are in the unconscious survival patterns of our childhood, we are on relationship auto-pilot. When we are reactive instead of present to what is happening in the moment, we are on auto-pilot. When we are anxiously trying to meet our needs through compulsive actions, we are on auto-pilot. When we are detached and isolating, we are on autopilot. When we are screaming, shutting down, accusing, ignoring, escaping, criticizing, abandoning, avoiding, and submitting, we are on auto-pilot. We are unconsciously living out our childhood in our adulthood.

Self-awareness is what stops us in our tracks and gives us options. We consciously think, "Oh, I'm doing _____ again. I know why I do this. I know what need I'm trying to meet. I'm choosing to stop this behavior. I have a better tool to meet this need." We gain more control over ourselves through the compassionate understanding of our own story. That which is shrouded in shame controls us, through the unconscious mind. That which has been exposed to the light, to love, to understanding, compassion, forgiveness, and acceptance, has the potential for transformation.

Self-awareness is what enables us to grow, not merely change. Change is a shift in behavior, and sometimes that is the best we can do. Growth is a shift in consciousness. Growth is an internal transformation of how we see ourselves. If we see ourselves in overly simplistic terms and describe our lives in overly simplistic terms, we will never know our potential or our strength because we have effectively overly simplified ourselves. We become partners who oversimplify the other, and we lack patience for the complexity of another human being. Self-awareness is what expands our self-concept and therefore expands us. We can love more, feel more, care more, and conversely, we can hurt more, fear more, and desire more.

This is to be alive.

Our potential for connection will always reflect our level of self-awareness. Denial, defensiveness, and avoidance are enemies of self-awareness. Curiosity about ourselves, remembering, processing, talking, feeling, identifying behaviors in the past and the present, eventually having compassionate understanding about who we are -- this is the path of the self-aware.

IT ALL STARTS IN CHILDHOOD

Mirroring is a vital developmental interaction in childhood. This is the experience adults and caregivers give to babies and children when they reflect back gestures, expressions, emotional states, and sounds to the little one. Baby looks surprised, and mom instinctively reflects the expression back. Her eyebrows rise and her eyes are wide open, mimicking the infant's face. Baby cries, and dad's face changes immediately from neutral to sad, concerned, and compassionate. While infants cannot communicate verbally, they communicate with expressions, gestures, and sounds. They are aware of the connection or the lack of it immediately. When babies are properly mirrored, they feel safe, known, seen, and loved. When they are not mirrored, they feel distressed, anxious, fearful, and alone.

A famous experiment by Dr. Edward Tronick (this video is available on YouTube) shows a mother interacting with her infant. The child is engaging playfully and joyfully with the mother, who is mirroring the child. Their bond is warm and loving. The mother turns her face away and when she turns back to her baby, her expression is blank. The baby is immediately confused, tries to win her back, begins to squirm uncomfortably, and eventually cries out in distress, all while the mother keeps a blank, expressionless face. The baby went from joyful and secure to distressed and desperate in under two minutes, solely dependent on whether her mother was mirroring her or not. This is the power of mirroring.

What does mirroring have to do with self-awareness? The emotional attunement babies and children receive from their parents gives the children an externalized experience of themselves. It essentially says, "You are a person, and I see you. I'm connected to you, and I'm with you." Many factors may inhibit proper mirroring: self-absorption on the part of the parents; lives that are too busy to stop and focus on the emotional states of the child or children; or even mental/emotional distress or pathology in parents that inhibits them from offering their attention to their children in this way. Without the emotional experience of mirroring, children lose a sense of themselves. They internalize feelings of aloneness and self-reliance and struggle to form close relationships.

While humans actually crave mirroring experiences for the entire lifespan, what eventually takes the place of parent-infant mirroring is parent-child empathy. When children express emotional states, particularly painful ones, self-aware parents are able to empathize. The message is identical to mirroring: "You are a person, and I see you. I'm connected to you, and I'm with you." Many well-meaning parents seek to change or resolve painful emotional states for their children. This is understandable; no parent wishes to see their child in pain. However, if normal emotions are viewed as problems that need to be fixed rather than a normal part of life, children develop shame around their emotions and begin to edit.

"Confidence is okay; fear is not."

"Happiness is okay; anger is not."

"Success is okay; failure is not."

This emotional editing is how kids control interactions with their parents. If they keep their emotions in the realm of what is acceptable and wins approval, they will feel less disconnection. This is their goal. Again, no child has the emotional wisdom or self-awareness to say, "Dad, please don't try to fix this right now. My best friend betrayed me, and I'm really heartbroken. I just need a hug and some time to grieve." Instead, dad instructs the child to put on a happy face because "you don't need those kinds of friends anyway" and the child, unable to advocate for their own emotional needs, smiles, suppresses the pain, and goes into denial. Dad has likely not felt or grieved his own betrayals in life, and so he does not know how to empathize with his child.

If we did not receive mirroring and empathy, we will likely lack self-awareness, particularly around our emotions and needs. Without mirroring, we grow up without the internalized relational experience of being seen, we do not know ourselves, and we do not know how or why we relate as we do. We grow older, but we don't grow up. We may mature intellectually, but our emotional lives are stunted.

We may frequently describe our emotional state as "fine." We may have lost a sense of how our emotions feel in our bodies. We lack an emotional vocabulary. We don't know if we are happy or sad, and because we don't know how we feel, we don't know what we need. We cannot express emotion, and we therefore can't ask for what we want in an appropriate, responsible way. We may become anxious and search for someone, anyone who can and will mirror us. We may develop low self-worth, not truly believing ourselves to be someone worth engaging. We may become demanding, critical, and contemptuous of our partners without acknowledging that the hurt we are feeling is as old as we are. We hold them accountable for what we did not receive as children, and this is an unwinnable war. When we don't know our stories and our feelings, we blame and then blame some more.

We lack self-awareness.

When we ignore or deny our feelings, our needs go unmet. We miss opportunities for the rich intimacy that gives our lives meaning and fulfillment. If we do not mirror our partners or feel seen by them, it could be because, unused to the feeling and experience of mirroring, we have chosen partners who do not instinctively or intentionally do this. Without the early childhood experience of someone communicating, "You are a person, and I see you. I'm connected to you, and I'm with you," we don't seek it out as adults. We are entrenched in our unconscious survival patterns. That means if we suppressed emotions and needs in our family home, we often choose a partner with whom we must suppress emotions and needs. This is our wheelhouse.

There is hope. We can learn, and so can they. We must have compassion with ourselves: we were never taught to know ourselves. It takes self-aware parents to raise self-aware children.

Parents who mirror their children, beginning in infancy, and walk humbly and responsibly through the ages and stages of childhood raise children who have a sense of their own humanity in all its power and brokenness. These parents apologize to their children when they hurt them or fail them, as all human beings will do from time to time. These parents do not overly value emotions, allowing their children to act out in the name of emotional expression, nor do they suppress their own emotions or their children's, rearing children who are not free to be emotional beings. They walk through emotions with maturity and encourage authentic, appropriate expression. These children become adults who hold a realistic view of themselves, who have learned how to be emotionally, relationally responsible individuals who know and have taken responsibility for themselves and can navigate life with balance between self-compassion and self-accountability. These are adults who can apologize because they heard apologies given. These are adults who can forgive because they have been forgiven and have forgiven others. These are adults who know their own hearts – their healthy reactions and unhealthy reactions. Both are present; both have been mirrored. These adults seek out relationships with people who can and do give them a realistic experience of themselves in all their beauty and brokenness, as their earliest mirroring experiences did. Life and love are authentic.

SELF-AWARENESS IN ACTION

Growing in self-awareness begins with desire. We must want to know ourselves to engage the work because the work is hard and emotionally taxing. The rewards are worth the effort, but we begin with desire. The pivotal scene in *The Matrix*, when Neo must choose between the red pill or the blue pill, is a perfect cinematic representation for the choice before us. We can choose autopilot and settle for lives of comfortable convention. We may live out our days enjoyably and likely without much upheaval. We will not feel bliss, nor will we feel our existential angst. We will not connect deeply with our loved ones, but we likely won't feel an excruciating distance either. We are too lukewarm to feel passion or hatred. We pose no threat. We are well-liked, comfortable, and middle of the road. Perhaps we live life on autopilot by endlessly complaining about problems and relationships that never improve. We are habituated to misery, never able to see our part in it, never believing that we truly deserve happiness, and we therefore never able to create it. We blame others for our pain and avoid responsibility for our own lives.

If we desire self-awareness, we begin with one deep breath. As a mountaineer looks upward at a foreboding peak, we assess the trek before us and breathe deeply. It's going to take effort, perseverance, courage, and determination. But it's possible. One breath at a time, one day at a time, one moment at a time, we begin connecting our present and our past. We begin to feel again. We begin to know ourselves.

Relationships are nothing more than a million tiny moments. When the majority of those moments are pleasant, we have a satisfying relationship. When the majority of those moments are unpleasant, we understandably want out. In the absence of self-awareness, we resort to blaming our partner or ourselves. This guarantees dissatisfaction. If we are pursuing self-awareness, we are interested in why we are doing what we are doing, why we chose the partner we chose, and how the past may be playing out in the present. We are taking responsibility for our choices and patterns, and we are apologizing and healing the wounds between us.

QUESTIONS FOR INCREASING OUR SELF-AWARENESS:

- How would I describe my childhood?
- What childhood needs were met? Which went unmet?
- Did I experience abuse or trauma? (It is vital to name this.)
- How did I survive the pain I experienced during childhood? (If you still believe there was no pain, keep working on feeling your feelings.)
- What childhood patterns of survival am I in today?
- How do I avoid my own feelings?
- What tactics do I employ to avoid pain?
- What area(s) of my life need(s) attention? Am I approaching this daily? Weekly?
- What attracted me to my spouse/partner/lover?
- What do I love about myself? Hate about myself?

- Do I love myself in general? Why or why not?
- How do I do this practically? Is it a feeling? A practice?
- What do I believe it means to love myself?
- How do I spend my time? (It may be helpful to write out a daily schedule.)
- How do I feel about how I'm spending my time?
- What is my life's purpose?
- Does how I spend my time reflect my sense of purpose?
- Where is my energy drained?
- Where is it renewed?
- Who drains me?
- Who uplifts me?
- What do I need to feel connected to myself?
- When do I feel most connected to myself? Most disconnected from myself?
- How does my body feel around my mother? My father? My children? My friends? My coworkers? Am I tense? Relaxed? On edge? Safe?
- How does my body feel at work? During sex? In church? In nature?
- What feelings are connected to these sensations?

When we gain answers through brave self-examination, we are becoming self-aware. Apologies are not terribly difficult for the self-aware. We know what we do and why we do it, and we can offer ourselves compassion because we understand our own stories and what patterns we developed to survive. When faced with our failures, we aren't surprised. We know ourselves. We aren't threatened when others can see us. On the contrary, we treasure feeling known.

The self-aware are the adventurers of the soul. We are those who hunger to know ourselves as an explorer is hungry to know the seas or new lands. We come to realize that all the outer experiences in the world pale in comparison to the inner landscape of a human being. The more we learn, the more we share. The more we connect with ourselves, the greater our connection with others.

The deeper our awareness of ourselves, the greater our capacity to love.

• • •

Alexa never returned to therapy.

Her desire that I collude with her in blaming Brandon for every issue in their marriage went unmet, and her aggression went unresolved. In the absence of a deeper desire for self-awareness, Alexa ironically missed out on the only power she truly has: the power to know herself.

Her false sense of power enacted through rage, aggression, anger, demand, criticism, and contempt were repeats from her childhood, and they masked the victim stance she had adopted. "My problems are someone else's fault, and if only they would change, I'd be fine." This is the mindset of a victim, true in childhood, untrue in adulthood. Alexa could not see how even though she is a woman, a wife, and a mother, she is still a child emotionally. And sadly, her marriage will reflect this level of maturity.

Self-awareness may have been the vital difference. It may have slowed her down enough to see, really see, herself. And if she'd been able to see herself, she likely would have been able to see Brandon too.

TOOL TIPS:
SELF
AWARENESS

- Self-awareness is knowing and understanding our story from childhood to adulthood.
- The three stages of self-awareness are: (1) telling your story, (2) allowing yourself to have the feelings you had then now, (3) identifying which behaviors you employed to cope with your feelings then and now. (We are looking for patterns.)
- Our childhood behaviors for coping with our emotions form our original toolbox.
- Self-awareness allows us to participate in our relationships consciously.
- As adults, our potential for intimate connection will be commensurate with our level of self-awareness.
- Self-awareness requires desire and courage.
- Our capacity to love will match our level of self-awareness.

QUESTIONS
FOR
DISCUSSION

1. Am I curious about knowing myself more deeply? What about me interests me? What about me bores me?

2. Have I shared my life story with anyone? If not, why not? If so, how was the experience for me?

3. Which parts of my story do I leave out? Why? Which parts do I always include? Why? What do I believe this says about me?

4. Do I understand why I do what I do? Name an example of an adult behavior and the childhood root.

5. How do I perceive myself? Name 10 attributes. How do I believe others perceive me? Name 10 attributes. How do I want others to perceive me? Name 10 attributes.

Conclusion

Twelve tools.

Which tool felt the most native? Which felt the most foreign?

Which one will we pick?

WILL WE CHOOSE THE RIGHT MINDSET?

If so, we are done with excuses and blaming others. When we accept the challenge of working with and mastering this tool, it means we shift the focus off of our partner as the source of our problems and refocus on ourselves. We take our personal inventory and get busy! We stop thinking and speaking critically of others and take a long, honest look in the mirror. We face the great question: do I love the person I see staring back at me? We accept that without this step, our relationships just won't work. When we feel more concerned with our own growth than the faults of others, we are ready to love.

WILL WE CHOOSE LISTENING?

If so, we are ready to learn. A lot. We take a deep breath. We do it again. We are about to become learners in life. We are letting go of the false belief that it is more important to be heard than it is to hear others. We are ready to embrace other's perceptions, stories, and experiences. We are refusing to interrupt. We are rejecting the old behavior of shutting down and walking away. We are making the courageous decision to remain present: attuned, attentive, and available. We are ready to listen, and we are even more ready to learn.

WILL WE CHOOSE EMOTIONAL EXPRESSION?

If so, we are ready to open up. We are staring down the lie that we had to "toughen up" to be strong. We are seeing past the ridiculous belief that emotions don't matter. Of course they do! They aren't precise indicators of truth (that's not their job), but they are important signals as to whether or not our needs are being met. We are ready to say: I have needs and I have feelings. I'm tired of being a human robot. I wasn't an emotionless robot as a child, and I'm done acting like one as an adult. I'm learning that rational thought isn't always what my relationship needs. I am ready to be open. I am willing to be vulnerable.

WILL WE CHOOSE VALIDATION?

If so, we are ready to really *see* our partner. We will expand ourselves by developing the ability to perceive the world through others' eyes. We are done with the "my way or the highway" approach. We accept that others want to be understood and respected as much as we do. We see how afraid we've been of ceding ground. We didn't realize that by rigidly holding our position, we were unintentionally remaining isolated. We are ready to accept the obvious truth that perceptions differ and therefore emotional experiences do too. Validation is the glue that keeps us united when our differences arise. By acknowledging our partner's experience, we become an irreplaceable part of it.

WILL WE CHOOSE GRATITUDE?

If so, we are ready to be thankful. We got too comfortable, too demanding, and too lazy. We stopped appreciating every day, every smile, every task, every gesture, every gift. We've been busy expecting more while ignoring what's been right in front of us. We are done living this way! We are ready to be *moved* each and every day by the goodness and beauty around us, starting with our partner. We got lost in striving, attaining, and wanting more. We became numb with greed. We are ready to STOP, notice, and say thank you. Again and again. Each and every day. Starting now.

WILL WE CHOOSE COMPASSION?

If so, we are ready to feel pain and connection. We are going to remember what it felt like to be in pain and have that pain ignored or overlooked. We remember how desperate we felt for someone, *anyone* to notice that we weren't okay. We became hard-hearted. We erroneously thought no one cared, so why should we? But our pain matters. We start there. We affirm this first. And then we focus on our partner... *their* pain matters. We are ready to come out of denial. Life is hard and filled with challenges. We are ready to offer our hearts and our willingness to sit with others in pain, even if they've hurt us too. We see compassion as a way of life, not something to be earned or given based on merit. (We can now count ourselves among the world changers.)

WILL WE CHOOSE BOUNDARIES?

If so, we are ready to feel in control of ourselves. We are exhausted from feeling resentment. We are admitting that we have limits, and those limits do not mean we are weak. They simply mean we are human. We are ready to see ourselves as flesh and blood, not machines. We can stop the crazed pursuit of trying to please and impress everyone. We can own what we want, and we are ready to start advocating for ourselves. We would rather face our fear of abandonment than keep driving ourselves into the ground. We are ready to say "yes" when our bodies say yes and "no" when our bodies say no. We are willing to work on doing this gently and firmly when necessary.

WILL WE CHOOSE HUMOR?

If so, we are ready to laugh at life appropriately. Maybe our joking has been immature or hurtful. Our relationships aren't connected, and we are finally owning that we've been using humor to avoid pain. We've been using humor to cut people down and then ignoring their hurt feelings. Maybe our lack of humor has put everyone around us on edge. We are tired of the tension. We've been using seriousness to control others into taking us as seriously as we take ourselves. We are ready to laugh! Really laugh. Healthy, robust laughter. Everyone is in on the joke, including us. We are ready to face challenges appropriately, and we are

ready to let things go when we can't control them. We are
remembering: it's only life.

WILL WE CHOOSE EMPATHY?

If so, we are ready to connect! If we are a "Natural," we
own that constant, full-blown empathy has been draining us
and creating unrealistic expectations for our relationships.
No one can be emotionally attuned to us constantly. We are
accepting the limits of others and granting them the space
to be in their own energy. We are practicing self-love by
blocking. We cannot and do not have to be available all of
the time. If we are an "Intentional," we are ready to explore
and feel our own unfelt pain. We are ready to connect to
others emotionally, because we are *remembering* our feelings.
We are rejecting the erroneous belief that we can think
our way out of every problem in life. We are starting to
grasp the power of empathy. When the heart cries out and
the head answers, disconnection ensues. When the heart
cries out and another heart answers, connection is made.

WILL WE CHOOSE CONFRONTATION?

If so, we are ready to stand up for ourselves with
peaceful maturity. If we've been avoiding confrontations,
we are ready to be heard. If we've been bullies in
confrontation – dominant and unbending – we are ready
for a different approach. We see how disagreements are
inevitable, but if we can remain respectful and connected
in our disagreements, they have the unique power to teach
us about one another and draw us into closer connection.
We are ready to master Confrontation as the tool that
promotes and protects our individuality without damaging

another person's. We see that both are essential.

WILL WE CHOOSE APOLOGIZING
AND FORGIVING?

If so, we are ready to heal wounds. We are done with shallow relationship. We want *real* connection and *real* passion. We have buried too much, and we feel the need to clean the slate. We didn't realize how important apologizing was. We didn't realize that by not apologizing, we were failing to acknowledge our partner's right to be treated with dignity, respect, honesty, kindness, and fairness. We are accepting that we make mistakes, and we are ready to face the shame of admitting them. If we are focusing on forgiveness, we are tired of carrying around the crippling weight of anger and hurt. We aren't victims, and we don't need to act like the hurts and harms committed against us define us. We are ready to let go of the anger while still holding onto our dignity. What happened was wrong, but we deserve to be free. We are ready to breathe some fresh air!

WILL WE CHOOSE SELF-AWARENESS?

If so, we are ready for the adventure of a lifetime. We are tired of living disconnected from ourselves. We don't know what we feel, why we do what we do, why our lives look the way they look, why happiness eludes us, and we're sick of it. We're tired of being clueless and therefore powerless to direct ourselves in our relationships with intention and clarity. *We want to know ourselves.* Perhaps we became who we were taught to be without much questioning or resistance, but we are ready to wake up and see who we are.

We are ready to bring our True Selves to our relationships.

A final word, my friends: Try.

Don't expect perfection. No one has advanced skill with a new tool immediately, but each one of these tools is worth an honest try. Each one has the power to transform a relationship. Each one is essential, even in a small amount.

Relationships *are* hard. They become impossible when we attempt the impossible: changing someone else. But if our sole focus is on bringing the healthiest version of ourselves to our relationships every day, we are in the realm of the possible and the empowered.

We are now the builders.

Appendix A: Self-Inventory

Use this list periodically – once a year is a good cadence – to assess how you're doing in your life and where your growth areas are. Without an inventory, we typically pursue growth in some areas and leave others unattended. This takes a toll on our relationships and our overall health. A good exercise is to complete this inventory by yourself and have your partner do the same. Then share your answers with one another and what you have both decided is an area of growth. Be supportive and encouraging of one another.

- How are my relationships?
- How is my relationship with myself? Do I like myself? Love myself?
- How is my relationship with my ex/exes? Do I have peace in my heart about those chapters of my life? How are the boundaries?
- Do I have healthy relationships with my children? (A good marker is: do I mostly enjoy them?)
- Have I forgiven those who have harmed me? Am I bitter? Who have I not forgiven?
- Am I close to my parents? Too close? Too distant? Is it appropriate?
- Do I have friends I trust and rely on? Am I truly

honest with anyone in my life?

- How are my finances?
- Do I have debt? What kind of debt is it? Do I have an organized plan to get out of debt?
- Do I have a budget? Do I need a budget?
- What are my spending habits? Am I reckless and impulsive? Am I stingy and tightfisted? Am I disciplined? Can I have fun?
- Am I financially independent? Do I rely on my ex or my family in exploitative ways? To what extent? Is it healthy?
- Am I up-to-date with my taxes?
- What is my living situation?
- Do I like where I live? Is my home reflective of my values?
- Is it clean? Dirty? Messy? Filthy? What is my preferred standard of "lived-in?"
- How is my professional situation?
- Do I enjoy my work? Am I satisfied with the pay?
- Do I dream about doing something else?
- What holds me back?
- What are my career goals?
- How is my physical health?
- Am I addicted to a substance? Nicotine? Alcohol? Narcotics? Marijuana?
- Am I overweight? Am I working on that? Do I want to?
- Do I exercise? Am I compulsive? Is my workout routine about self-care or vanity?
- Do I like the way I look?
- How is my mental health?
- Am I addicted to a behavior? Sex? Work? Masturbation? Gambling? Eating? Pornography?

- Am I generally content? Do I experience joy?
- Am I depressed? Suicidal? Miserable? Is melancholy a habit?
- Am I anxious, worried, and insecure?
- What am I doing to improve my mental state?
- Do I have any secretive behaviors or addictions that I hide from others?
- How is my emotional health?
- Can I name my feelings?
- Can I share my feelings with others?
- Do I feel shame when I do this?
- Do I view emotions as weakness or immaturity? (If so, this needs an adjustment.)
- Can and do I connect emotionally with others?

Appendix B: List of Emotions

∽

This is a list of normal, human emotions or "feelings." Use this list to find the right word to describe what is going on inside of you emotionally. This is how we build our emotional vocabulary, without which we cannot accurately describe what we feel and will therefore not know what we need. The category of emotion is in bold and after that there are more refined words that fall under that spectrum. Take out this list and use it any and every time you need to describe your emotional state until the words become your own.

The goal is twofold:

1. We will begin to identify our feelings and have words for them

2. We will be able to share our emotional state confidently and accurately with our partner and other relationships

WHEN OUR NEEDS ARE SATISFIED

Affectionate... compassionate, friendly, loving, open hearted, sympathetic, tender, warm

Confident... empowered, open, proud, safe, secure

Engaged... absorbed, alert, curious, engrossed, enchanted, entranced, fascinated, interested, intrigued, involved, spellbound, stimulated

Excited... amazed, animated, ardent, aroused, astonished, dazzled, eager, energetic, enthusiastic, exhilarated, giddy, invigorated, lively, passionate, surprised, vibrant

Glad... blissful, ecstatic, elated, enthralled, exhilarated, exuberant, radiant, rapturous, thrilled

Grateful... appreciative, moved, thankful, touched

Hopeful... expectant, encouraged, optimistic

Inspired... amazed, awed, wonder

Joyful... amused, delighted, glad, happy, jubilant, pleased, tickled

Peaceful... calm, clear headed, comfortable, centered, content, equanimous, fulfilled, mellow, quiet, relaxed, relieved, satisfied, serene, still, tranquil, trusting

Refreshed... enlivened, rejuvenated, renewed, rested, restored, revived

WHEN OUR NEEDS ARE NOT SATISFIED

Afraid... apprehensive, dread, foreboding, frightened, mistrustful, panicked, petrified, scared, suspicious, terrified, wary, worried

Annoyed... aggravated, dismayed, disgruntled, displeased, exasperated, frustrated, impatient, irritated, irked

Angry... enraged, furious, incensed, indignant, irate, livid, outraged, resentful

Averse... animosity, appalled, contempt, disgusted, dislike, hate, horrified, hostile, repulsed

Confused... ambivalent, baffled, bewildered, dazed,

hesitant, lost, mystified, perplexed, puzzled, torn

Disconnected... alienated, aloof, apathetic, bored, cold, detached, distant, distracted, indifferent, numb, removed, uninterested, withdrawn

Disquiet... agitated, alarmed, discombobulated, disconcerted, disturbed, perturbed, rattled, restless, shocked, startled, surprised, troubled, turbulent, turmoil, uncomfortable, uneasy, unnerved, unsettled, upset

Embarrassed... ashamed, chagrined, flustered, guilty, mortified, self-conscious

Fatigue... beat, burnt out, depleted, exhausted, lethargic, listless, sleepy, tired, weary, worn out

Pain... agony, anguished, bereaved, devastated, grief, heartbroken, hurt, lonely, miserable, regretful, remorseful

Sad... depressed, dejected, despair, despondent, disappointed, discouraged, disheartened, forlorn, gloomy, heavy-hearted, hopeless, melancholy, unhappy, wretched

Tense... anxious, cranky, distressed, distraught, edgy, fidgety, frazzled, irritable, jittery, nervous, overwhelmed, restless, stressed out

Vulnerable... fragile, guarded, helpless, insecure, leery, reserved, sensitive, shaky

Yearning... envious, jealous, longing, nostalgic, pining, wistful

Appendix C: List of Needs

∽

This is a list of normal, human needs. Use this list in conjunction with the List of Emotions (Appendix B). When you feel joy or satisfaction, notice which need is being met by scanning the list below. When you feel distress of any kind or dissatisfaction, notice which need is going unmet by scanning the list below. The category of need is in bold. The following words and phrases are needs that fall under that general category.

The goal is twofold:

1. consciously making the connection between your emotions and your needs

2. learning to ask for what you need in relationship with confidence and specificity

Autonomy... choice, freedom, independence, respect, space, spontaneity

Beauty... delight, complexity, fascination, simplicity, variety

Connection with others... acceptance, affection, appreciation, belonging, cooperation, communication, closeness, community, companionship, compassion, consideration, consistency, curiosity, empathy, inclusion, intimacy, love, mutuality, nurturing, respect/self-respect, safety, security, stability, support, to know and be known, to see and be seen, to understand and be understood, trust, warmth

Connection with God/Higher Power/the Divine /Spirit... awe, community, discipline, faith, growth, mystery, prayer, quietness, revelation, smallness, solitude, teaching/teachers, transcendence, transformation

Connection with self... curiosity, patience, self-compassion, self-exploration, self-knowledge, solitude, time

Honesty... authenticity, consistency, integrity, presence

Meaning... awareness, celebration of life, challenge, clarity, competence, consciousness, contribution, creativity, discovery, efficacy, effectiveness, growth, hope, learning, mourning, participation, purpose, selfexpression, stimulation, to matter, understanding

Peace... communion, ease, equality, harmony, inspiration, order, reliability

Personal power... competence, confidence, desire, direction, efficacy, expansion, instinct, respect and self-respect, self-knowledge

Physical well-being... air, clothing, food (healthy), exercise, movement, rest, sexual expression, safety, shelter, sleep, touch, water

Play... creativity, humor, joy, laughter, lightness, spontaneity, taking turns/fairness

Safety... attachment, boundaries, known environment, non-threatening presence, order, predictability, protection, quietness, reliability, trustworthiness, truth telling

Appendix D: Glossary of Terms

Abandonment... the act of withdrawing our love, affection, presence, or resources from another person who is dependent or reliant on us for some or all of the above

Anger... the emotion that signals that a boundary has been crossed or our rights/personhood have been violated

Apology... a verbal acknowledgement that we have failed to treat another human being with dignity, respect, honesty, kindness, and fairness

Attuned... making eye contact, turning our bodies (hips and shoulders) toward our partner, slowing our breathing

Autonomy... a state of self-direction, self-ownership

Autopilot... living and loving unconsciously; not paying attention to feelings; not making choices from conscious awareness but rather unconscious beliefs and patterns

Aware... reacting appropriately to sensitive, vulnerable disclosures

Available... removing or turning off all distractions, including phones, televisions, reading materials, projects, etc., in order to fully listen to our partner

Blindness... the inability to see the good in another person

Blocking... for natural empaths, this is the act of

intentionally withholding emotional connection through empathy for the purpose of maintaining healthy boundaries and preserving energy

Boundary... the line we draw in relationship that delineates what we will and will not accept or tolerate

Bundling... grouping several emotions together into one emotion

Clean anger... the emotion that signals that a boundary has been crossed or our rights/personhood have been violated

Compassion... the impulse to move toward another person with the goal of alleviating their suffering

Conflict... the state of seeing the same situation through differing lenses and having strong emotional attachment to one's position

Confrontation... the act of thoughtfully bringing our thoughts, feelings, and needs to another person with the purpose of understanding their position and finding resolution in conflict

Crassness... a style of humor that lacks sensitivity and ignores complexity

Deep listening... the act of turning toward our partner, meeting their eyes with our eyes, putting aside all distractions, and offering attunement, awareness, and availability

Denial... the intentional or unintentional act of not seeing

Ego... the part of us that wants to be perceived as right, good, smart, successful, beautiful, etc.; the need for recognition that drives us to value power (winning) over connection

Embarrassment... the emotion that signals that we've been exposed in a way that does not feel safe

Emotional diet... the elements of relationship necessary to foster and nurture optimum emotional growth and maturity; includes acceptance, affection, compassion, expression, patience, gentleness, kindness, validation, play, and empathy

Emotions... the body's reactions to the environment based on how the environment is perceived

Empathy... the experience of feeling what another person is feeling

Entitlement... a state of mind due to inexperience with suffering that causes us to take gifts for granted

Fantasy... a dream (either waking or sleeping) in which all of our needs are met and it is not required that we grow

Fear... the emotion that signals that danger or threat, real or perceived, is imminent

Forgetfulness... the failure to show gratitude because our lives are overbooked

Forgiveness... the act of releasing the anger we feel toward another person who failed to give us the love (dignity, respect, honesty, kindness, and fairness) we deserve

Gladness... the emotion that signals that our needs have been met successfully or satisfactorily

Gratitude... the act of noticing another person's goodness and gifts and verbally expressing our appreciation

Hurt... the emotion that signals that our personhood has been disrespected

Ingratitude... the failure to show gratitude usually based on forgetfulness, blindness, resistance, or entitlement

"Intentional"... a person for whom empathy must be consciously practiced through remembering one's own feelings and then allowing connection to another person through a shared emotional state

Light listening... the act of hearing our partner share logistical or non-sensitive information and offering a response as a confirmation that we have heard them

Listening... the act of giving another person our attention for the purpose of hearing and understanding them

Loneliness... the emotion that signals our need for connection

Mocking/mockery... a style of humor that uses cruelty to make fun of another person

"Natural"... a person for whom empathy is innate and automatic

Polyanna... someone who is endlessly chipper and well-meaning

(the) Presumption of good intent... a belief that our partner has ours and the relationship's best interest in mind; an assumption that hardship does not arise from malice or malicious intent

Protective anger... anger that masks more vulnerable emotions like hurt, embarrassment, or fear

Relational Tennis... the act of talking back and forth without truly listening

Resistance... the willful refusal to see and acknowledge another person's goodness

(the) Right mindset... a mindset of realism, self-accountability, and personal responsibility in our lives and relationships

Sarcasm... a style of humor that utilizes mockery or contempt to communicate irony, often stemming from a place of unresolved anger; a passive-aggressive means of communicating anger

Self-awareness... the state of being in a consistent process of knowing oneself more deeply and without judgment

Self-deprecation... a style of humor that focuses on the faults and flaws of the self

Self-validation... the ability and act of connecting our present pain, patterns, and beliefs with our past in informed compassion

Sorrow... the emotion that signals that something of value has been lost

S.T.E.P.... a method of apologizing in which apologies are Specific, Thoughtful, Empathic, and Personal

Story... the events (including feelings, thoughts, beliefs, behaviors, traumas, and formative experiences) of one person's life from childhood to present

Thoughts... an idea that originates in the brain based on learning, processing, or inspiration

Tool... an action or pattern utilized in relationship for connection or self-protection; can be conscious or unconscious

Validation... the act of declaring that given another person's perspective, personality, and history, what they are perceiving and feeling makes sense

* These terms are defined as they appear and function in this book. Other, more generalized, definitions exist.

References

CHAPTER 4

"Episode 297." *Saturday Night Live*, created by Lorne Michaels, performance by Al Franken, season 16, episode 11, SNL Studios, 19 January 1991.

CHAPTER 6

Annie. Directed by John Huston, performances by Aileen Quinn, Carol Burnett, Ann Reinking, Bernadette Peters, Tim Curry, and Albert Finney, Columbia Pictures, 1982.

Pollyanna. Directed by David Swift, Buena Vista Distribution Company, 1960.

CHAPTER 8

Modern Times. Directed by Charlie Chaplin, performances by Charlie Chaplin, Paulette Goddard, Henry Bergman, Tiny Sandford, and Chester Conklin, United Artists, 1936.

"Job Switching." *I Love Lucy,* created by Desi Arnaz, performances by Lucille Ball, Desi Arnaz, Vivian Vance, and William Frawley, season 2, episode 1, Central Broadcasting Station, 15 September, 1952.

CHAPTER 12

The Matrix. Directed by The Wachowskis, performances by Keanu Reeves, Carrie-Anne Moss, Laurence Fishburne, Hugo Weaving, and Joe Pantoliano, Warner Bros., 1999.

The Golden Girls. Created by Susan Harris, performances by Beatrice Arthur, Betty White, Rue McClanahan, and Estelle Getty, Buena Vista Television, 1985-1992.

Acknowledgements

~

A book is a collective work, and this book is no different. From the spark of an idea to a perfectly bound copy, a book passes through so many hands before it's actually held in hand. My heartfelt gratitude goes out first to my clients whose bravery, vulnerability, and determination to improve their relationships gave me the real life, real time proof that better tools mean better relationships. Thank you M.P. for being the inspiration for this book. May your road lead you to a love that doesn't need a lot of repair. Thank you Ruben Estevez, Brian Hooper, Lydia Cox, and Hillary Humphreys for tackling the first draft. Your faith in this project kept me going. Ruben, thank you for your constant belief in me and for seeing a writer in a therapist. Brian, thank you for legitimizing this project in our field. Lydia, thank you for keeping my feet squarely in reality with your feedback. Hillary, thank you for showing me that this would and could be relevant to the people for which it's written. Thank you Collin Peterson for the selfless time you gave the first edits of this book, for the lengthy conversations on the world of publishing, and for making me laugh at every place of fear. Thank you Linda Bordeaux for the exceptional work on the cover design and the early text edits. Thank you Chuck Hargett for pulling it all together and modeling for me what self-publication looks like in the real world. To everyone at Book Baby, specifically Matthew Idler, thank you for the ongoing support and endless explanations. Navigating self-publishing is a bit like steering your ship toward the open seas for the first time, and your guidance provided me a map of the stars. A huge debt of gratitude is owed to my mother who taught me to dream, believe in myself, and travel through life with diehard grit and determination. And thank you, Jared Bentley, for nurturing a love with me that is worthy of the best tools I have.